Romancing Ribbons Into Flowers

ELLY SIENKIEWICZ

Editing by Mary Coyne Penders.
Technical editing by Darlene Zimmerman.
Book and cover design by Kajun Graphics, San Francisco.
Illustrations by Lorelei Brede.

Photography by Linda Clausen, pages 19, 20, 22, 23, 64; Lorraine Fukuwa, pages 110–111; Gary McKinstry, page 57; David Michels, pages 18, 148, 150, 157; Sharon Risedorph, pages 10, 16, 17, 21, 30, 32, 33, 58, 71, 75–77, 79, 83, 88, 93, 97, 102, 103, 112, 115, 122, 123, 127, 132, 133, 132; and Alan Stephens, pages 7, 13, 22, 26, 36, 38, 40, 45–48, 50–54, 56, 59, 61, 64, 66, 67, 116, 128, 140–142, 150, 154.

Printed in Hong Kong.

First Edition

Library of Congress Cataloging-in-Publication Data
Sienkiewicz, Elly,
Romancing ribbons into flowers
       p.   cm.
1. Crafts and Hobbies   2. Appliqué   3. Quilt Design
ISBN 1-881588-16-5

EZ International
Quilt House Publishing
95 Mayhill Street
Saddle Brook, New Jersey 07663

I'll tell you how the sun rose,
A ribbon at a time,
The steeples swam in amethyst,
The news like squirrels ran.

—Emily Dickinson

ACKNOWLEDGMENTS

Ribbonart is ancient and shared. I am indebted to seamstresses, milliners, costume-makers, embroiderers, quiltmakers, authors, teachers, and students—fanciers all—from centuries past and present. Eleven contemporary ribbon artists share unique pieces herein. To all these needlewomen, the nameless and forgotten, no less than the noteworthy, thank you!

Thank you to the publishers, Joe Mishkin and Chuck Sabosik; and to the editors, Mary Coyne Penders, the executive editor, and Darlene Zimmerman, the technical editor; to the illustrator, Lorelei Brede; and to the designers Pat Koren and Laurie Smith of Kajun Graphics. Without your faith, support and input, this book would not have been. Stan Sienkiewicz, too, has edited and cheerfully done "whatever it takes." Thank you to my colleague, Denise Scott, for all. And to my husband, forever.

DEDICATION

To Alex Corbly Sienkiewicz, who excels. You were my first stitcher-child, now become a wrestler-scholar. You were always a maker of things: my fixer, my artist, my companion, my historian, my philosopher, and our most sociable family member. You are sunlight and shadow with your love and warmth, joy and sorrow; all so quiet, but so close to the surface. I cannot think of your middle name without thinking of "your" Corbly ancestors and our walks on the West Virginia hills. When not so little, you insisted—with a stubborn smile—that you would never leave this home. In a sense you never will. You will always live here in our hearts, will always be welcomed back with joy, will always be Our Alex.

Flora's Album

Pansies, pl. *from the French* pensées, *thoughts…" I am filled with thoughts of you."*

What memories does a pansy bring? For each of us, a pansy is never about just one flower. It's about accumulated anecdotes and memories that deepen all flowers' meaning over time. Like a breeze bearing petals, thoughts transport. In recollection, we breathe a scene's fragrance, feel the sun's warmth on our cheeks, or savor the memory of the cool garden loam between our fingers. This afternoon, fashioning flowers out of ribbon, my thoughts fall open to pansies pressed between life's album pages, long, long ago.

Grandma Hamilton loved flowers. When we visited her in Flushing, New York, she took us to walk the Bronx Botanical Gardens. Each Easter, when we were little, she gave my sister and me a flat of pansies to plant. Her home was turn-of-the-century dark, and smelled of boiled cabbage. I remember a snake plant (that draught-tolerant Victorian) set primly on a doilied side table, so stark that it must have been mission oak. I remember a terrarium under glass. I understood that the glass preserved an ecosystem. Though young, I sensed a mystery there, knowing that as long as the glass world remained closed, the plants needed no watering. On tip-toe, I would slide the terrarium top aside and breath deep the moist aroma of ancient soil. The world I peered into was mossy and pulsing with budding life. I can almost smell that moment now; sense its wonder still. When I think of the droplets, vapor condensed on glass, I know magic, and think of life's mysterious journey. A religious woman, Grandma conveyed an abiding joy in flowers, those mirrors of Creation's miracle. However, hers was also a scientist's fascination.

A botany teacher, May Davina Ross Hamilton was tall, dignified and stately. She was compassionate at the same time that she was tireless in her convictions, and her motives were entirely noble. Nonetheless, I remember her as "not a child's person." Mother of four, she worked hard as the wife of a young Vermont circuit minister. She worked even harder when he died, leaving her eldest, Donald Ross Hamilton, my father, just thirteen years old, and the youngest, my Uncle John, just two. My father survived the same mastoid infection which, in an adjoining hospital room, killed his father. May Davina sat by my dad's bed for another two days until he was well enough to come home. During that time she never told him his father had died. After she brought her recovering first-born home, she packed him,

his siblings and all their belongings onto the train which would take them and my grandfather's coffin to Flushing, New York. There her immigrant Scot uncle, Donald Ross, ran a nursery. There her bachelor brother and maiden sister lived. There, she had decided on a dime, she would make her family's new life.

Grandma Hamilton buried her husband in Flushing Cemetery, then took a job teaching botany and biology at Flushing High School. Grandma taught me about Mendel's Law and cross-pollination, and instructed me to pick my pansies at full bloom, before they went to seed. Her observation that, if allowed to go to seed, they would cease to produce so many flowers, impressed me. I "dead head" my porch plants to this day. Grandma taught me that the goal of all flowers is to reproduce. From her I learned flora's facts of life, without much romance. Somehow her son, my father, conveyed both the facts of life and love for the universe, which is our home, and for his wife, my mother. In their separate ways, both he and Grandma instilled in me a sense of wonder in the natural world, and an abiding love for it.

Pansies of wired ribbon and vintage rayon adorn a Mokuba striped velvet ribbon necklace fashioned by the author.

My British grandmother, Eleanor (née Virginia) Thora Griswold Ferris Clare-Patton Broy Crowley, was bright, driven, and emoted romance. Her garden was the quintessential English garden though it bloomed in Madison, New Jersey. Madison is a few hours from Princeton, where I grew up. Nana—as I called her—sent us summer, fall, and spring flowers from her garden. She packed tall-stemmed gladiolas in waxed paper layered with wet handfuls of ice. Those floral offerings arrived fresh and fragrant back then in the late 'forties, when the mail was delivered twice a day. I loved a visit from Nana. In between visits, I loved her notes to me and her flowers to my mother. I was both a bit afraid of her and adored her. My mother named me Eleanor after her.

Uncle Jack, Nana's third husband, was my step-grandfather. Tall, Irish-American, and a bit withdrawn, he had hired Nana as a housekeeper when his first wife died in childbirth. He did Nana's bidding. He built low rock walls, a carriage house, a fish pond, a fountain, and laid a footpath to Nana's Shakespeare Garden. In the wet cement, Nana quoted Shakespeare with a pointed stick. When I was in high school, she had a severe heart attack. She and Uncle Jack gave up the garden and retired to Cape Canaveral, where she couldn't keep from cultivating the soil. She turned the sand fertile and, around her Florida home, made the earth bloom. As she had in Madison, she started a garden club and reigned over yet another group of admiring ladies.

A second heart attack killed her, but she and Uncle Jack had seemed much happier together in those years which were her last. For burial, he brought her by train to New York where they had married. When we looked at her birth certificate, it read that her name was Virginia and that she had been born in County Clare, Ireland. Nana remains the most fascinating woman I have ever known. Flowers *en masse*, flowers in full glory, flowers from dirt-rooted seedlings to summer garlands, to flowers delivered at the door—they all remind me of her. Every time I pin a flower to my clothing or pat a floral scent behind my ear, I smile, recalling my mother's mother.

Flowers En Masse

Nana walked her Madison gardens, and brought me to visit with her flowers. She was far too heavy. I remember her at home, a smutsy apron over her round tummy. She wore an apron when she cooked (exquisitely!) and an artist's smock in which to garden. Then I remember her swathed in silk and cashmere, trailing the scent of Maillot's *Crêpe de Chine* when she came to visit us. Even when she was white-haired, I—a teenager— noticed that men stole glances at her as she passed by. She had style and that appeal which the French mischievously dub "elle a du chien."

Everything she did was in excess. She taught me the names of the flowers— nicotiana, snapdragon, baby's breath. (Consider how a child could dream on such names!) She told me stories. Her grandmother, after all, had been Lady-in-Waiting to Queen Victoria. Her father's ships plied the English Channel and, their mother dead, he made his daughters wait hungrily as he ate the first course, mushrooms under glass, alone. At seventeen, Nana met her first husband on the tennis court. She, just graduated from the Sacre Coeur Convent School in Paris, was contemplating a return to become a nun. He, honors in hand from Edinburgh University, had been around the world as a nobleman's touring physician. With that expedition's earnings, the handsome Reginald Clare Patton purchased his medical practice in Brixham. Side-stepping her stern father, the couple eloped. Reginald gave Nana *Mrs. Beaton's Guide to Household Management* as a wedding present and established her as the young mistress of their estate, Cross Parks, with its retinue of servants. All too soon the Colonial Service called Dr. Patton to West Africa to research the "Bang Panga" disease. Though he won several awards in Applied Histology for this work, he himself contracted malaria and longed for home and his small family. Appointed chief medical officer on a troop transport ship, he shepherded a load of German prisoners of war (all sick with Black Water Fever) to England and into hospitals. Only then, increasingly ill, did he return to Cross Parks where he died, widowing Nana, now nineteen.

While Eleanor had remained behind in Brixham, she had sent her husband formal photographs: uniformed nanny by her side, there is Nana (a thick chestnut braid wrapped round her head) holding my wee mother cradled in white lace. She married her second husband when my mother was five. He was the American Consul to Cherbourg, France, insanely jealous and abusive. With the help of officer friends in the American Army of Occupation, Nana fled to refuge in the Koblenzehoff Hotel in Germany. Months and many adventures later, Nana pawned the last of her jewels for first class passage for two. She and my mother, age seven, sailed aboard the Berengeria to seek their fortune in America. Eleanor, now wife of Bell Telephone engineer Jack Crowley, toiled to save some semblance of that gracious life to which she had been born decades ago; two husbands ago; almost a lifetime ago—on another continent, across the wide ocean.

Uncle Jack was one of four orphaned brothers, intellectual, industrious, devout and awkward. He called her "Nell" and was in awe of her. They were both stubborn and fought terribly over money. She created old world elegance on a Bronx housewife's budget and I know he was proud of her. Who knows why we are pulled more to one relative than to another? The fact remains that even at time's distance, I cannot but admire Grandma Hamilton. But by Nana, one of memory's brightest flowers, I remain enthralled.

A Yellow Rose

Thus it is more Nana's romance of flowers than Grandma's lessons in genetics and flora culture that have lead to this book. What other memories fill my Flora's Album? There is one from January, 1964. My boyfriend of three years had declined my invitation to Senior Prom at Wellesley, citing his senior thesis that would keep him eight hours away at Princeton. On prom night, in loneliness, I telephoned and reached him at his eating club, where he was watching a movie. It would take more youthful heartbreak to realize this was not a man I wanted to marry. Come Valentine's Day that year, I posted this note: "Dear John, Thank you for the beautiful yellow roses. How did you know yellow is my favorite color? I was so disappointed that you could not come for prom, but this gift was such a Valentine's Day surprise. Thank you again. All my love, El." There had been no prom date, no phone call, and... in truth, no flowers. In retrospect, John's contrite reply was as agile as it was charming: "Dear El, While I didn't send you the roses, I wish I had. Love, John".

The stuff of floral memories is the stuff of life, an engaging mix of the memorable and the forgettable. Ribbonwork invites you to smell the flowers bordering Memory Lane. Please, let's accept the invitation together.

Table of Contents

A Fancywork Odyssey

There is no occupation so essentially feminine, at the same time so truly lady-like, as needle work in every branch, from the plain, useful sewing that keeps household and person neat and orderly, to the exquisite, dainty fancy work that adds beauty to every room.

—Annie Shields, *The Ladies' Guide to Needle Work, Embroidery, Etc./Being a Complete Guide to All Kinds of Ladies' Fancy Work/With Full Description of All the Various Stitches and Materials, and a Large Number of Illustrations for Each Variety of Work (1877).*

Even at noon on this July-hot day, the Library of Congress's reading room is stone-cool. Books ordered earlier are arriving at my desk. There are books on fancywork, embroidery, histories of ribbon and the Lyon silk trade, costume, millinery, ribbonwork: art needlework in all its page-pressed grandeur. Vintage ladies' magazines are among the first arrivals, their sequence reflecting stylistic evolution. Some books turn out to be pamphlets so fragile they come encased in envelopes. One is neither stapled nor stitched, but tied with pink silk, laid flat by time. The cover price is 35¢. Most books I skim; in some I mark designs for photocopying. Always I read the Introduction. Why, so long ago, did the author write this book? What purpose did she intend? For whom did she write? Regrettably, these questions are seldom answered.

Many of the oldest needlework manuals seem impersonal, written at the behest of a manufacturer desirous of selling his product. Early twentieth century ribbon books tediously teach the tucks, pleats, and cockades of an outmoded couture. Dramatic ribbon blossoms are there too, precious blooms from weedy beds of fussier lingerie and millinery flowers. I grow impatient. What of the romance that inspires fancywork? The real fancy, the image created in the stitcher's mind, shows only in the needlework pictured. In those illustrations, one senses a kindred passion: for fancywork is ornate, painstaking, and intensively stitched. Fancywork is fashioned by an adventurous soul on an imaginative voyage.

Fancywork flowers resemble reality, but do not imitate it. Like poetry, they are born of romance. It is the Victorian accent, in particular, that I long to hear echoed in these old volumes. But here, in this marble columned hall, amidst a throng of scholarly types, I want more than pictures and instructions. I yearn for the voice of a needlewoman. I want some hint of what compelled her to share her passion in

The author fashioned a unique folded and rolled rose (Lesson Six) by keeping the wired ribbon's edge prominent. Its kimono fold leaves and knotted Mokuba ribbon overlays are also taught in Lesson Six.

ink as well as in thread. I feel her here beside me, a fellow traveler on a fancy-work odyssey, and I want to know her better.

The books continue to arrive at my desk. My research becomes a peaceful visit with the needlework we love. We are creatures of our past, I muse, and our tastes reflect our culture. Were my love *Ikebana*, "flower arranging" in Japanese, I would stitch traditional stem positions into my fancywork. I would contemplate what "intermediaries" would best fill the empty spaces. The Japanese aesthetic calls for simplicity and purity. It eschews the elaboration beloved of the Victorians. *Ikebana* is arrangement by rule so the flowers appear natural, as though growing. A potent word in the art is *furyu* (flowing wind), the antithesis of elaborate. In ribbonart's felicitous way, the occidental and the oriental, the Victorian and the modern, blend, their vitality renewed. Some of the most luxurious modern ribbons, for example, are Japanese. Models in this book showcase exquisite Mokuba velvets, satins, and organdies. Some even give the affectionate nomen "kimono pleat" to the neat folds and pleated petals of Lesson Six. There, petals seem politely to press their hands before them, and as though kimono-clad, to bow.

The attraction between Victorian decorative arts and Japanese folk art is fabled and worth exploring. *Ikebana* is an awareness of nature. Plants and flowers nourish this quality of spirit in us. Buddha taught that like man plants have a spiritual life and thus a soul. Naturally, then, the study of flowers increases this harmony and fellow-feeling between man and nature. As needleworkers romance ribbons into flowers, our skills increase, ease ensues, and thoughts are freed to a more contemplative level. This close communion with flowers, with the omnipresent beauty around us, makes us grateful. Optimism lifts our spirits. So many who love flowers feel a friendship, and yes, a kinship with them. Flowers, wrote one naturalist, are "friendly signposts" in our neighborhood. They become a welcome part of the scenery, like someone we make time to visit when we are in town.

Ancient mythology personified the botanical world, peopling it with mortals metamorphosed into flowers. Narcissus of the drooping head so stared at his reflection that he fell into the pool, becoming the deep-rooted daffodil with the delicately down-turned face. The lovely Iris once traversed the rainbow bearing decisions divine. The persistently pursued Rodanthe, Queen of Flowers, gained eternal respite, though no less ardent attentions, as the rose. Were man's memory that long, we might know of flowers picked and praised, laid on a rock-mounded

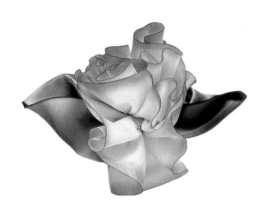

grave or ceremonially twined in a cave-dwelling maiden's tousled hair.

We people our homes with house plants. While I scarcely notice them in the summer, my winter-flowering Amaryllis and the sweetly dogged African violets lift my spirits when the days are grey. They are my friends and friendship is something Victorians cherished. So we've the Buddhist perception of a flower's soul, the Greek humans in floral form, and the Victorian high-valuing of friendship. Small wonder fashioning ribbons into flowers leads us down a garden path! Some stitch their blooms with restraint, *Ikebana*-like, using "... no more than three materials in one arrangement." Others luxuriate in an opulence of techniques and textures. All are less lonely for it; all feel beauty's flowering.

*H*ere in the nation's library, my research continues on flowers pressed paper-thin. A tune of cultivated tastes plays softly around the tomes piled beside me. My predecessors have become more familiar, as though we are observing each other, silently. Suddenly, a unique book has arrived. This morning, in the thickly varnished file, an age-darkened card had seemed significant. Its penciled cursive script reads: "Shields, Mrs. Annie S. (Frost), *The Ladies' Guide to Needle Work, Embroidery, Etc.*". The 1877 publication date had whispered romance. Book in hand now, a gold title imprints the Moroccan binding which opens to marbleized end-papers. Engravings illustrate that the work is fancy indeed! A strong-minded stitcher penned the Introduction and allows us a glimpse of her soul:

"There is no occupation so essentially feminine, at the same time so truly ladylike, as needle work in every branch, from the plain, useful sewing that keeps household and person neat and orderly, to the exquisite, dainty fancy work that adds beauty to every room…Fancy as well as fact dates the use of the needle to remotest ages, for the rivalry of Minerva and Arachne, and the wondrous webs they wove, are in every mythology…

Martha Washington received her lady friends, rising from her knitting or sewing, and resuming the work of her fingers while conversing, and there are specimens of her skill still treasured… . Too much cannot be said in favor of this branch of feminine education, and it is a grievous error to allow girls to arrive at maturity ignorant of the full use of the needle."

A good marketer, Mrs. Shields concludes that this sewn beauty can easily be accomplished: "But while the variety of form and use is endless, close examination will generally prove to the expert needlewoman that the most complicated and bewildering combinations reduce themselves to some simple stitch or rule perfectly familiar to them."

For we who would now fashion ribbons into flowers, a handful of simple techniques—folding, rolling, gathering, pleating—each perfectly familiar, will create brilliant botanical ornaments. That we learned these basics in childhood is our secret. From time immemorial, needlewomen have coupled simple skills with imagination, and practice with patience. You readied yourself for this ribbon flower adventure a lifetime ago. Savor it: observe nature and imagine that you are a botanist, hybridizing ribbon cultivars all your own. The Japanese word "kado" means the way of the flowers. Listen to the kado, catch the gesture of the blooms, arrange them in their way. Enjoy the process; savor the happiness. How natural to repeat that which we do when we are peaceful and happy together, like a marriage that wants to work. Devote yourself to needleart and your life itself will beautify all that it touches.

Each of us learns differently. Some will first read this book through. Others will delve into this teach-yourself course, one lesson at a time. Like a skillful tutor, the chapters teach you what you need to know, only as you need to know it. Each refers back to terminology, tools, and basic techniques taught in Part One. Heed the call of romance. Now softly, now more clearly, the melody invites you to follow your own fancy. Lush, luminescent ribbons; plush velvet ribbons; ribbons ruffled, tucked, pleated, painted, and hand-dyed. In chorus, they sing a siren song, beckoning you to wrap your days in "ribbands".

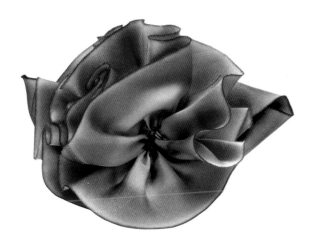

Original hand-embroidered silk ribbon designs center each block in the machine appliquéd quilt,
Rosa Rugosa—Victorian Beach Roses, *by Ruth Meyers.*

Cultivating a Ribbon Garden

HOW TO USE THIS BOOK

Romancing Ribbons into Flowers is a guide to fashioning flowers from ribbon, a workbook of step-by-step lessons, and a source of inspiration. Flowers are both Beauty's message and her medium. Some ribbon flora bear botanical names, so closely do they resemble their natural sisters. Others will be more impressionistic. Less namable still is the effect upon the gardener herself: quite magically, sowing ribbon flowers cultivates a bloom of spirit. Six lessons develop the requisite skills for making flowers from ribbon.

Each lesson specifies which ribbons to use and suggests you re-read *Getting Started* before starting. The lessons teach flower making methods as well as projects. Many of these projects take only a few hours to make.

To learn ribbonart most easily, follow the lessons sequentially. The course progresses quickly, leading from simpler to fancier florals, including ribbons blooming in heirloom quilts. These teach-yourself lessons contain the wings to set your ribbonry free. Artful ribbonwork photographs inspire; clear illustrations instruct. And if you are curious about the contributing designers, read *About the Needleartists* in Part Three.

Christa Lynn Brown's brooch exemplifies the elegant, romantic style she has originated for Honey Moon French Ribbon Roses.

You'll also find classes there, and a comprehensive *Resource Directory*. The directory walks you through retail and wholesale purveyors of ribbons, trims, notions, dyeing supplies, pleating services and bead suppliers, and tells you where you can take ribbonwork classes.

Since initially one learns by imitation, many projects use readily available materials. When the yen grows for lush ribbons from far-off places, the *Resource Directory* brings ribbonart's exotica directly to your armchair.

WHERE DOES TODAY'S FLOWER-MAKING RIBBON COME FROM?

Ribbons come from long ago and far away. Some exquisite ribbons are Japanese: Midori and Mokuba of Japan fabricate a wonderland of sumptuous satins, silks, velvets, polyesters, acetates, rayons, cottons, organzas and georgettes.

Luminescent colors, rich prints, and gradated shades are finished with edges both plain and fancy. The French, who excel in silk flowers, also make ribbon. Theirs is the most supple of the wired (wire-edged) ribbon and their color range in this ribbon is the widest in the world. Popularly called *ombrés*, these ribbons shade from selvage to selvage in decreasing intensities of hue.

Vintage ribbons are surprisingly plentiful and their vendors are found in the *Resource Directory*. Finely woven of rayon, these decades-old ribbons have a silken hand and stunning hues. Each type of ribbon serves a special need, so *Romancing Ribbons* teaches techniques tailored to all manner of ribbons. From the satins and grosgrains of our youth, to rediscovered wired ribbons, to opulent Japanese ribbons, there are flowers here to be made and pleasure to be had in the making!

Generally, the fineness of the ribbon is related to its cost. The more finely woven, the more malleable the ribbon, the fancier the coloration (complexly woven hues, overdyed, or airbrushed shades), the more costly the ribbon. Most ribbon is mass-produced. Today, though, a home-based industry in hand-dyed ribbon flourishes. Because natural fibers best accept dyes, imported silk and cotton ribbon, or vintage rayon velvet, are best for painting, dyeing, and over-dyeing. Of the ribbon imports, the Japanese and French are collected, but beautiful domestic ribbons are sought as well. A good value wired ribbon is Offray's line, also sold as Lion Ribbon.®

Many of this book's floral pieces draw heavily on Mokuba's vast line. This sets the models in *Romancing Ribbons* apart from much of the ribbonwork being done today. Discerning shops carry the Mokuba ribbons (see *Resources*). Worth the additional expense are French wired Elégance Ribbons from Quilter's Resource and those from Vaban, Inc., to name just two. While those brands are made in France, today even domestic wired ribbons tend generically to be called French ribbons. Think of French as in French fries which, as McDonald's® has proven, can be made anywhere in the world! With that domestic thought, let's look more closely at ribbonart's materials, tools, and techniques. This information lays the groundwork for making the projects and leads on to the Lessons.

RIBBON AND ORNAMENT MATERIALS

RIBBON CHARACTERISTICS

Types of Ribbon

Ribbons include rayon, straight or bias-cut silk, metallic, velvet, wired ombré acetate, polyester, georgette, organza, plain-bound and pleated satin, and grosgrain. Which ribbon do I use where? How do I use them? The answer is found in the ribbonart photographs. Each lesson lists suitable ribbons for that lesson, then cites ribbon selected for a specific project.

Malleability

This property is important for sculpting ribbon flowers. Seek a silky hand, even in wired ribbons. Avoid stiff "craft ribbons" heavy with sizing, for their wire is too thick for the fine scale of this book's ribbon blooms.

Washability

We each have our own level of acceptable risk. For you, how washable must your ribbonwork be? Pre-test if washability concerns you. If your project is an Album block on pale cloth, pin the pre-washed ribbon to the background cloth and test this combination for washability. For Ribbon Appliqué® in quiltmaking, I require stable color in dampness or when water is spilled, but I don't intend washability. And the wire in French ribbon? A metallurgist notes that like surgical steel, stainless wire left in ribbon will not corrode. Copper-wired ribbon, he cautioned, may develop a patina "in ninety years or so—especially if left outside".

Evening purse by Suzanne Charleston, showing her signature details: ribbon straw and puffed and stuffed buds.

Ironability

Wired ribbon can also be ironed (synthetic setting) after washing. You can iron ribbon flat or texture it by ironing dry the still crumpled ribbon. Experiment with effects achieved by crimping dampened ribbon with a hair-curling iron. Craft stores specializing in flower-making supplies sell "flower irons". Electric flower irons have interchangeable shaping attachments for cupping and veining, for example. Use such irons with caution. Most have no thermostat and get scorching hot the longer they are left on.

Ribbon Stiffeners

I love the corsage-like delicacy of narrow Japanese ribbons looped lavishly as a backdrop to my ribbon flowers, but such fine ribbon eventually flops. To be kept fresh-looking, it should be stiffened. While craft stores carry commercial ribbon/cloth sizings, even the most inexpensive hair spray is an excellent stiffener. Hair spray's critical ingredient is resin, that sap which, over eons, nature hardens into semi-precious amber. Hold that romantic thought while you spray-stiffen your ribbonart! Wired ribbon will hold any shape it is molded into while wet with hair spray. This is a boon, especially when edge-pleating petals.

Protective Sprays

Krylon®, a clear acrylic fixative, comes in a spray can and is available at art supply stores. Scotch Guard® is a widely available spray-on moisture repellent. Both sprays protect ribbonart from dirt and damage. Read their labels for specific properties and applications.

DEVELOPING AN HEIRLOOM RIBBON COLLECTION

Like gloves, scarves, buttons and postcards, ribbons are collectibles, kept for sentiment's sake from one generation to another. While some types of ribbon can be purchased inexpensively, luxurious ribbons and the sum total of a ribbon artist's palette are costly. Initially, you'll gather ribbon in a wide variety of colors,

Bonnie Campbell and Katya Sienkiewicz, childhood best friends, pose accommodatingly in paired pansy hats.

widths, types and textures. As you fashion ribbon into flowers, you'll develop a style with particular ribbon types, sizes and colors.

Janet Stauffacher, an acclaimed ribbon professional, uses only Size 5 ribbon for every component. Limiting ribbon use to a single size focuses her investment so she can spend more on broadening her selection in type and color. This systematic approach also leads to a well-defined style. As recognizable, but strikingly different, is Lorraine Fukuwa's ribbon jewelry *(Lesson 4)*. Lorraine focuses on velvet and organza flowers. When the thick plush dictates it, she keeps the petals to a low number. Thus, economics, taste and the nature of the ribbon affect the art of these professionals.

STORING A RIBBON COLLECTION

Creating with ribbon can produce a jumble! Establish a storage system for accessibility, for ease in returning ribbon to its place, and for preservation of its appearance. The dedicated ribboneuse needs permanent storage and portable current project storage. For permanent storage, I recycle any long, deep cardboard box roughly 15″ wide to accommodate legal size file folders. Then I store my ribbon in files alphabetized by color. Files of metallic ribbon, diaphanous ribbons (sheers), and velvets are labeled by type rather than color. Green requires augmented storage: a resealable plastic bag right behind the "Green Ribbon" folder.

These cardboard file boxes are portable within my home, since I work all over the place. When I travel, I follow Martha Pullen's advice and pack ribbon pre-selected for a special project into a Bass Pro® bait bag, a tidy soft-sided zippered case of see-through compartments. A sporting goods department offers inexpensive plastic fishing tackle boxes. These multi-compartmented boxes are excellent for storing ribbonry tools and equipment, ribbons, beads and other embellishments.

Wired Ribbon

This stores best wrapped around a paper towel tube. This avoids kinks in the wire. Second best is to fold it in figure eights, folding its packing paper along with the ribbon. I have made my peace with the tiny wire kinks, and even

On an Indian Summer afternoon, Katya Sienkiewicz wears the fuchsia necklace and earrings her mother designed as Project 5, Lesson Two. More fuchsias adorn her Memory Purse, also fashioned by the author.

find charm in this visible evidence of the ribbon's magical properties. My over-riding goal is to store a large ribbon collection compactly, and in a retrievable way.

Velvets and Satins

Like wire ribbon, velvets and satins can be wound around four fingers into small packets, then pinned.

Silk Ribbon for Embroidery

This stores well by color in re-sealable plastic bags—as does most ribbon. (Hefty One-Zip™ freezer weight bags are ideal!) Multiple shades of a hue can be kept in separate bags which have been hole-punched and threaded onto a steel key ring. Bead and craft stores as well as large office supply stores carry multi-sized re-sealable plastic bags.

BASES FOR RIBBON ORNAMENT

Buckram or AidaPlus®

Traditionally, buckram was the preferred foundation onto which ribbon flowers were stitched. In antique costume, the flowers were buckram-backed. They could thus be removed and switched, like jewelry, from one garment to another. I use a Zweigart product called AidaPlus (available in craft stores) to back my ribbonwork. It is stiffened Aida cloth (cross-stitch canvas in a range of colors) and cuts easily with scissors. Because it is backed with a fiber coating, the raw edges won't ravel.

Glue-stiffened Ribbon

Professional ribboneuse Lorraine Fukuwa folds a 6½″ length of size 9 ribbon into a loop, gluing it into a stiffened rectangle with its raw edges tucked under at the back of a floral piece. Again by gluing, she attaches this foundation to the appropriate finding.

Findings

Findings for ribbon art include pin and earring backs, hair combs, barrettes, shoe clips, mitten clips, earrings and necklaces. Floral ribbon corsages look elegant held by a simple 2″ hatpin. To my eye, no necklace is quite as romantic as the sim-

ple bow-tied ribbon. A notions catalogue like Clotilde's® will inspire you with products to ornament with ribbon flowers. Stationary departments may also offer something which, by the addition of a ribbon flower, can be made into a handsome gift. So might the clothing or sporting goods department. I purchased a fishing vest and aspire to decorate its multiple pockets into an enviable stitcher's vest.

Other Objects for Ribbon Ornament

Only your imagination sets limits here! Obvious ribbon flower sites include more substantial ready-made objects like pillows, mirrors, curtain tie-backs, purses, jewelry and cosmetic cases. Similarly suited are photo or other album books, picture frames, boxes, key chains, umbrellas, totes, eyeglass cases, sewing kits and purses. Ready-to-wear (from sweaters to sweat togs, from vests to aprons, and on to shirts, hats, ties, gloves and scarves) becomes boutique material when adorned by ribbon flowers.

EMBELLISHMENT FOR RIBBON ORNAMENT

Signature Touch

An artist's unique style is often characterized by her embellishing touches. Look through the pictured ribbonwork for glued-on glitter, buttons, charms, silk buds, and wisps of silk ribbon stiffened to look like fern or moss. Gold metallic ribbon, frayed out so that it looks loose and straw-like, is an appealing embellishment which catches your eye in Suzanne Charleston's work (page 8).

Fancy Touches

In a file so named, I keep evocative odds and ends for possible use in ribbonwork: raffia (looped as though straw behind a sunflower brooch, for a country look), old lace, bits of embroidery, vintage handkerchiefs, and wire a-twinkle with metallic stars from a party hat.

Coiled Wire Tendrils

On a spool, store the copper wire pulled from ribbon. To curl it into a tendril embellishment, coil it around a narrow cylinder, like a crochet hook handle. For green tendrils, use floral tape-wrapped stems from manufactured leaves or flowers. Bead wire, 28 gauge, (purchased by the spool) can attach a flower to a comb or other finding. It can also be coiled into tendrils.

Feathers

Feathers both found and purchased may inspire a ribbon flower piece. I keep one peacock feather to incorporate in something opulently Victorian. A second one remains in my embellishment box for me to dream on.

Silk Flowers

Commercial silk flowers also have potential. They make good samples for translating into ribbon and can occasionally be incorporated into a ribbon piece.

Leaves

Collect manufactured leaves from silk flowers, or those purchased separately as trims from craft, millinery, and fancy-work suppliers. I love the fronds of velvet rose leaves and the silk maidenhair fern from Lacis, and velvet pods from Dawn's Discount Lace (see *Resources*).

Beads

Seed beads and bugle beads (tubular beads) are a natural embellishment for ribbonwork. The combination of a bugle bead topped off by seed beads makes a fine flat-laying stamen. Notice in the photographs how differently each ribbon artist uses beading.

Stamens

This botanical detail defines many flowers. My favorite double-ended stamens come from Lacis. You can also make stamens with beads, or with embroidery thread or silk ribbon floss, finished into French knots. Stamens can be fashioned from yarn loops, shorn off, or they can be made like pods, stuffed ribbon circles. Any of the new age modeling materials: Fimo®, Cernit®, Pro-Mat®, and Formello® can be molded into flower centers and oven baked to ceramic hardness. Great for a dramatic sun-

flower or daisy center, you'll find these clays in art and craft stores.

Trims and Passementeries

Passementeries are trims made of gimp, cord, braid, or beads. Trims are classic milliner's embellishment when used in combination with ribbon flowers. Collect old trims and exquisite contemporary imports. Paulette Knight has enviable French metallic lace edgings (see *Resources*).

TOOLS AND EQUIPMENT FOR RIBBON ORNAMENT

Ruler

A 6″ plastic ruler marked in inches, centimeters, and millimeters is handy. A tape measure is the most compact tool to measure long lengths.

Template Material

Contac® paper or other sticky-backed self-adhering paper makes convenient template material for Ribbon Appliqué. Plastic-coated freezer paper also makes good templates. It is translucent enough to trace through, and a freezer paper pattern adheres when ironed to cloth.

Needles

Sharps size #10–#11. These are good for gathering and excellent for attaching ribbon and doing beading.

Milliner's Straw Needles size #10–#11. Often called simply milliner's needles, these fine, long needles originated for stitching flowers to straw hats. They are my favorite all-purpose ribbonwork and Ribbon Appliqué needles.

Chenilles size #22–#26. These are sharp pointed, large eyed, good for heavier threads and embroidery. My favorites for narrow silk ribbon embroidery are the extremely fine chenilles #26. For wider ribbon embroidery use the lower chenille numbers (#24 or #22). Their larger eye pokes a bigger hole in the cloth so that the ribbon passing through frays less. (If fraying is a problem, use Mokuba's Heirloom Sylk®, rather than 100% silk.) Have a mixed size set of chenilles to adjust the needle's size to the ribbon's width.

Needle Threader

A fine needlethreader is sometimes

She Wore a Velvet Ribbon, *a tailored rose necklace to be tied in a bow at one's nape, fashioned of Elégance and Mokuba ribbon by the author.*

Elly is pictured enjoying flowers, both fanciful and natural. Pansies from Lesson Two adorn a Mokuba striped velvet ribbon necklace, fashioned by the author.

The ribbon pansies on Katya's hat (fashioned by the author) rival the garden flowers.

critical, so keep one handy. For silk ribbon or floss, fold a 1/8″ x 2″ piece of scrap paper in half lengthwise and push it through the chenille needle's eye. This makes an easily threaded paper loop by which to pull the thread back through the eye.

Thread

A strong thread is needed for gathering and securing ribbon. Milliner's thread is ideal. Nymo®, a Belding Corticelli thread, is particularly durable, though fine. Bead stores, many quilt stores, and large fabric shops carry it. Strong hand-sewing thread works well. While too slippery to hold ribbon gathers in place well, silk thread is excellent for stitching a flower or for appliquéing. My favorite "invisible" thread for those tasks is Sulky's® 100% polyester.

Beeswax

Beeswax stiffens thread so it tangles less, coats it so it frays less, causes the thread to drag slightly so it holds gathers better, and protects the thread against the cutting edge of bugle beads.

Thimble

Keep a thimble on hand for those times when you need a mighty push to get the needle through multiple ribbon layers, or to protect your fingertip from the fine sharps and milliners' needles.

Pins

Silk pins or the Japanese glass-headed pins, each about 1″ to 1½″ long, are excellent for ribbonwork. They must be fine enough not to damage the ribbon or leave a visible hole.

Scissors

Wire-cutting Scissors: use utility scissors or a child's craft scissors for cutting wired ribbons. The wire dulls scissors!

Embroidery Scissors: keep embroidery scissors near at hand for cutting thread and non-wired ribbons.

5″ Sewing Scissors: use these for cutting cloth and UltraSuede shapes.

5″ Paper Scissors: use these for cutting templates and paper bases for flower centers such as Lesson Six's sunflower.

Embroidery Hoop

Use an embroidery hoop when doing Ribbon Appliqué or silk ribbon embroidery. A 6″ diameter hoop holds the cloth taut, and allows both hands to function.

Pens and Colored Markers

Few of ribbonry's stitches actually show in the end. I use a neutral colored thread like white Nymo throughout. I then camoflage any stitches which do show with fine-pointed colored markers matched to the ribbon. Pigma Micron .01 pens in assorted colors are permanent and ideal for this, but inexpensive fine tip watercolor markers also work well.

I also use watercolor markers to add subtle color to ribbon flowers. Pigma .01 pens in black can add spots to the throat of a foxglove or jet streaks to a pansy. A superfine Pigma .005 black pen is useful for marking measurement dots on ribbon, or for noting the measurement on the underside of work in progress.

Beading Wire

A medium weight beading wire (28 gauge) is useful for beading stand-up stamens, or for wrapping blossom bases, rather than sewing them. Bead wires naturally form a stem when incorporated in Suzanne Charleston's Puffed and Stuffed Buds, for example(see page 138). When wrapped with green floral tape, these stems look realistic and fit easily into a ribbon flower arrangement.

Bead wire can be purchased by the spool and used to attach a flower to a comb or other finding.

Floral Tape

This is a stretchy paper tape available at craft stores or floral suppliers. Fully extended, it lies almost flat and binds fabric, ribbon ends, or wires into stems. To save time, buy stem green tape.

Crushers

After decades of non-crushable velvet and perky polyesters, the rumpled look of natural fibers has a longed-for familiarity. Rayon ribbons (both flat and velvet), silk, and lustrous georgette ribbons all nestle down, timelessly, against a back-

One of the author's gentleman neighbors sports a Lesson Two pansy on his fishing hat.

ground and settle into old-fashioned light-catching folds.

More recent synthetics take less gracefully to the prospect of generations in a trunk. When crushed, even these ribbons will take on the fragile aspect of pressed flowers. Moisture (water or steam) and applied pressure romanticize a modern ribbon into vintage grace.

It is easier to crush the ribbon before you make the flower. However, if you make a flower, and then decide to wrinkle its ribbon as an afterthought, use hemostats or a pair of larger needle-nosed pliers. Each of these tools crushes damp ribbon into softer folds.

Hemostats

This scissor-handled medical clamp works to some extent like craft tweezers, but has a stronger grip. Its scored edges clutch the ribbon, then lock. Hemostats can pull the wire out of the selvage to begin gathering or sculpt tight whorls at a rose's center.

Long-Handled Craft Tweezers

These are the kind used by stamp collectors. Like a hummingbird's bill, they can reach down into a rolled flower's center and beneath tight petals to shape the finished flower.

Needle-Nose Pliers

Fine pliers are useful in shaping ribbon flowers, edge-pleating wired ribbon, or tugging silk ribbon-threaded chenille needles through finely woven cloth. In 1995 Fiskars came out with both a tweezer/magnifier tool and bent-tipped pliers ideal for ribbon flower making.

Round Pommeled Awl

Use the awl's point to score veins into velvet leaves. Use its round pommel to press a concave curve into acetate ribbon which has been sized with hair spray.

Pleaters

Clotilde's Perfect Pleater® and the Pullen Pleater®, both designed for smocking, also pleat ribbon. Wired ribbon is easy to pleat at quarter-inch intervals without a special tool, while some ribbons (including Mokuba) come pre-pleated. See the *Resource Directory* for businesses which will pleat your ribbon by the yard.

Iron

For ribbonwork you need an iron which irons synthetics without melting them. But you also need one which can get searing hot. An old, pre-1980's iron will sear the raw edge of synthetic ribbon. When compared with other modern irons, the Bernette® from your Bernina dealer or the Black and Decker Classic Iron® both get very hot—a plus for craft work.

Ideally, have a modern iron for clean pressing ribbon, and an old iron for searing and other tasks which might dirty the ironing plate.

Glue

White Glue: Gem-Tac is a white glue which glues cloth to cloth, plastic, or metal and dries flexible. Perfect for ribbonwork!

Gluestick: keep a gluestick with your ribbonry supplies. Use it to hold Ribbon Appliqués together temporarily, prior to sewing. To prevent staining later, use gluestick where it will not wet through a visible, top layer in the end product.

Glue in a tube: Bond 527 is a multipurpose glue-in-a-tube for china, glass, metal, fabric and paper. It quickly dries clear and has a precision tip for fine work.

Glue Gun

The smallest size glue gun (used in conjunction with a toothpick) aids ribbon flower projects. Small ones are inexpensive and widely available.

Toothpicks

Keep these on hand for dabbing glue into hard to reach places.

Ribbon Squares

CONVEYING MEASUREMENT:
WHICH WAY WORKS BEST WITH RIBBON?

Ribbon Sizes

For centuries, ribbons have been woven to an old width unit called lignes (11 lignes per inch; 9 lignes per 2 centimeters). Ribbon widths are measured in millimeters (mm) and translate imprecisely into inches. In *Romancing Ribbons,* the most commonly used widths are size 3 (⅝˝), size 5 (⅞˝), and size 9 (1½˝ wide). Silk embroidery ribbon is sold by its mm width, while wider ribbons are sold by sizes or by their widths cited in fractions of inches. A ribbon's width is measured from bound edge to bound edge.

Measurement

Each ribbon flower in this book is taught to a specific size. It is liberating to realize that virtually any flower can be made from more than one size of ribbon. Think of ribbon measurements as proportions, rather than in inches. Therefore, measure a ribbon's unit length by multiples of its width.

In the Lessons, the ribbon width always precedes its length. The length can be given in various ways. Length can be cited in inches, or it can be given as a multiple of ribbon widths (RWs). For example: "Make a 1½˝ x 6˝ (4RWs) cut of ribbon." The RWs number tells you how many ribbon-widths must make up the cut unit's length. The proportion of width (RW) to length (repeats of RWs) is the key to making that flower from ribbon of any width.

There's an easier way to measure! Because the translation from millimeters to inches to RWs rarely comes out precisely, the easiest way to calculate required ribbon length is in terms of ribbon squares. A square is formed when you fold the raw edge (a ribbon's width) down on the diagonal—like a turnover—to lie on top of the adjacent selvage *(GS-1)*. The ribbon's raw edge is also the width of the square thus formed when you open the turnover back up *(GS-1)*. Thus, if you measure a ribbon's length by "SQs" (squares), you don't have to deal with disconcerting fractions. One square—or even ¾, ½, or ¼ square is close enough to make any flower come out right!

Convey ribbon flower formulas most quickly not by citing measurement, but by citing a ribbon's size and its length in either RWs or SQs. Example: "Cut a (1½˝ x 6˝) ribbon piece" means the same as "Cut a (sz9 x 4SQs) ribbon piece." To teach this mode of expression, *Romancing Ribbons* presents ribbon cuts in inches followed parenthetically by ribbon size and number of squares.

COMMON RIBBON WIDTHS

Size #1H = ⁵⁄₁₆˝ (8mm)

Size #2 = ⁷⁄₁₆˝ (11mm)

Size #3 = ⅝˝ (16mm)

Size #5 = ⅞˝ (22mm)

Size #9 = 1⁷⁄₁₆˝ (cited in inches as 1½˝; or as 35mm)

Size #16 = 2˝ (49mm)

Size #40 = 2¾˝ (67mm)

Size #80 = 3⅛˝ (79mm)

Size #100 = 4˝ (98mm)

Ribbonry's Law of Relativity

The wider the ribbon, the longer its gathering unit will be; the narrower the ribbon, the shorter its gathering unit will be. Gathering units are the patterns (triangles, rectangles, and crescent-shapes) in which gathering stitches are taken. The gathering unit length is always measured from widest point to widest point *(GS-2)*. In general, a gathered petal takes three ribbon squares, so a five-petaled flower, with seam allowance, would take 15½ squares.

A.

(RW)

RIBBON WIDTHS (RWS) AND
RIBBON SQUARES (SQS)
A ribbon's width (RW) is the same size as a ribbon square (SQ). It simply takes the odd math out of ribbon measuring if you talk of a ribbon's length in terms of squares.

EXAMPLE: When a sz5 x 3SQs of ribbon is needed:
1. Fold the sz3 ribbon's raw edge down to get the square (B).
2. Fold the square 2 more times to get 3 squares (C).

B.

Fold corner down to see the ribbon "square" (SQ).

C.

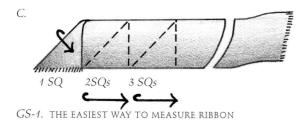

1 SQ   *2SQs*   *3 SQs*

GS-1. THE EASIEST WAY TO MEASURE RIBBON

RAKE RUCHING BEING DONE AT 3RWS PER PETAL

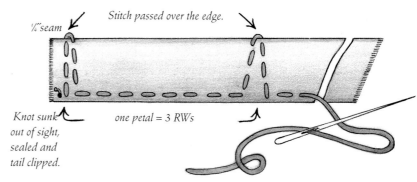

¼" seam   *Stitch passed over the edge.*

Knot sunk out of sight, sealed and tail clipped.   *one petal = 3 RWs*

GS-2. GATHERING UNIT

Gift wrap ornament featuring a Cabbage Rose *from Lesson One.*
This is fashioned by the author, using Lesson One's fringed ribbon center and purchased velvet leaves.

Wooden Clamp Clothespins

Wooden clothespins serve as a third hand for such ribbonry tasks as holding fuchsia stamens while the glue dries.

Hair Wave Clips

Another third hand, these clamps hold ribbon flowers in progress. Longer than clothespins, they can hold larger flowers or multi-folded ribbon.

Clear Nail Polish

In its handy brush-cap container, clear nail polish is a quick-drying sealant. It seals ribbon's raw edges against fraying, ensures that a thread knot stays tied, and hardens thread ends to ease threading. Always seal wired ribbon cuts of 6″ length or less. Use clear, colorless, quick-drying polish and wipe the brush almost dry against the lip of the bottle.

Double-stick Tape

Keep this handy office tape among your ribbon tools. It pastes cloth and ribbon layouts quickly. For example, a collage made with ribbon flowers and UltraSuede can be stuck together with gluestick or double-stick tape. Double-stick tape aided in covering the sunflower's base *(Lesson Six)* and arranging the petals around it.

Design Board

Collect several cardboard fabric bolt sleeves as design boards. The ideal design board holds the flower tidily every step of the way as you fashion it from cut ribbon segments to prepared units to the finished flower, leaves and bud. Especially for assembly line production, some method for holding the unit parts becomes critical.

Ribbonry units contained in sealable plastic sandwich bags, for example, are more quickly accessible when pinned sequentially onto a design board. The Felsan Board (felt holds the ribbon on one side, sandpaper covers the other side) is convenient, and comes in a handy travel size and in a generous board large enough to hold production work (see *Resources*).

FLOWER-MAKING TECHNIQUES

Right-Handed and Left-Handed

Please note that for right-handers, the term "starting end" means the right-hand end of a ribbon length. (A right-hander will stitch-gather a ribbon length or roll a ribbon length from right to left.) For left-handers, the term "starting end" means the left-hand end. (A left-hander will stitch-gather a ribbon length or roll a ribbon length from left to right.) Given the simplicity of this book's flowers, the directions and illustrations are all for right-handed stitchers unless otherwise noted.

Antiqueing Wired Ribbon

Fold one yard of French wired ribbon (any width) into a square. Run hot tap water over it. Scrunch the wet square tightly in your fist; then leave it folded in a heap to dry overnight. The next morning

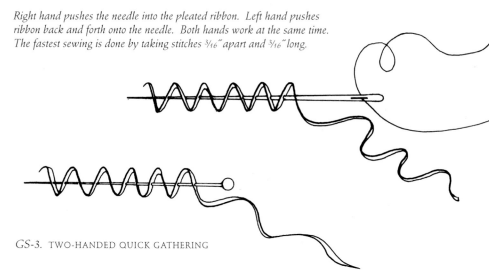

Right hand pushes the needle into the pleated ribbon. Left hand pushes ribbon back and forth onto the needle. Both hands work at the same time. The fastest sewing is done by taking stitches 3/16″ apart and 3/16″ long.

GS-3. TWO-HANDED QUICK GATHERING

the ribbon length will have changed into a linear landscape of folded hillocks whose angles catch the light and set it a-dance.

This ribbon looks elegantly olde—a wrinkled thing, long cherished. You'll feel the stir of long-forgotten memories. Try antiqueing other ribbons as well. While modern polyester velvet resists crushing, steam ironing can crumple 100% rayon velvet pile into the lustrous stuff of childhood recollections.

Gathering on the Wire

Gathering can be done by pulling the wire in wired ribbon. You can pull the wire in the bottom edge of the ribbon, the top edge of the ribbon, or both. Avoid pulling the wire out of the opposite end or even breaking the fragile copper wire. To gather the full length of one ribbon edge, gather from the top of the ribbon to its center, and then from the bottom of the ribbon to its center.

U-turn Gathering on the Wire

This term denotes both ends of a single wire pulled simultaneously. U-turn gather shorter ribbon cuts to avoid pulling the wire out of reach on the end not pulled. U-turn gathering is also efficient for gathering small pieces. Pinching the two wires with a hemostat, then pulling the ribbon down in the opposite direction simultaneously, facilitates gathering a small (up to 12″ long) length of ribbon.

Stitch-Gathering

Gathering can be done with a needle and thread, taking a running stitch. When you gather flowers, keep your stitches relaxed and relatively long: a generous 3/16″ in length, front and back *(GS-3)*. To quick-gather: push the fabric with one hand, folding it on to the needle, while you rock the needle through the folds with the other hand. Why not tiny stitches? Imagine if you took tiny stitches on the sewing machine, then pulled the bobbin thread to gather. Little gathering would occur, because there is virtually no up space or down space between such tiny stitches.

☆ Miniature Memo: On short lengths, or to gather narrow ribbon, closer stitches are required to create finer ruffles.

Rolling

Gathering a length of ribbon into ruffles, then rolling the length concentrically around a stem-center, is how roses, peonies, carnations and camellias are made.

Twisting

A wire-gathered ribbon can be twisted a full turn every 2 to 3RWs to form scalloped petals. A 5/8″ wide wired ribbon makes charming roses when twisted into scallops and wound into a flower. To make a particularly voluptuous rose, take a 1½ yard length of 1½″ wide wired ribbon and twist it into petals, using 2½ RWs per scallop.

Swirling

Lesson One teaches straight line gathering. If a length of wire ribbon is folded in half lengthwise and gathered along that fold, the two wired edges almost automatically swirl into cupped shapes (see page 37). By sculpting with tweezers, the swirls can be emphasized. Swirls make beautiful flowers rising from a drooping stem or hanging down from a stalk.

Heat-Shaping

Moderate heat can shape a ribbon petal. A curling iron, crimping iron, or flower iron can all shape acetate ribbon. Acetate ribbon can be shaped over the point of an iron. A cut petal shape, for example, can be pressed convexly into a curve. A longer piece of ribbon can be pulled over the iron's tip to curve the center of the strip. Test the iron's heat to shape, not sear, the ribbon. You can also pressure-shape ribbon. To do this, lay a hair spray soaked ribbon on cardboard and press a shallow hollow into it with the pommel of an awl or the bowl of a tablespoon, pulled down and towards you. You can also resort to a heat-pressing method to crush an already shaped flower, but with caution, since a flower is more fragile than flat ribbon.

Heat-Sealing a Ribbon's Raw Edge

A dry, hot (linen setting) iron can sear the cut edge of acetate ribbon. An iron several decades old will get the hottest and work the best for this. Set the iron upright and cautiously use both hands to guide the ribbon edges over the tip of the iron. Ribbon can be cut into non-linear shapes (circles for centers, petals) and the edges heat-sealed. (This makes stitch-gathering the edge of small circles much easier.) Use caution to avoid burning fingertips and soiling the iron. Experiment to see what other ribbon fibers can be heat-sealed.

Alternatively, any raw edge can be sealed with clear nail polish. Consider! If you can seal cut ribbon, you change the very nature of the material. Like leather, any shape can now be cut from it. Ribbon flowers edge-sealed (compared to those edge-hemmed) are less bulky, more delicate and realistic.

Wire-Wrapping

Wrapping with wire quickly secures multiples (petals, looped ribbon floss or silk embroidery ribbon for stamens, or concentric rolls of a ribbon). Use the copper wire pulled from ribbon to wrap around the base of the multiples, or purchase fine spool wire from a bead store or a craft shop which specializes in flower-making supplies.

Tacking

Ribbon can be shaped by rolling its edges and tack-stitching them down. Early in this century, this was a popular way to make separate petal roses like the Cherokee Rose. When separate petals are made today, they are stitch-gathered into a curve *(Lesson Three)*, then tack-stitched into a fan of overlapping edges. A single length of wired ribbon is an easier rose-making method. With the latter, tacking is used to hold the final shaping of the rose in place. The tack stitch is a sturdy all-purpose stitch for appliqué and ribbon flower construction.

Assembling Techniques

To assemble a compound flower like a pansy, the separate units must be sewn together. If you have a good thread match, use a tiny tack stitch over the ribbon edge to attach one flower part to another. If the thread does not match the ribbon color well, use the pointillist appliqué stitch. Face the front of the flower and take the pointillist stitch out of and back into the same hole. On the flower's underneath side, carry the thread forward for ⅛″ before taking the next stitch. Virtually no thread will show on the front side. The secret? It is almost impossible to stitch in and out of the same spot, so the stitch is quite tiny.

Gluing

Quicker than stitching, gluing secures one element to another. Glue stamens to flowers, leaves to flowers, flowers to fabric, and finished ribbonwork to a base. Combined with stitching, it ensures stability. For production work, gluing is essential.

A Road Map to the Lessons

*T*he preceding wealth of information equips us well for our ribbonry journey. Instructions here in *Getting Started* are not repeated, but should be reviewed before beginning each new lesson.

Six lessons follow to guide you along the ribbon garden path. At each stop along the way, redolent flowers bloom. By Eden's end, your dreams will be a-blossom—and you'll know exactly how to bring them into flower, one petal at a time. Each lesson teaches projects easily made, suggests how you can hybridize the basic flower, and inspires with colorful models. All conspire to set your flower-making fancies a-dance! Here's a road map to the lessons:

Lesson One uses the simplest flower gathering pattern of all—a straight line. From this basic beginning, bouquets of flowers can be made.

Lesson Two features flowers gathered in three unique patterns. The first line bends sharply in a diamond pattern and makes flowers reminiscent of fuchsias, clematis, azaleas, fruit blossoms and trumpet flowers. The second bends gently into a U-shape, then adds two crescent moons to magically produce perfect pansies. The third gather line is asymmetrical and looks like a check mark or the silhouette of a sugar scoop. From such humble beginnings come an elegant, slender petal to enhance many a flower.

Lesson Three studies curved line gathers from shallow crescent moons to the shape of halved oranges; and from single petals to petals made all-in-a-row.

Lesson Four instructs in mountain/valley ruching and rake ruching. It waxes romantic about flowers gathered in the steep peaks of the Tetons or in the sparsely spiked outline of an old iron garden rake.

Lesson Five names a cluster of techniques Ribbon Appliqué. Because this method establishes ribbon flowers firmly in the lexicon of late twentieth century quiltmaking, it ensures ribbon blooms an heirloom role. The basics of silk ribbon embroidery are taught here as well, for this lesson integrates ribbon flowers, silk ribbon embroidery, and classic Album Quilt appliqué.

Lesson Six crescendos with flowers fashioned from ribbons tied, knotted, pleated, looped, folded and folded-and-rolled. Thus are made some of ribbonry's simplest yet most spectacular flowers.

Our "map" shows the lessons' main roads: the side roads you'll discover by exploring. Enjoy the journey!

An original Album block design by Wendy Grande from her quilt, Ribbon Appliqué.

The Garden in Bloom

In art the hand can never execute anything higher than the heart can inspire. —Ralph Waldo Emerson

Who will disagree? Flowers are symbols, visible signs of invisible things. We are attracted to flowers by their beauty and for many this is enough. Some sense in these wildings a freedom, an unexpectedness, a gift. Where flowers flourish, we know the land is healthy. Even without giving it much thought, this comforts us. Though they bloom only briefly, we get to know them. Quickly they become part of our neighborhood, part of our world. Some we cultivate, and like friends they become important to our lives. After all, we gather pictures of persons dear to us and carry their likenesses in our pockets. How understandable then, this urge to capture floral images, to attach these ancient and communal beauties to our lives. To fashion blooms pays them homage; to wear flowers from our hand acknowledges our indebtedness to all flowers. Consider: what would life be without flowers? Flowers, sewn, grace the spot on which we place them; stitching them invokes a blessing.

Then, too, we are not so far removed from our Victorian foremothers who, with floral bouquets, spelled out specific messages. Even late in the twentieth century, we understand flowers as eminently expressive. Thus stitched, flowers can formulate a thought, reflect a mood, convey even our deepest feelings. Ease in floral expression comes with the practice of it. We feel this as we fashion an ornament to give to another. After all, the most hopeful thing for any of us is the beauty of the world around us; that and the love of the people around us. Thus making ribbon flowers, then sharing them as gifts, cultivates beauty both of this world and of the spirit.

The cultivars these lessons teach sprout from seeds of promise. Can you doubt that to make them will bring you peaceful, happy moments? Like nature's flowers, the memory of their making will become a timepost, keeping you in touch with the seasons. Weave these ribbon flowers, then, into the tapestry of your life. Romance them: follow your fancy, halo your days with them, enjoy the adventure! Take the stitcher's path to places old and unexpected, or to understandings fresh with wonder. These ribbon gardens will leave their memory with you, so that even cuttings given away are yours forever. A lifetime from now, someone admiring your everlastings will surely smile, remembering you—you who so romanced a ribbon that it turned into a rose.

Detail From Rosa Rugosa—Victorian Beach Rose

Flowers Made From Ribbon Gathered in a Straight Line

*R*ibbons, you'll find, can be folded, twisted, pleated, swirled, gathered—and gathered repetitiously in set patterns—all to fashion flowers. To begin our flower-making, the simplest pattern, straight-line gathering, is a fine place to start.

Review *Getting Started.*

RIBBON TYPES

Organza, raw-edged bias-cut silk, plus a gamut of bound-edge ribbons: wired ribbon, single or double-faced satin, grosgrain, velvet, rayon, silk, acetate, moiré and georgette.

RIBBON SIZES

From 8mm up to 2″ wide (size 1H up to size 16).

PROJECTS

Project 1: The pin-on fancy flower
Project 2: Three easy pieces—fancy silk
flowers
Fancy Flower #1—Edge-gathered
Fancy Flower #2—Two edge-
gathered
Fancy Flower #3—Fold-gathered
Project 3: A primrose necklace
Project 4: A miniature basket of blooms—
a brooch

RIBBON FLOWER TECHNIQUES

Lesson One's techniques make both impressionistic flora and flora reminiscent of their natural sisters: Anemone, Aster, Bachelor's Button, Begonia, Calendula, Camellia, Campanulate (bell-shaped flowers), Bluebell, Canterbury Bell, Carnation, Cornflower, Cosmos, Chrysanthemum, Clover, Daffodil, Daisy (or Marguerite), Delphinium, Foxglove, Fruit (Apple, Berry), Gaillardia, Grape Hyacinth, Heather, Hollyhock, Hyacinth, Larkspur, Lily of the Valley, Moonflower, Morning Glory, Mountain Laurel, Myrtle Pod, Narcissus, Pansy, Petunia, Pin-on Fancy Flower, Pink, Pompom, Poppy, Primrose, Ranunculus, Rose Hip, Rose (Bourbon Rose, Cabbage Rose, Cherokee Rose, Pillow Rose, Sweetheart Rose, Noisette Rose, Turncoat Tea Rose), Spider Mum, Sunflower, Tuberose, Tulip, Water Lily, Wisteria and Zinnia.

RIBBON LEAF TECHNIQUES

Boat prow leaf, super-fast boat prow leaf, and bud leaf.

1-1. *The* Pin-on Fancy Flower *fashioned by the author: Lesson One, Project 1.*

THE PIN-ON FANCY FLOWER

One of this book's delights has been not only the fashioning but the wearing of its ornaments. I made the Project 1 flower to wear while the book's other models were being photographed. Though fancy, this flower was particularly simple to make, and I came to love its elegance and soft swath of color. A nostalgic hat pin held this accessory, and the blossom traveled well, emerging fresh from a tightly packed suitcase. Because others also admired it, let's learn this bloom first.

SUPPLIES

This flower can be made in many ribbon types, sizes, and colors. The following supplies were used to make one organza pin-on fancy flower as pictured in photo 1-1.

One Flower

Mokuba No. 4563 Organdy Ribbon, 50mm width in color 10—Cut one 2″ x 1yd. (sz16 x 18SQs) length.

Stamen

Mokuba No. 1520 Organdy Ribbon, 15mm width in color 49—Cut one ⅝″ x 2½″ length. Pull out thread to create ½″ of fringe on both the ribbon's ends.

Five gold double-ended stamens No. 83 from Lacis.

Two Leaves

Mokuba No. 4595 Luminous Ribbon, 25mm width in color 5—Cut three 1″ x 6″ (sz6 x 6SQs) lengths.

Backing

3″ x 4″ rectangle of loden green UltraSuede.

Finding

2″ long hatpin (gold, silver, or pearl tear-drop topped).

Basic sewing kit and ribbon tools

PROCEDURE

The Pin-On Fancy Flower in Organza

1. Hem the raw edges by tucking them under ¼″ at the starting and finishing ends *(1-1)*. Then fold these ends each down at a 45° angle and pin to hold.

2. Thread a milliner's #10 needle with 36″ of strong matching thread, doubled to 18″, and knotted. With this thread, running-stitch the ribbon's bottom edge from starting end to finishing end.

3. Pull your thread to gather after stitching every 10″ or so. Gather ribbon to a 12″ length *(1-1)*. Secure thread and remove pins.

4. Roll this gathered strip into a spiral around the starting end. Slip two long quilter's pins under the jelly-rolled selvages. Pin from the outside row to the center, bringing each round of gathered edges to the same level.

5. With a freshly threaded milliner's needle, whip-stitch the back of the flower, catching just the gathered edge, from the outside to the inside. Secure thread, and remove pins *(1-2)*.

FIGURES 1–6. PROJECT ONE

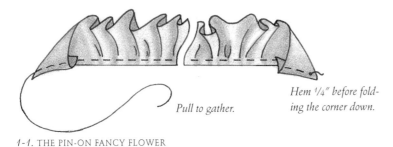

Pull to gather.

Hem ¼″ before folding the corner down.

1-1. THE PIN-ON FANCY FLOWER

A. Gold-edged organza, fringed

B. Five double-ended stamens, folded in half

Whip-stitch the spiraled selvages.

1-2.

C. Wrap ribbon around the stamens

1-3. STAMENS

Hybrids

To make a much fuller flower, cut a 2″ x 70″ (sz16 x 35SQs) length of Mokuba No. 4563 Organdy Ribbon and follow steps 1-5 above. Using a 3″ x 1 yd. (sz45 x 12SQs) length of Mokuba No. 4563 Organdy Ribbon, make this flower according to the Project 2 directions for Fancy Flower #2 and Fancy Flower #3.

Stamens

Fold the gold-edged organza ribbon in half, raw edge to raw edge (1-3A). Next, fold five double-ended gold stamens in half so that the gold heads are all together (1-3B). Wrap the ribbon around the stamens, making a bouquet of ten stamens surrounded by a silken fringe of brown and gold threads. Stitch to hold this bundle together (1-3C), then push it into place at the tight center of the flower. Stitch it into place. While I added my stamens as a finishing touch (1-4), they could have been incorporated at step 4, above.

Boat Prow Leaves

1. Fold ⅝″ x 6″ (sz3 x 9½SQs) ribbon in half lengthwise, laying cut edges one on top of the other (1-5A).

2. At fold #2, crease the corner up, mark a 45° angle at the fold end. When sewn, this crease forms a point: the boat prow leaf-tip.

3. Stitch-gather the ribbon from the point, down the crease, and along the bottom bound edge (1-5B).

4. Pull to gather to a 2″ long finished leaf. Secure the stitches and open the leaf (1-5C).

ASSEMBLY

1. Make three boat prow leaves and tack or glue them to the flower's underside.

2. Cut a circular backing of felt or UltraSuede. To finish the flower, glue this backing over the three leaf ends and to the flower's underside (1-6). Wear the flower pinned with a hat pin.

1-6. UNDERSIDE OF THE PIN-ON FANCY FLOWER

Insert stamens.

1-4. THE PIN-ON FANCY FLOWER IN ORGANZA

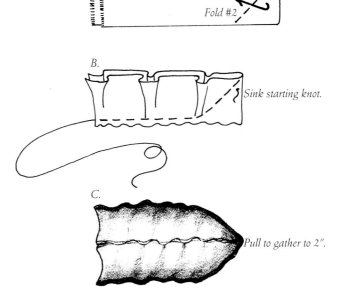

A.

Fold #1

Fold #2

B.

Sink starting knot.

C.

Pull to gather to 2″.

1-5. BOAT PROW LEAVES

1-2. Three Easy Pieces—Fancy Silk Flowers *fashioned by Diana Dickey: Project 2, Lesson One. (From top to bottom, left to right: Fancy Flowers #1, #2; #3, #1; #3,#2.)*

Project Two

3 EASY PIECES FANCY SILK FLOWERS

*S*o simple to make, so quick to stitch, these blooms become a signature accessory and a gift box staple. The flowers' flair is in the ribbon itself. For a tailored look, try plaid taffeta or grosgrain; for wintry elegance, use satin-backed velvet; for an artful splurge, use hand-dyed bias-cut silk or dye your own.

SUPPLIES

These Fancy Flowers can be made using many ribbon types, sizes and colors. The following supplies were used to make the Fancy Silk Flowers as pictured in photo 1-2.

Fancy Silk Flower #1

Bias-cut silk ribbon—Cut one 1½″ x 1 yd. (sz9 x 24SQs) ribbon length.

Fancy Silk Flower #2

Bias-cut silk ribbon—Cut one 3″ x 1 yd. (sz45 x 12SQs) ribbon length.

Fancy Silk Flower #3

Bias-cut silk ribbon—Cut one 3″ x 1 yd (sz45 x 12SQs) ribbon length.

Two Leaves

Bias-cut silk ribbon—Cut two 2″ x 6″ (sz16 x 3SQs) ribbon lengths.

Finding

Metal pin-back.

Hybrid

When you use narrower ribbon, you use shorter cuts.

PROCEDURE

Fancy Silk Flower #1—Single Edge-Gathered

This silk ribbon flower *(1-7)* is sophisticated and elegant. Diana Dickey fashioned it from Hanah hand-dyed silk, bias-cut (see *Resources*).

1. Stitch-gather one raw edge as in Project 1 *(1-1, again)*.

2. Roll gathered strip into a tight spiral with the gathered edges level and the back of the flower flat *(1-2, again)*.

3. On the flower's underside, whipstitch the whorl of gathered edges, to attach them, one to another *(1-2, again)*. The flower's diameter should be about 3″. Secure the stitches.

Bud-leaf

1. From the center, fold the left ribbon end down to the right, at an angle *(Fold #1, 1-8A)*. Next, fold the right end down to the left, over the first ribbon tail *(Fold #2)*. Pin to hold.

2. Running-stitch from **a** to **b** and pull stitches to gather. The distance from **a** to **b**, gathered, should be approximately 1″ *(1-8B)*. Secure the stitches.

ASSEMBLY

1. Tack two bud leaves to underside of flower *(1-7)*.

2. Align a pinback with the leaves and stitch in place.

☆ *Speed Tip:* Gathering can be done on the sewing machine. Final assembly can be done by gluing rather than by stitching. If glue is used, a backing is needed for stability. Glue a fabric backing over the leaves, then glue the pin-back to this backing.

Fancy Silk Flower #2—Two Edge-gathered

The two edge-gathered fancy flower is shown in *1-9*. Begin by folding the 3″ wide ribbon in half, from top to bottom, along its length *(1-10A)*. The fold line becomes the top edge of the flower. Fold the raw edges down as illustrated, then running-stitch the bottom edges and pull to gather both edges simultaneously. Roll the gathered strip in a spiral from starting end to finish to a 3″ diameter *(1-10B)*.

Fancy Silk Flower #3—Fold-Gathered

The fold-gathered fancy flower is much the same as the Fancy Silk Flower #1, but the petals are less deep while the flower itself is fuller *(1-11)*. To make it, fold the ribbon in half from top to bottom along its length, as in Fancy Silk Flower #2. This time, simply gather along the length-wise fold *(1-12A)*. The two bias-cut raw edges face upwards and swirl into petals as the fold line is gathered in tight concentric whorls.

Finish to a 3″ diameter as for Fancy Flower #1 and #2.

Hybrid

The begonia in *1-12B* was made from a 1½″ x 8½″ (sz9 x 5¾SQs) cut of vintage 100% rayon ribbon. Its edges are off-set by ¼″ *(1-13A)* and fold-gathered as in Fancy Flower #3. The ribbon's soft drape and luster promise abundant variations. Other ribbon types promise yet more hybrids, which is the glory of a ribbon garden. The narcissus-like flower *(1-13B)* is perkier, being made the same way, but out of shaded wire ribbon. Both blooms are about 1½″ in diameter.

FIGURES 7–11. PROJECT TWO

1-7. FANCY SILK FLOWER #1

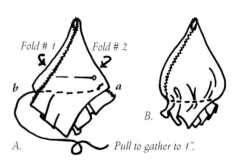

1-8. BUD LEAF

1-9. FANCY SILK FLOWER #2

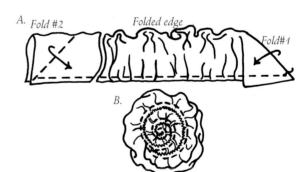

1-10. FANCY SILK FLOWER #2

1-11. FANCY SILK FLOWER #3

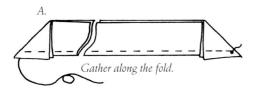

A.

Gather along the fold.

B.

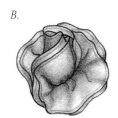

1-12. BEGONIA

A.

The back edge is ¼″ below the front edge.

Gather on the fold.

B.

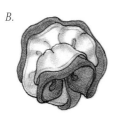

1-13. NARCISSUS

Project Three

A PRIMROSE NECKLACE

$\mathcal{O}$ld fashioned primroses are stitched to a ribbon worn around the throat. Though only several hours in the making, this simple jewel has almost infinite variations. For example, consider velvet flowers with metallic leaves, and bead or antique button blossom centers.

SUPPLIES

This necklace can be made in multiple ribbon types, sizes, and colors. The following supplies were used to make the primrose necklace as pictured in photo 1-3.

Single-layer Primroses

Wired ribbon—three pieces ⅝″ x 6″ (sz3 x 9½SQs) of Elégance ribbon, color #17, shaded yellow to lavender.

Boat Prow Leaves

Hanah bias-cut silk ribbon —eight pieces ⅝″ x 3″ (sz3 x 5SQs) of color FG (Flamingo Glacé).

Ornamental Vine

Mokuba No. 4599 Luminous Ribbon, 7mm x 1 yd. of color #5. (Pull a central thread down the ribbon's length to ruffle-gather it into a vine-like botanical element. Put a drop of clear nail polish at both raw-edged ends, to keep the gather thread from pulling back and allowing the ribbon to flatten again.)

Foundation

Cut three 1¼″ circles of AidaPlus coordinated to the flower ribbon color. (The model uses muslin color AidaPlus.)

Flower centers

1 yd. of 4mm overdyed silk embroidery ribbon in a yellow shade.

1-3. The Primrose Necklace *fashioned by the author: Project 3, Lesson One.*

Necklace ribbon

1 yd. of ⅝″ Elégance ribbon color #17, shaded yellow to lavender.

PROCEDURE

Primroses

Make three of shaded wired ribbon, the dark side being the flower's center. For each primrose:

1. U-turn gather a 6″ length of ribbon: pull the dark edge's wire up, both ends simultaneously (1-14A). Twist the wires together to hold the gathers. Coil the wires around a pin or pencil, then press them tightly to keep them out of the way (1-14B).

2. With ¼″ seam, stitch the raw-edged ends together. Secure stitches but don't cut the thread (1-14B).

3. With the same thread, whip-stitch gather the bottom edge and pull tightly to gather the flower center to ¼″ diameter (1-14C). Crush the flower tightly in your hand to antique it.

4. Tack-stitch the flower center to the foundation's center.

5. Use 12″ of 2mm silk ribbon per flower to embroider French knots on the primrose's center (1-15A).

Boat Prow Leaves

Make eight boat prow leaves as in Project 1. Four leaves surround the center flower and attach it to the outer two flowers (1-15B). The outer flowers each have two leaves.

ASSEMBLY

1. Stitch a row of three primroses, centered, onto the front of the necklace ribbon. Attach the flowers and leaves to each other and then to the ribbon by tack-stitching. Intertwine the ribbon vine as in 1-15C.

2. Clip the ribbon ends, so that the necklace finishes gracefully like a swallow's tail (1-15D). Seal the raw edges with clear nail polish.

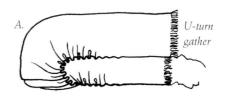

A. *U-turn gather*

B. *Coil the wires to keep them out of the way.*

Seam the raw edges together.

C. *Whip-stitch gather to pull the center more tightly.*

1-14. PRIMROSE

FIGURES 14–15. PROJECT THREE

A. French knot centers added

C. Ribbon Vine

B. Center flower with 4 leaves

D. Swallow-tail ends

1-15. PRIMROSE NECKLACE

MINIATURE BASKET OF BLOOMS—A BROOCH

*I*t takes only a couple of hours to make, but this basket pin (photo 1-4) overflows with charm. About the size of a pullet's egg, it is small enough to cradle in the palm of your hand and teaches miniature flower making. Almost any flower can be miniaturized simply by changing ribbon type and size. The basket pin's bloom is based on Project 3's primrose, but uses a shorter cut of narrower ribbon. The flowers' Lilliputian size calls for the fine hand of rayon or silk.

SUPPLIES

This brooch can be made in more than one ribbon type, size and color. The following supplies were used to make one miniature basket of blooms, Project 4, as pictured in photo 1-4.

Flowers

Mokuba No. 4882 Gradation Ribbon, color #5— Cut three 12mm x 3˝ (12mm x 6½SQs) lengths.

Leaves A

Mokuba No. 4595 Luminous Ribbon, color #5— Cut two 9mm x 2½˝ (9mm x 7SQs) lengths.

Leaves B

Mokuba No. 4599 Luminous Ribbon, color #5— Cut two 7mm x 2½˝ (7mm x 9SQs) lengths.

Leaves C

Shaded wired ribbon: Offray (Lion) Ambrosia Ribbon, color "fern", or Elegance Ribbon, color #186, "moss green to white"— Cut three ⅝˝ x 1¾˝ (sz3 x 3SQs) lengths.

Stamens

Gold seed beads.

Basket

French shaded wired ribbon, color "brown to beige". Cut one piece ⅞˝ x 3˝ (sz5 x 31⁄2SQs) wired edge ribbon.

Foundation

2½˝ square AidaPlus. (Heavy manila paper or file card can be substituted.) Cut Template C, the basket pattern shape, from this scrap of AidaPlus. Add no seam allowance.

Cloth backing

2½˝ square scrap of felt, UltraSuede, or fused cotton. Cut, using Template C, with no seam allowance added.

Finding

Pin-back to glue on.

FIGURES 16–19. PROJECT FOUR

1-4. The Miniature Basket of Blooms *(enlarged). Fashioned by the author.*

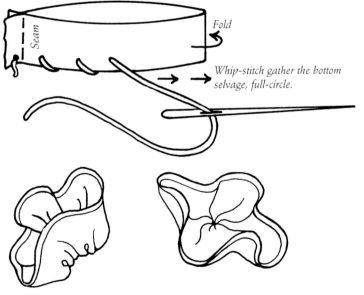

Seam

Fold

Whip-stitch gather the bottom selvage, full-circle.

1-16. MOON-FACED BLOOMS

PROCEDURE

Moon-faced blooms

These circles of softly gathered ribbon are so simple, so versatile, that you'll use them often. If for this reason alone, they need a memorable name!

Make three blooms. For each, seam the ribbon's raw edges together, then whip-stitch gather the bottom edge. Sew the single edge (not both bottom edges together) full-circle. Pull the thread tightly to gather the flower's center closed (1-16). Secure the stitches.

Leaves

1. Make two of leaf A and two of leaf B. For each, use the bud-leaf taught in Project 2. Do not gather the leaf's base. Simply tack the tail ends together so the leaf lies flat.

2. Make three of leaf C, using a version of Project 1's boat-prow leaf. Fold the ribbon in half from selvage to selvage (1-17A). Fold the right end up at a 45° angle. Running-stitch the fold line from **a** to **b**. Pull to gather and secure the stitches (1-17B). Fingerpress the leaf open (1-17C). When you tack-stitch this leaf to the basket foundation, glue or stitch to keep the point's seam hidden beneath the leaf.

Basket

1. To cover the basket (1-18, Template C): put a smear of gluestick across the bottom of Template C's AidaPlus basket cut-out. Center the length of the wired ribbon over it, leaving a 1/16" overlap to cover the bottom edge (1-19).

2. Fold the excess wired ribbon to the back of the foundation and secure it with gluestick (1-19, again).

ASSEMBLY

1. With gluestick, glue the blooms and leaves to the foundation. For layout, follow figure 1-20. Note that the leaf bases overlap, but are hidden under the blooms. Tack-stitch as needed, through all the layers.

2. Stitch on the seed bead blossom centers.

3. Using Gem Tac or other white craft glue, glue on an UltraSuede (or felt or fused cotton) backing, then a pinback.

☆ *Miniature Memo:* 12mm wide silk or rayon ribbon easily makes exquisite flowers. Seam the ribbon length's raw edges together. Then, from just above the bound edge, pull a thread along the ribbon's length, gathering it until the center closes. If necessary, lock the pull thread in place with a dab of clear nail polish.

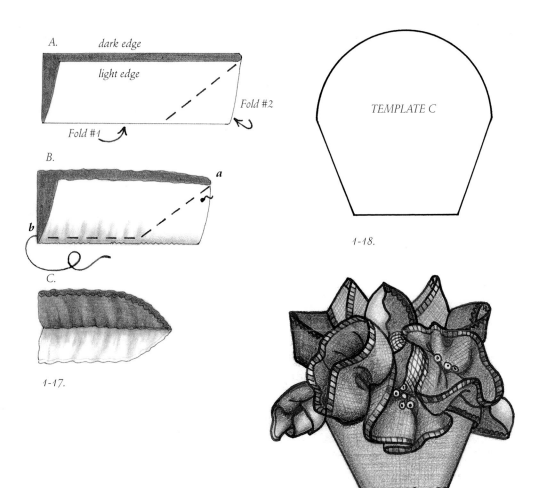

1-17.

1-18.

1-20. MINIATURE BASKET OF BLOOMS (actual size)

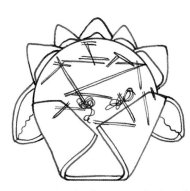

1-19. *Underside of* Miniature Basket of Blooms, *ready for backing.*

*From a ⅝" x 6" length
of shaded wire ribbon:*

Oval-centered

Circle-centered

*From a ⅝" x 8"
length of shaded
wire ribbon:*

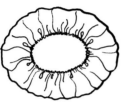

Oval-centered

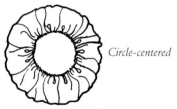

Circle-centered

1-21. SCULPTING BLOOMS WITH A STRAIGHT-
LINE GATHER

1-22. HYBRID #1
Bead center

1-23. HYBRID #2
Pansy center

Details Define Straight-Line Gathered Ribbons

*E*very type of ribbon can be stitch-gathered. Wired ribbon can be gathered on one or both wires. Or, when folded in half from bound edge to bound edge, it can be stitch-gathered the length of the fold. In addition to the methods already taught, see what blooms a straight-line can sculpt.

Stitch-gather a ribbon length along one edge, pull it into a circle, then view it from above (like a donut on a plate) to make any one of these highly stylized flowers.

Anemone, Aster, Calendula, Carnation, Chrysanthemum, Cornflower, Cosmos, Daisy, Gaillardia, Morning Glory, Narcissus, Petunia, Pink, Poppy, Rose, Spider Mum and Zinnia.

Can such different flowers be constructed so similarly? The answer is simple and lies in the ribbon itself. Read on.

TEN FABRICATION CHOICES

To emphasize the differences between one flower and another, change:
1. COLOR OF THE RIBBON
2. COLOR, SIZE, AND TYPE OF FLOWER CENTER
from a small center to a large one, from a flat center to a stuffed one, from a beaded center to one embroidered with French knots or shorn loops, from a knotted ribbon to a button center, or from a round center to an oval center.

Hybrid Centers

These simple circular flowers become unique when a different center is used. The following are just a few possible centers:

• Hybrid #1: Bead Center

For a simple center, stitch a size 5 (approximately ⅛" diameter) brown wood bead into the center, or fill the center with tiny seed beads.

• Hybrid #2: Pansy Center—Experiment with 8" and 10" ribbon lengths.

This is a ⅝" x 8" (sz3 x 13SQs) length of antiqued shaded wired ribbon. The primrose's steps 1-3 (page 29) were taken, then the outer edge was gathered slightly by pulling its wire. The flower's margin was pushed into a pansy-like shape. Lines in black Pigma pen draw the pansy face around its wood bead center.

- ***Hybrid #3: Overhand Knot Center***

Tie a ⅝″ x 4½″ (sz3 x 7¼SQs) length into an overhand knot. (Overhand knot is shown on page 56). Push the knot from the underside *(1-24A)*, up through the center to the front. The knot can be the same color as the petal wreath *(1-24B)*, or be a yellow *(1-24C)*. For quite a different look, make the knotted center from a wider ribbon *(1-24D)*.

- ***Hybrid #4: Cupped Center***

A ⅝″ x 3½″ (sz3 x 5½SQs) ribbon has been U-turn gathered on the bottom wire, raw edges seamed together, and appliquéd to a petal wreath.

- ***Hybrid #5: Frilly Cup Center***

After making the cupped center for Hybrid #4, running-stitch ¼″ below the rim. Pull the thread to gather into the frilly cupped center.

3. NUMBER OF LAYERS GATHERED

The petal wreaths were made from a single ribbon layer. A double ribbon layer can be made from a wider ribbon folded off-center and fold-gathered *(1-27)*. Or it can be made from three layers of separate ribbon wreaths, each decreasing in length and width from bottom to top *(1-28)*.

4. WIDTH OF RIBBON

5. LENGTH OF RIBBON

6. WEIGHT OF RIBBON

7. TYPE OF RIBBON

8. EDGE FINISH OF THE RIBBON

Within one ribbon type, satin for example, change the edging: from straight-bound *(1-29)*, change to machine-pleated *(1-30)*, to picot-edged, to ruffled. A softly pleated edge imitates a poppy. A deeply pleated edge recalls a marigold. When a velvet ribbon's outer edge, for example, is stitch-gathered just enough to roll it under, it can look like a many petaled flower *(1-31)*. Make a petal wreath of ½″ x 8″ (sz2 x 4SQs) wired ribbon, then gather its outside edge, pulling it in. This edge makes it look like a petunia or morning glory. Every time you embark on a flower, consider these eight options. Ask yourself what ribbon color, what number of layers, what length, width, weight, type, ribbon edging and center best personify this particular flower. There are two more choices to consider:

9. PRESENTATION OF THE FLOWER —single-stemmed or clustered.

10. PERSPECTIVE FROM WHICH THE BLOOM IS VIEWED

A. *Underside of bloom*   B. *Same color center*

C. *Yellow center*   D. *Knot made from wider ribbon*

1-24. HYBRID #3 *Overhand knot center*

Edge of petal wreath folded under for perspective   *Edge crimped*

1-25. HYBRID #4
Cupped center   1-26. HYBRID #5
Frilly cup center

1-27. HYBRID #6
Two layers   1-28. HYBRID #7
Three layers

1-29. HYBRID #8
Double-faced satin   1-30. HYBRID #9
Pleated satin

1-31. HYBRID #10
Velvet ribbon, edges slightly gathered   1-32. HYBRID #11
PETUNIA OR MORNING GLORY

*A. 5/8″ x 9″ shaded
wired ribbon, edge-
gathered and crimped;
then the petal wreath
is folded, front to back.*

*B. 7/8″ x 10″ shaded
wired ribbon edge-
gathered, outer edge
crimped; then the
petal wreath is folded
into quarters.*

1-33. SIDE VIEWS

*A. 1¹/2″ x 4¹/2″ shaded
wired ribbon, wires
removed, folded
lengthwise off-center
and fold-gathered.*

*B. ¹/2″ x 5¹/2″ length,
same as A, but with a
puffed center added.*

 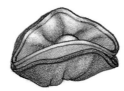

*C. Unusual angle of same
flower as B, but with both
edge wires left in.*

1-34. SIDE VIEWS OF FOLD-GATHERED FLOWERS

BOLD BLOSSOM OR SHY VIOLET?

In *Ikebana*, flowers are said to have faces, centered on the bloom. Personify your flowers; befriend them and view them sympathetically. Your flowers can look you squarely in the eye, glance down shyly, or stare off into the distance. To present your flowers in different poses, to view them in all their moods from straightforward to contemplative, is to romance them.

To emphasize the difference between one sort of flower and another:

• You can view a flower from the side.

To make the following highly stylized flowers, stitch-gather a ribbon length on one edge or on the lengthwise fold. Then pull it into a circle and press the front half up so that its rim just misses covering up the back rim *(1-33)*. Depending on size, center, color, and type of ribbon, this view might evoke one of these blooms:

Anemone, Canterbury Bell, Poppy and Water Lily.

A ribbon length stitch-gathered along the fold *(1-34)*, pulled into a circle, then viewed from the side, could be made to evoke these stylized flowers:

Bachelor's Button, Camellia, Petunia, Pom Pom, Chrysanthemum, and Pink.

• You can view a stalk of blooms from above. A ribbon length stitch-gathered along the fold and draped so that you see it swirl down its axis and about itself *(1-35A)* makes these highly stylized flowers:

Canterbury Bell, Delphinium, Foxglove, Hollyhock and Wisteria.

• You can view cluster flowers from above. A ribbon length stitch-gathered along the fold and wound in a concentric circle *(1-35B)* makes these flowers:

Begonia, Ranunculus and Tuberose.

*A. 5/8″ x 6″ length of
shaded wired ribbon,
edge-gathered and
swirled.*

*B. 1¹/2″ x 12″ of shad-
ed wired ribbon, stitch-
gathered up the center
and swirled.*

1-35. FLOWERS VIEWED FROM ABOVE

Flora Sculpted by Two Straight-Line Gathers

A. 5/8″ x 3″ length of shaded wired ribbon U-turn gathered, seamed, and sewn to the background in a cup shape.

B. 5/8″ x 2½″ U-turn gathered wires twisted together to hold the gathers.

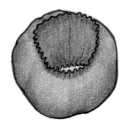

1-36. CUPPED FLOWERS

1-5. *A detail of a purse fashioned by the author. The apples are made by two straight gathering lines, a technique from Lesson One.*

A. 2″ x 5″ shaded wired ribbon, U-turn gathered as tightly as possible, then seamed at **b**.

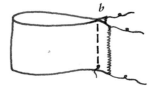

C. Stitch gather ¼″ below top rim.

B. Stuff from bottom.

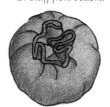

1-37. BERRIES, PODS AND POPPY CENTERS

Cupped flowers

A ribbon length tightly gathered into a circle along its bottom edge, then gathered less tightly along its top edge to form a cupped shape *(1-36A)* makes these flowers, viewed from the side:

Clover, Heather, Tulip, a Narcissus or Daffodil Trumpet, Lily of the Valley, Mountain Laurel and Grape Hyacinth.

Berries, pods, and poppy centers

A ribbon length tightly gathered into a circle along its bottom edge and then gathered tightly along its top edge forms a spherical shape *(1-37)*. The round can be stuffed before the top is gathered, or left empty. This method makes a shape which could represent:

An Apple, Berry, Myrtle Pod, Rose Hip and Poppy Center.

MORE FLOWERS GATHERED ON THE CENTER FOLD

BELL-LIKE FLOWERS

Fold wired ribbon in half lengthwise, then stitch-gather the fold. This causes the unstitched wired edges to ruffle freely and swirl into cupped floral-like shapes. With tweezers, emphasize the swirls by sculpting them into graceful curves. Because two examples of these flowers are pictured in this book's photographs, directions are given here. The first is a highly stylized flower shown in photo 1-6. Figure *1-38* shows these swirled blooms from Project 8, *Pennsylvania Dutch Nouveau*. To make one stalk of these flowers:

1. Cut a ⅞″ x 10″ (sz5 x 11½SQs) length of overdyed wired ribbon.

2. Fold it in half, lengthwise (*1-39A*). Next fold the beginning and ending raw edges to the back and down at a 45° angle (*1-39B*). With a knotted thread, running-stitch the length of the fold.

1-6. *Detail of* Pennsylvania Dutch Nouveau, *Project 8, Lesson Three. These bell-like flowers are fashioned by the author, using Lesson One's swirling and straight-line gathering.*

3. Pull the thread to gather the total length down to 2½″.

4. Appliqué the gathered fold to the background. Figure *1-38* shows the up-turned flowers on a gracefully arched stem of couched bead cord.

WISTERIA

Wisteria cascades below softly looped Mokuba ribbon in photo 1-7. Framed by boat prow leaves, moonflowers from Project 4, French knots, and grape-like clusters of beads, the wisteria ornaments an opulent brooch. To make the wisteria:

1. Cut two ⅞″ x 10″ (sz5 x 11½SQs)

lengths of shaded wired ribbon and one 1½″ x 18″ (sz9 x 12SQs) length of shaded wired organza ribbon. Then follow steps 2 and 3, above. Clustered short/long/short, the three lengths of swirled ribbon convey wisteria's graceful character.

2. On a collaged background like that of the Wisteria Brooch (photo 1-7), the fold-gathered edges can be glued or appliquéd to the pin base. The Wisteria Brooch's pin base is a 2″ x 4½″ rectangle (with the top and bottom rounded) of grey AidaPlus, covered by a wrap of wider ribbon. Both the wisteria and the other ribbon botanicals were arranged on the base, then glued. Next the bead and silk ribbon embroidered embellishments were sewn. The soft fall of Japanese ribbons —rayon, cotton, and metallic-edged organdy— folds to the back of the foundation where stitches secure it. A glued-on UltraSuede backing, cut to the finished shape, completes the piece. It is worn held by two corsage pins.

DAISY OR MARGUERITE

1. For the stuffed center, cut one 1½″ x 1½″ (sz9 x 1SQ) length of shaded wired ribbon.

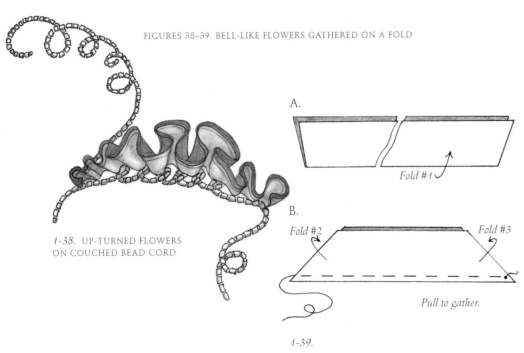

FIGURES 38–39. BELL-LIKE FLOWERS GATHERED ON A FOLD

1-38. UP-TURNED FLOWERS ON COUCHED BEAD CORD

A.

Fold #1

B.

Fold #2   *Fold #3*

Pull to gather.

1-39.

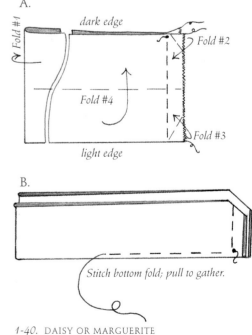

A.

Fold #1   *dark edge*   *Fold #2*

Fold #4

light edge   *Fold #3*

B.

Stitch bottom fold; pull to gather.

1-40. DAISY OR MARGUERITE

2. For the petals, cut one 1½″ x 6″ (sz9 x 4SQs) length of shaded wired ribbon.

3. Fold the ribbon in half from selvage to selvage (1-40A).

4. Take a ¼″ seam through the two raw edges. Fold the upper and lower corners of the seam down and in, to get the raw edges out of the way (1-40A, Fold #2 and #3).

5. Now fold the light (bottom) edge up to ⅛″ below the dark (top) edge, seams folded inside so that the raw edges lie on top of one another. (1-40A and B, Fold #4).

6. Running-stitch the bottom fold, full-circle (1-40B). (Do not stitch the front and back halves together.) Pull the thread to gather the ribbon into a tight petal wreath (1-41). Secure the stitches, clip the thread.

7. Center: with a circle template, draw a 1″ diameter circle centered on the 1½″ x 1½″ ribbon length (1-42A). Running-stitch, then pull to gather the ribbon into a shallow pouch. Stuff this pouch with the ribbon excess from outside the circle, then pull the gathering thread tightly to form a puffed center. Secure the stitches; clip the thread.

☆ *Tip:* Try a stiff ½″ circle (like a stick-on pricing dot) adhered to the center of the 1″ circle.

8. Sprinkle the stuffed center with a scattering of seed beads (1-42B), choosing their color, like the ribbon's, by the natural flower.

9. Stitch the puff center onto the double ruff of gathered petals (1-43), or use a decorative button center.

FIGURES 40–43. DOUBLE PETALED FLOWERS, GATHERED ON A FOLD

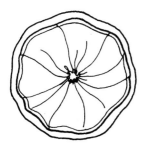

1-41. GATHERED DOUBLE PETAL WREATH

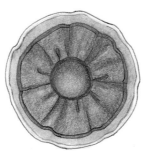

1-43. DAISY OR MARGUERITE

A. Pull thread to gather to ½ circle. Stuff.

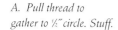

B. Add beads or French knots.

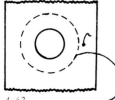

1-42.

1-7. Linda's Wisteria Brooch *is fashioned by the author. Its swirled and fold-gathered ribbon is a variation of Lesson One's straight-line gathering.*

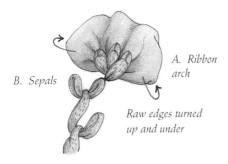

1-8. *Detail from Pennsylvania Dutch Nouveau, Project 8, Lesson Three, fashioned by the author.*

FIGURES 44–46. ONE SIMPLE METHOD MAKES THREE DIFFERENT FLOWERS

B. *Sepals*

A. *Ribbon arch*

Raw edges turned up and under

1-44. CALIFORNIA POPPY

1-45. *Daisy with an UltraSuede calyx*

1-46. *Petunia with a folded ribbon trumpet*

THREE ONE-EDGE GATHERED FLOWERS

CALIFORNIA POPPY

Painted with artistic license, this California poppy is gathered on one edge and viewed from the side (photo 1-8 detail). It couldn't be simpler to make!

1. Cut a ⅝″ x 4″ (sz3 x 6½SQs) length of shaded yellow to lavender wired ribbon.

2. U-turn gather the bottom edge tightly, reducing the length to 1″. Allow the gathered ribbon to form a gentle arch *(1-44A)*.

3. Tuck the raw-edged ends up at an angle behind the arch *(1-44, again)* and appliqué the flower to the background.

4. *Sepals* If you are making this poppy as part of Lesson Three's pattern, *Pennsylvania Dutch Nouveau,* then leaf-stitch the three sepals in 10mm Mokuba No.1512 Fashion Tape, color 49. The sepals *1-44B)* top the stems which are feather-stitched in the same ribbon.

5. *Hybrids* Consider an UltraSuede half-circle of sepals for a daisy-like flower *(1-45)*. Or view a petunia from the side *(1-46)*. To make its cone-shaped base, tuck the corners of a ⅞″ x 1¼″ (sz5 x 1½SQs) ribbon under to form a triangle.

EVERYFLOWER

Straight-line sewn, and curvaceously full, this ribbon bloom seemingly has no natural sisters. But doesn't it remind you of flowers just beyond memory? Thus it is given a poetic name and represents all flowers!

1. For the lower petal, cut a ⅞″ x 3½″ (sz5 x 4SQs) length of rayon, organza, or French wired ribbon (wires removed).

2. Fold the ribbon in half, lengthwise, so the two bound edges lie, one on top of the other. Running-stitch from the fold *a*, across the bottom, and on to *b*, leaving ¼″ seam allowance at both ends *(1-47A)*.

3. Pull tightly to gather *(1-47B)*. Tack-stitch *a* to *b*.

4. For the flower's cup, cut a ⅝″ x 3¼″ (sz3 x 5SQs) length of rayon, organza, or French wired ribbon (wires removed).

5. Fold the ends down as in figure *1-47C* and running-stitch the length.

6. Pull to gather the cup *(1-48A)*. Leave the needle threaded while you fold an 8″ length of 9mm silk embroidery ribbon into five loops. Tack-stitch across the bottom *(1-48B)* and insert into the cup .

7. To finish *Version I,* appliqué the cup to the petal base *(1-48C)*.

8. *Version II* is the petal base itself, made from a ⅝″ x 6″ (sz3 x 9½SQs) length of shaded wired ribbon, gathered as in *1-47A,* but not folded lengthwise. It

Barrette with unique flowers, made by Katie Scott, using Lesson One's straight line gathering technique.

makes an appealing petal wreath, ready to be centered with artificial stamens or French knots *(1-49)*.

9. *Version III* is the petal base itself, made from a ⅞″ x 8″ (sz5 x 9SQs) length of shaded wired ribbon, gathered as in *1-51*, but not folded lengthwise. It makes an appealing petal wreath, centered with an overhand knot tied from a ⅝″ x 4½″ (sz3 x 7¼SQs) length of satin ribbon *(1-50)*.

FIGURES 47–50. A UNIQUE METHOD MAKES REMINISCENT FLOWERS

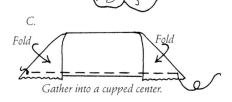

A. *Pull to gather the base petals.*

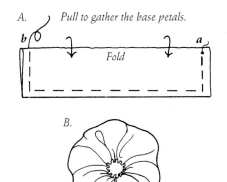

B.

C.

Fold   *Fold*

Gather into a cupped center.

1-47. "EVERYFLOWER"

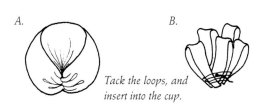

A.

B.

Tack the loops, and insert into the cup.

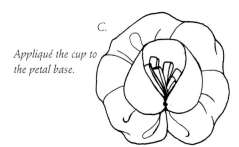

C.

Appliqué the cup to the petal base.

1-48. "EVERYFLOWER", VERSION I

RANUNCULUS OR TRIPLE BEGONIA

1. For one flower, cut three lengths of rayon or wired ribbon.

For the bottom petals, cut a piece 1½″ x 8″ (sz9 x 5½SQs).

For the middle petals, cut a piece ⅞″ x 7″ (sz5 x 8SQs).

For the top petals, cut a piece ⅝″ x 6″ (sz3 x 9½SQs).

2. For each layer of petals, fold the ribbon in half lengthwise and seam the raw edges together *(1-51)*.

3. Gather each layer of petals tightly *(1-51)*.

4. Stack petal layers A, B, and C *(1-52)*, from bottom to top, in that order. Pin to hold.

5. *Center:* tie an overhand knot in the middle of a 7mm x 12″ length of silk or organdy ribbon.

6. Using a chenille #22 needle, thread the knot-center's tails down through the three stacked center holes.

7. With a milliner's needle and matching thread, stitch the tails down to the back of the flower, close to its center. Stitch through all layers, using the pointillist stitch to stabilize the flower. The finished flower is plump and perky *(1-52)*. To hybridize it, use any one of the three petal layers as a single flower.

1-49.

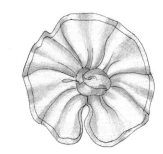

1-50. "EVERYFLOWER" VERSION III, centered with an overhand knot.

FIGURES 51–52. LAYERS OF PETALS MAKE A FAMILIAR FLOWER

Seam   *Fold*

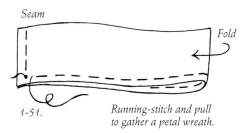

1-51.   *Running-stitch and pull to gather a petal wreath.*

A. Bottom petal

B. Middle petal

C. Top petal

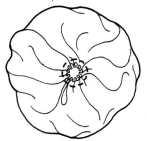

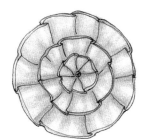

1-52. RANUCULUS OR TRIPLE BEGONIA

1-9. Joen's Birthday Corsage, *a cuffed variation of Lesson One's Cherokee Rose, fringe-centered with pinked cotton leaves (from Dimensional Appliqué)* and ready-made velvet leaves.

FLOWERS GATHERED ON ONE EDGE AND ROLLED

Gathered and rolled flowers can be made from any of the ribbon types listed at this lesson's opening. Several of the directions which follow specify wired or other ribbon. While wired or organza ribbon give the drawn model a characteristic look, try substituting other ribbons as well—you may celebrate the difference!

THE CABBAGE ROSE

The cabbage rose is the first ribbon rose I learned to make. I love to pin one on! Some of my corsages are pictured in this lesson. They are a pleasure to make, to wear and to give. *Dimensional Appliqué* teaches this rose in depth and is worth reviewing. Anyone who loves a style learns its potential by working in it. Innovations on my original follow.

1. Cut ⅞″ x 30″ (sz5 x 34¼SQs) length of shaded wired ribbon. For a lush old-fashioned rose, use imported French wired ribbon and extend this length up to as much as two yards. Antique the ribbon as taught in *Getting Started*.

2. Gather the bottom (the darker edge's) wire until the gathered ribbon is ⅓ its flat length. Move the finishing end wire out of your sewing's way by coiling it around a pencil (1-53A).

3. At the starting end, pull the top edge wire out for 3″ or so. Then twist the top and bottom edge corners together (1-53A, again). Wind the loose wires around the twist to hold it.

4. Roll the starting end down the ribbon's length until a bud center begins to form (1-53B). Continue rolling a whorl that opens up a bit more on each round—like the spiral of a snail's shell. Most needlewomen err by pulling this around too tightly, preventing the rose from opening up. Relax and roll the rose gently around. Resist looking at the front until you've taken step 5.

5. At the ribbon's finishing end (1-54A), take Fold #1, hemming the edge under ¼″. Turn the corner down with Fold #2, laying the hem fold directly over the ribbon's bottom selvage. Pin to hold temporarily.

6. When the full length is wound, slip

1-10. *Corsage made by the author from a Lesson One Cabbage Rose, cuffed and fringe-centered.*

three long quilter's pins under each selvage whorl, lifting them all to the same
level *(1-54B)*.

7. Turn to the front and check the
rose's size *(1-55)*. If it is too small, let the
whorls out a bit on the back. If it is too
large, cup it in your palm and squeeze it.
For an even more compact rose, tighten
the whorls from the back.

8. On the underside, whip-stitch to
hold the selvages in place *(1-54B, again)*.
(Persevere! After you have made a dozen
roses or so, skip this stitching of the
underside and proceed to step 9. This
leap constitutes Expertise.)

9. The rose you've made *(1-55, again)*
will delight you. But it has fascinations
not yet explored. Become the botanist,
idealizing the strain. All manner of sculptural options follow. Name your rose in
honor of someone you love. Tack its
petals down while still in your hand, and
then appliqué just its outer edge to the
chosen base.

1-11. *Necklace pendant by the author. The center flower is of Mokuba satin velvet, using Lesson One's two-edge gathered technique. The two smaller flowers of Mokuba luminous velvet are gathered down the center only.*

FIGURES 53–55. A UNIQUE ROSE FROM START TO FINISH

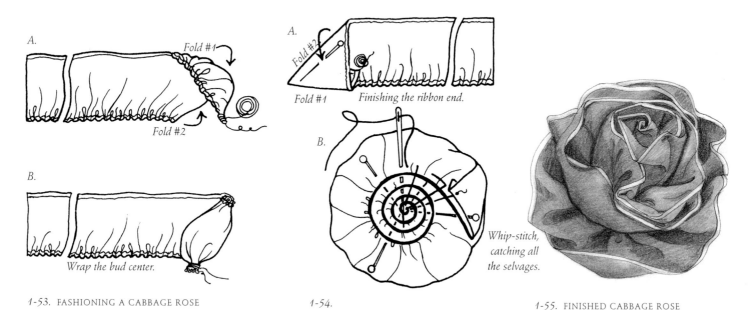

A.

Fold #1

Fold #2

B.

Wrap the bud center.

1-53. FASHIONING A CABBAGE ROSE

A.

Fold #2

Fold #1   *Finishing the ribbon end.*

B.

Whip-stitch, catching all the selvages.

1-54.

1-55. FINISHED CABBAGE ROSE

Eleven Rose-Sculpting Finishing Touches

1. **Whorl the center.** With tweezers or hemostats, twist the center into a tight whorl. *(1-56)*

2. **Cuff the petals.** Fold the ribbon's outer edge forward and to the front *(1-57)*. Finger-press a cuff of about ⅛″, the full length of the ribbon. For more control, cuff this edge before you roll the rose.

3. **Create a cup and saucer.** Push the center of the rose away from you, towards the upper edge. *(1-56)* Then do as your great-grandmother was taught when she learned to paint roses on fine china: "Fashion the bud center to sit, a floral cup, ensconced on a petaled saucer." In shaded ribbon, this exposes the ribbon's darker inner edge, adding depth to the rose.

4. **Add a diagonal.** Shape the outer whorl of the bud center so that it crosses the layer just beneath it at a diagonal, from upper left to lower right *(1-57)*. Nature's diagonal line is unstable and carries the eye with it, making your rose less static, more intriguing and romantic!

5. **Mold the petal edges.** Gently fingerpress occasional petal points into the outer edge of the rose *(1-58)*.

6. **Crinkle the petal tips.** At the very beginning, pull the outer edge wire, gathering the petals down to ¼″ of the flat length. (Pull gently, so as not to break the wire.) Then fingerpress—or even iron—a crimp into the edge. Pull the ribbon back out again, then proceed to gather the bottom edge and roll the rose. This exercise will leave the crinkled outer edge pictured in figure *1-59*.

7. **Curl the outer petal under.** Turn to the underside of the rose and pull the outer edge wire, forming gathers around its perimeter, creating the full-blown rose's characteristic backward curl *(1-56 and 1-57)*.

8. **Watercolor the rose.** Try this on a pale to mid-tone ribbon. With water on your fingertip, wet the central whorls of the rose. On one side only, touch the petals with a fine-tipped washable felt marker. Try a touch of green, then blend its edges with a marker of the same pale color (yellow, for example) as the ribbon. With a smile, you'll recall that touch of green on a rose you met in a garden somewhere, long ago.

9. **Add stamens.** Add the Fringed Blossom Center, shown on page 60.

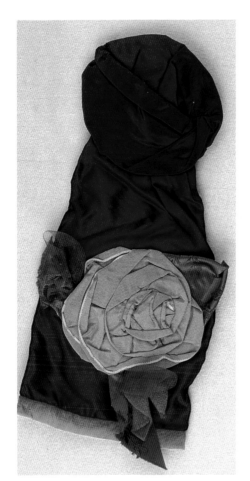

1-12. Purple Necktie for Linda, *fashioned by the author from 6″ wide luminous wired ribbon. The Lesson One Cabbage Rose rests on Mokuba ribbon leaves.*

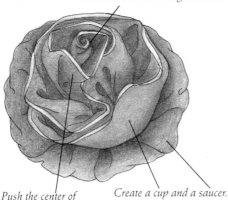

Twist the center into a tight whorl.

Create a cup and a saucer.

Push the center of the rose away from you, towards the back.

1-56.

Cuff the petals

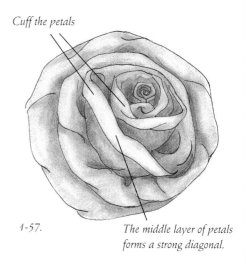

1-57.

*The middle layer of petals
forms a strong diagonal.*

10. ***Flatten the rose.*** Press the rose against the table with the flat of your hand. Surprisingly, this often improves its appearance and always gives it a vintage "pressed in the trunk" character.

11. ***Antique the rose.*** Crush the rose in your palm, squeeze it tightly, squishing it in different positions; then open it to relax it. Or wet it, using the more thorough pre-crushing taught in *Getting Started*. Now iron it dry between two paper towels. Figure *1-59* shows a rose crushed by the latter method.

Unless the rose is to be stiffened into rigidity with hair spray, then worn and stored with care, tack it down sufficiently so that it won't wilt in the trunk. Use a milliner's needle and a fine single thread in a matching color. If the color match is not good, use the pointillist stitch, going in and out of the same hole, through all the layers. I prefer using Sulky's translucent 100% polyester thread and the tack stitch done over the bound edge, working from the center outward. When you come to the "cup", blind-stitch its base to the gathered edge of the petal layer beneath it.

Mold the edges.

1-58.

1-13. *This crushed Cabbage Rose from Lesson One was fashioned by the author from two yards of wired ribbon, fringe-centered and ornamented with vintage trim and Mokuba jacquard satin ribbon.*

*Crinkle the petal tips.
Antique the rose.*

1-59.

THE SWEETHEART ROSE

A Sweetheart Rose is made like the Cabbage Rose, but with narrower ribbon. Use a ⅝″ x 18″ (sz3 x 29SQs).

THE CHEROKEE ROSE

Early in this century, milliners fashioned the Cherokee Rose from separate petals, each a ribbon rectangle with corners rolled, then hemmed. Nameless, the rose we are about to learn (1-61) was also shown—but unheralded—in the same vintage ribbon manuals as the Cherokee Rose. Done in today's wired ribbon, it re-creates the individual petals and so inherits the Cherokee Rose's romantic name.

1. Cut 1½″ x 36″ (sz9 x 24SQs) length of shaded wired ribbon. Fold the beginning and ending raw edges in and down at an angle, so that they fall a bit below the bottom selvage (1-60).

2. Gather the bottom (darker edge) wires until the gathered edge is between ½ and ⅓ of its original flat length (1-60).

3. Mark (by pin or pen) consecutive intervals along the ribbon's ungathered edge. Beginning from the starting end, mark off point *a* six inches to the left of the raw edge, point *b* six inches to the left of *a*; point *c* ten and a half inches to the left of *b* (1-60).

4. At point *a*, take 5″ of fine wire (bead or ribbon-edge wire) and wrap the ribbon's outside edge to its gathered edge (1-60). Do this to points *b* and *c* as well. If no wire is handy, thread-wrap this valley and secure the thread. Clip the tails off.

5. Next, roll the bud end from right to left, lightly, until the gathered length is all wound around and all the selvage edges are level. Finish as in steps 6 to 8 of the Cabbage Rose. The finished flower (1-61) is quite puffy and more scalloped than the Cabbage Rose.

1-14. Holiday Corsage, *hybridized by the author from* Lesson One's *Cabbage and Turncoat Tea roses.*

FIGURES 60–61. PETALS BEING SCALLOPED AND FASHIONED INTO A CHEROKEE ROSE

1-60.

1-61. FINISHED CHEROKEE ROSE

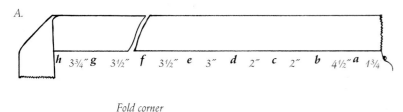

A.

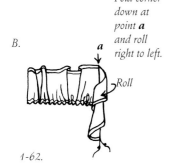

*Fold corner down at point **a** and roll right to left.*

Roll

1-62.

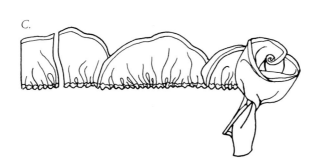

C.

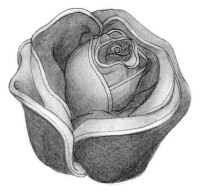

1-63. FINISHED TURNCOAT TEA ROSE

A TURNCOAT TEA ROSE

Once upon a time, in far-off magical China, were bred the ancestors of all the Tea roses…From their blood has sprung a race of roses, once designated as Tea-Scented China roses…Throughout the literature of roses are to be found tributes to this most elegant, most refined, most delicately beautiful and aristocratic of all roses.

– Judyth A. McLeod,
Our Heritage of Old Roses

1. Cut a ⅞″ x 24″ (sz5 x 27½SQs) length of shaded wired ribbon.

2. Mark (by pin or pen) consecutive intervals along the ribbon's ungathered edge. Beginning from the starting end, mark off point **a**: 1¾″ to the left of the raw edge (point **a** marks where you fold down to make the stem); point **b**: 4½″ to the left of point **a**; point **c**: 2″ to the left of point **b**; point **d**: 2″ to the left of **c**; point **e**: 3″ to the left of **d**; and point **f**: 3½″ to the left of **e**; point **g**: 3½″ further; and point **h**: 3¾″ further still (total marked units = 24″ ribbon length).

☆ *Art Tip:* Pen marks will show on the finished rose if marked boldly and on the front ribbon surface. To prevent this, mark the backside of the ribbon, or use just a dot of soft pencil.

3. Proceed as in steps 1 and 2 for the Cabbage Rose, gathering the bottom (darker edge) wire until the gathered edge measures 12″ long.

4. Fold the starting end forward and down at a 45° angle *(1-62A)*. Its raw edge hangs close to ¾″ below the gathered edge, forming a stem.

5. Roll the stem toward point **b**, rolling relatively tightly and wrapping the gathered edge around and around so that the bound edges lie one right on top of the other. You'll reach point **b** with about eight rolls of the handle, forming the rose's rolled center bud *(1-62B)*.

6. Hold the rolled center between your thumb and hand, so that point **b** is at the tip of the thumb, held between the right-hand thumb and forefinger.

7. Just to the left of point **b**, pinch the ribbon between the left thumb —pressed to the back of the ribbon— and the forefinger pressed to the front. (Your right hand will be palm down; your left hand, palm up.) Next you twist a Turncoat into this Tea Rose.

8. With the left hand still pinching it, roll the ribbon forward, down (so the petal stands on its head), then around to the back and right side up again.

9. Make petals with the turncoat twist at points **c**, **d**, **e**, and **f**.

10. Continue rolling, now loosely, in a jellyroll pattern. Keep the gathered edges flat and on one level. Twist the finishing edge's wires together at **g**. Tuck the tail out of sight, tacked under the rose.

The Turncoat Tea Rose illustrated in *1-63* finishes at 2¾″. A smaller version made from a ⅞″ x 18″ (sz5 x 20½SQs) length of ribbon finishes to a 1½″ diameter.

1-64. THE PILLOW ROSE

THE PILLOW ROSE

As its name suggests, this rose is pillowy, but surprisingly sturdy and needs little stitching down (1-64). To wear it, sew three leaves to the back and stiffen the rose with hair spray. Back the rose with a circle of AidaPlus or UltraSuede. This rose is made much like the Fancy Silk Flower #2, but out of wired ribbon. Refer to that flower's diagrams to reinforce the following written instructions:

1. Cut a 1½″ x 36″ (sz9 x 24SQs) length of shaded wired ribbon.

2. Fold the ribbon from top to bottom, so the two bound edges lie one on top of the other.

☆ *Design Detail:* The secret to successful gathering on two edge-wires is to have both sides of the ribbon stay together and gather as though one. You need to pin the finger-pressed lengthwise fold at 5″ intervals. Then pull the two edge-wires to gather the ribbon on both simultaneously until the ribbon, gathered, is one-third its length when flat.

3. Fold the beginning end forward towards yourself and down at a 45° angle. Let its raw edges hang ¾″ below the gathered edge to form a stem by which you can hold it.

4. Roll the ribbon towards its length.

☆ *Design Detail:* The most common short-fall is to wrap the rose too tightly. Consider whether you need to loosen up!

5. Halfway through, add a turncoat twist (steps 7 and 8) to the gathered length. Turn to the rose's underside and slip three long glass-headed pins under the gathered edges and into the stem-

1-15. *This necklace pendant is a sz9 x 12SQs version of Lesson One's Pillow Rose.*

center. This lifts the whorled edges so they are flat, all on the same plane.

6. Resume winding the ribbon concentrically around itself, letting the gathered edge out a bit further with each whorl, like a chambered nautilus shell. Make one more turncoat twist before you come to the last 6″.

7. To finish, fold the raw edge end forward at a 45° angle, tucking it out of sight beneath the rose.

8. Pin to lift the remaining whorls to the same flat level as those closest to the center.

9. Whip-stitch the underside of the rose and cut off the stem-center.

THE NOISETTE ROSE

A favorite! The petite Noisette Rose (2″ in diameter) is shown in photo 1-16 and in figure 1-65. Use ⅝″ x 24″ (sz3 x 38½SQs) shaded wired ribbon. Gather the ribbon on its darker side (1-65), remembering that old fashioned roses fade to the sunlight. Follow the previous directions for the Turncoat Tea Rose. Whorl the center tightly, pushing it towards the back of the bloom. Then shape each petal, stitching each down, using the pointillist stitch. This rose is quick to make and almost fail-proof.

☆ *Art Tip:* As you develop an original style, push its possibilities. When your work becomes uniquely expressive of you, it also becomes recognizable to others. By so sharing something admired, you will have made the world a happier place.

Look closely at all the ribbon ornaments pictured in this book. You'll soon recognize that something which looks fresh and intriguing represents a new twist on one of the methods taught herein. It is just this vivacity which keeps ribbonart thriving and ready to bloom again in the new millennium!

1-65. THE NOISETTE ROSE

1-16. *Noisette Roses fashioned as pin-on corsages by the author.*

1-17. *Susan Duffield's* Ribbons and Roses *plants Lesson One's Cabbage Rose into a magnificently original machine-stitched quilt.*

Hummingbirds and Fuchsias, *an original Album block design by Wendy Grande*
from her quilt, Ribbon Appliqué. *With wondrous innovation, Wendy combines broad Ribbon Appliqué*
and Lesson Two's silk ribbon embroidery!

LESSON TWO

Flowers Gathered in Three Unique Patterns

*I*ntroducing ribbonry's trio of versatile gathering patterns:
1. Diamond-shaped gathering pattern.
2. U-turn and Crescent Moon gathering patterns.
3. Sugar Scoop gathering pattern.

Review *Getting Started*.

RIBBON TYPES

Shaded wired ribbon, bias-cut silk, contemporary or vintage rayon ribbon. The shaded wired ribbon is ideal for the fuchsias. Both shaded wired ribbon and vintage rayon ribbon evoke a pansy's characteristic coloration and have the requisite hand. Wired ribbon also suits petals gathered along the sugar scoop path.

RIBBON SIZES

⅝″ wide up to 1½″ wide (Sizes 3, 5, and 9).

PROJECTS

Project 5: Fuchsia necklace and earring set.
Project 6: Pansy barrette or bar pin.

RIBBON FLOWER TECHNIQUES

Lesson Two's techniques make both impressionistic flora and flora reminiscent of their natural sisters: Azalea, Begonia, Bloodroot, Bluebell, Bluet, Buttercup, Columbine, Clematis, Cyclamen, Dogwood, Four O'Clock, Foxglove, Fruit Blossom, Fuchsia, Gentian, Harebell, Hepatica, Hollyhock, Honeysuckle, Hydrangea, Japanese Iris, Lady's Slipper, Lilac, Lilium, Marsh Marigold, Mayflower, Nicotiana, Orchid, Pansy, Petunia, Phlox, Poinsettia, Rhododendron, Snowdrop, Star of Bethlehem, Sweet Alyssum, Thorn Apple, Trumpet Flower, Rockrose, Snapdragon, Tulip (with separate petals), Violet and Water Lily (with separate petals).

RIBBON LEAF TECHNIQUES

Rounded leaves, U-turn gathered leaves, and echo leaves.

BLOOMS STITCHED BY LINES THAT BEND

Three unique stitch patterns make the flowers that follow. Each one performs a small miracle, for the blooms shaped seem far removed from the path pulled by the gathering thread.

1. *The first line bends sharply into a diamond* to form flowers reminiscent of fuchsias, clematis, azaleas, fruit blossoms and trumpet flowers.

2. *The second line bends gently into a U-turn* which flips right-side out for three front petals. This combines a shorter ribbon length stitched with two crescent moons to make two back petals. The five combined comprise a perfect five-petaled pansy.

3. *The third line is asymmetrical, like the profile of a sugar scoop viewed sideways.* Gathered, it makes a graceful elongated petal, the stuff of lilies and poinsettias, Japanese iris and gentians. When large, the versatile sugar scoop petal forms water lilies, when medium it fashions tulips, and when petite it makes the five petals of a Star of Bethlehem. This same off-center line also shapes the slender, pointed petals of compound

2-1. *Delicate fuchsias drop from a ribbon necklace of Mokuba frill satin, fashioned by the author. Even when paired with earrings, a set of these Project 5 jewels takes under two hours to make.*

flowers like lady's slipper or an orchid. When foreshortened, it reads as begonia or hollyhock-like blossoms. All these blooms are yours when you fertilize them with some imagination!

Project Five

FUCHSIA NECKLACE AND EARRING SET

What romantic has not admired the Gibson girl ribbon worn around the neck? I thought my own ribbon-at-the-throat days had slipped away, but now I find ribbons worn thus still most becoming. When the weather becomes too hot for collars, a ribbon tied at the nape prettifies. Like cologne, a ribbon necklace makes one feel quite the lady, as will fashioning this project in which five fuchsia blossoms are carried by an elegant ribbon, while two more dangle delicately from earrings. The beauty is in the ribbons used and in the magic by which an angular stitch-pattern transforms flat ribbon into fairyland flowers.

SUPPLIES

This necklace can be made in multiple ribbon types, sizes and colors. The following supplies were used to make the fuchsia necklace as pictured in photo 2-1.

The necklace's three center fuchsias are made of a longer ribbon rectangle whose raw edges were folded in to overlap. Slightly larger, the center blossom is made out of a wider ribbon than the others. The outermost fuchsia blossoms and those on the earrings are fashioned from unhemmed ribbon rectangles with raw edges sealed to prevent fray. The sealed-edge blossoms have a fragile look while the hemmed-edge flower is sturdier. Though delicate, these blooms show well even when nestled into the busier backdrop of a ribbon collage (see photo on page 10).

Hemmed-edge fuchsias

Wired shaded ribbon or vintage rayon ribbon—Cut one 1½″ x 4¾″ (sz9 x 3¼ SQs) piece each for the two smaller inner blossoms; one 2″ x 4½″ (sz16 x 2¼SQs) piece for the bigger center blossom.

Sealed raw-edge fuchsias

Wired shaded ribbon or vintage rayon ribbon—Cut one 1½″ x 2¼″ (sz9 x 1 ½SQs) piece for each of four blossoms: the two outer necklace flowers and the earring flowers. The raw edges can be heat-sealed or acrylic-sealed with clear nail polish.

Artificial stamens

No. 83 (gold) and No. 730 (pink) double-ended stamens from Lacis, three of either color per flower folded in half, tips together.

Necklace ribbon

Mokuba No. 4895 Frill Satin Ribbon, 21mm width in color No. 3—⅞″ x 1yd. (sz5 x 57½SQs), ends clipped on the diagonal and acrylic-sealed.

Findings

One pair of hook earrings in gold or silver.

Basic sewing kit and ribbon tools, including white glue.

PROCEDURE

Fuchsia from a hemmed rectangle of ribbon

1. Fold the raw edges of the ribbon inward, letting one raw edge overlap the other by ¼″ (2-1A). Secure the overlap with a gluestick.

2. Mark the mid-point of each side of this ribbon rectangle.(2-1B)

3. With strong matching thread, stitch-gather a diamond shape running from mid-point to mid-point on all four sides of the ribbon rectangle. Figure 2-1B points out that the starting knot should be below the ribbon's edge so that it is hidden within the finished flower. At each corner of the diamond, pass your thread over the ribbon's edge to begin the next row of stitches by inserting the needle into the opposite ribbon surface (2-1B).

4. When you reach the knot where the sewing began, put the needle down temporarily. Put a drop of white glue at the ribbon's center (2-1B). Press three double-ended stamens (folded in half) into it. Allow glue to dry.

☆ *Art Tip:* Play with the stamens. Mix two varieties; use more, use less.

Glue them to the center (2-1B, again) or glue them closer to the bottom edge (2-2A).

FIGURES 1–2 SHOW METHODS FOR MAKING FUSCHIA BLOSSOMS

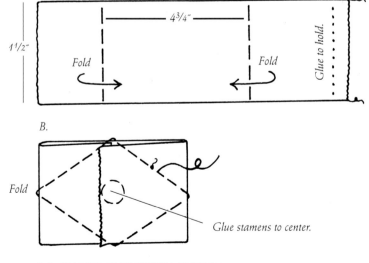

2-1. HEMMED-EDGE FUCHSIA BLOSSOM

5. Pull the thread, gathering the ribbon tightly into a trumpet with four petals *(2-2B)*. Secure the thread, clip it off and seal the end with a dab of clear polish. This side is the blossom's underside.

Fuchsia from an edge-sealed rectangle of ribbon

1. Seal the ribbon rectangle's two raw edges. Follow the directions for heat-sealing in *Getting Started*, or seal with clear acrylic nail polish.

2. Proceed as in steps 2 to 5, (page 50), for a fuchsia from a hemmed rectangle of ribbon.

☆ *Speed Tip:* These flowers lend themselves readily to mass production. Make several more while the glue dries! While a few minutes of drying time are also needed for the edges to seal on unhemmed fuchsias, those blooms are even quicker than the hemmed fuchsias and thus are ideal for assembly line manufacture.

More cautious sewing is required when you glue the stamens before stitching the blossoms *(2-2A, again)*, but I prefer this when I want to make many at one time.

ASSEMBLY

1. With a fine silk pin, mark the necklace ribbon's bottom edge at the center. Place two more pins 1¼″ to the left and right of the center. Pin-mark the place for the two outermost blossoms 1⅛″ beyond each of the previous pins.

2. Attach each fuchsia blossom to the ribbon with a buttonhole bar *(2-3)*. Use a matching thread (ideally silk), doubled. Beginning with a knot on the underside of the blossom, take two ¼″ long loops of the doubled thread, attaching the top back of the blossom to the neck ribbon.

3. With the thread still attached, blanket-stitch from the neck ribbon back down to the blossom. When the anchoring loop is covered with a tight wrapping of blanket stitches *(2-3)*, secure the thread on the underside of the blossom and clip. Seal the securing stitches with a tiny drop of polish. This completes the

bar, which though blanket-stitched, is called a buttonhole bar or a bar buttonhole!

4. Attach the five fuchsias to the neck ribbon from right to left in this order: sealed-edge blossom, hemmed-edge blossom, largest hemmed-edge blossom in the center, then the second hemmed-edge blossom, and finally another sealed-edge blossom as in photo 2-1.

5. With several small looped stitches taken one on top of the other, fasten the top back of a sealed-edge fuchsia bloom to each of the hook earring findings.

2-2. *Delicate fuchsia earrings fashioned by the author.*

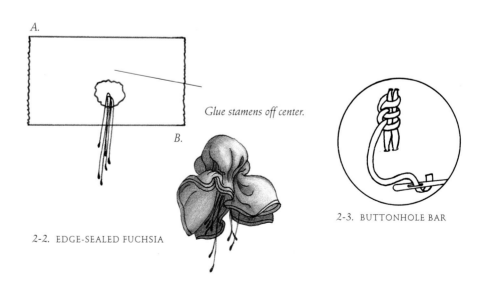

A.

Glue stamens off center.

B.

2-2. EDGE-SEALED FUCHSIA

2-3. BUTTONHOLE BAR

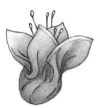

2-4A. AZALEA

2-4B. FRUIT BLOSSOM

*Mark a heavy circle
on ribbon with black
to make stamen tips.*

2-4D. FRUIT
BLOSSOM CENTER
*1½″ circle fringed
and folded in eighths*

2-4C. CIRCLE TEMPLATE

A.

B.

2-5. BLOSSOMS WITH BEADED CENTERS

2-6. VIOLET WITH
EMBROIDERED
CENTER

2-7. ROCKROSE
WITH STUFFED
CENTER

The Bloom of Many Faces

Though simple, the diamond-shaped gathering of ribbon rectangles has magical potential. Delight in how quickly these ribbon snippets are transformed into a bouquet of blooms. By changing just one or two aspects, you can stylize each gathered rectangle into a different flower.

Gathered Rectangle with Up-turned Sealed-edge Petals.

To make this bloom into an Azalea, choose ribbons shaded from white to pink to salmon to red. Place the bloom petals up and center it with artificial stamens *(2-4A)*.

Round-off a Rectangle's Corners by Cutting, Edge-sealing, and Diamond-gathering the Ribbon.

1. To make a fruit blossom (apple, cherry, plum, or peach), choose a ribbon shaded from white to pink, place the bloom round petals up. Center it with stamens or a fringed ribbon circle *(2-4B)*.

2. To make the fringed blossom stamens, draw a heavy circle onto a 1½″ x 2″ length of shaded wired ribbon. Draw with a black or brown Pigma Micron .01 pen around a 1½″ diameter template (2-4C). Cut out the circle to include this darkened rim. (When you fringe the circle, each thread will have a dark dot at the top of it, reminiscent of a fruit blossom stamen.) Fringe (by pulling out threads) ¼″ of the ribbon at each compass point.

Fold this fringed circle in half, then fourths, then eighths *(2-4D)*. With embroidery scissors, push this folded wedge down into the gathered blossom, leaving its dot-topped fringe peeking out as a soft brush of stamens.

Hybridizing the Diamond-Gathered Rectangle with Different Centers.

1. *Beaded centers*: Cluster seed beads in a ring *(2-5A)* or center the flower with three to five bugle beads, each topped by a seed bead *(2-5B)*.

2. *Embroidered centers*: Embroider 2mm silk ribbon single twist French knots or, for a violet, four French knots taken in gold sewing thread*(2-6)*.

3. *Stuffed circle centers*: Cut a 1½″ circle from ribbon, edge-gathered and

stuffed to form a round puff. Tuck this into a diamond-gathered ribbon rectangle with rounded corners *(2-7)*. The British call this a rockrose. Can you make a more familiar snapdragon or a bread and butter by manipulating this combination?

Gathered Rectangle Flower with Sealed-edged Petals Hanging Downwards.

1. To make a bluebell, round the rectangle corners, but leave a point at each tip, then seal. Cut a prominent sepal-shape from edge-sealed shaded wired ribbon or UltraSuede. Cap the bell with the sepals and let a single orange stamen hang from between the petals *(2-8)*.

2. To make bluets, use shaded grey wired ribbon. With white sewing thread, French-knot a white circle center around a wee yellow bead.

3. To make an eight-petaled bloodroot, combine a 2″ wide sealed-edge rectangle with a 1½″ wide rectangle, putting the smaller inside the larger after diamond-gathering. Off-set the eight petals and embroider a yellow center *(2-9)*.

4. To make nicotiana, fashion a sealed-edge diamond-gathered rectangle. Twist its trumpet to narrow it, then have it rise from the stem just above the horizontal *(2-10)*.

2-8. BLUEBELL   2-9. BLOODROOT

2-10. NICOTIANA

Do you see any of these other flowers in this lesson's gathered rectangle blooms?

Columbine, Cyclamen, Four O'Clock, Gentian, Harebell, Hepatica, Honeysuckle, Hydrangea, Marsh Marigold, Mayflower, Petunia, Rhododendron, Snowdrop, Thorn Apple and Lilium.

A ribbon rectangle with its corners rounded off and gathered in a square makes orchard blossoms, and also these highly stylized flowers, viewed petal side up:

Buttercup, Clematis, Dogwood, Hydrangea, Lilac, Phlox and Sweet Alyssum.

For one small bloom to have so many faces surely suggests adventure!

PANSY BARRETTE
OR BAR PIN

*I*n vintage needleart's repertoire, pansies are played to all sorts of tunes. From that plenty, this lesson's two-step pansy is my favorite. This project includes a ribbon pansy, leaves and a bud, all sewn to an AidaPlus base, backed with same, then glued to a purchased barrette back. A relaxed morning will take this accessory to completion.

This romancing of ribbon is so tidily productive, such relaxing fun, that you'll want to share it. Why not put on a Floral Tea? Remember childhood birthday parties, annual with ice cream, cake and festivity? Recreate that innocent pleasure for a handful of friends: favor them with a pansy kit, then sit together, stitching pansies into bud over tea and crumpets! Your gift will be enduring, for nothing lasts like a happy memory.

SUPPLIES

The pansy barrette or bar pin can be made in many ribbon sizes and colors. The following supplies were used to make a pansy barrette as pictured in photo 2-4. All the wired ribbon used in these models is Lion Ribbon by Offray. The embroidery ribbon is Heirloom Sylk by Mokuba.

Flower (three petals)
Wired ribbon—Cut one piece ⅝″ x 8 ½″ (sz3 x 13½SQs).

Flower (two petals)
Wired ribbon—Cut one piece ⅝″ x 5″ (sz3 x 8SQs).

Flower center
Mokuba Heirloom Sylk embroidery ribbon—Cut 1 yd. of 4mm.

Bud
Wired ribbon—Cut one piece ⅝″ x 2 ½″ (sz3 x 4SQs).

Bud calyx
Fern green shaded wired ribbon—Cut one piece ⅝″ x 1½″ (sz3 x 2½SQs).

Leaves
Wired ribbon—fern green shaded wired ribbon—Cut one piece ⅝″ x 4″ (sz3 x 6½SQs) for each of two leaves.

Foundation
1″ diameter circle of AidaPlus for the pansy; one 2″ x 4″ rectangle of AidaPlus to be trimmed to the flower arrangement's finished shape.

Finding
Metal barrette-back from craft suppliers.

Basic sewing kit and ribbon tools, including Gem Tac or a similar white glue, which will adhere cloth to metal.

2-4. *Pansy Barrette or Bar Pin fashioned by the author: Project 6, Lesson Two.*

2-5. *Pansy Brooch, antiqued and streaked with jet by the author.*

PROCEDURE

The Pansy

1. Fold the 8½″ length of ribbon into thirds, lengthwise. Fold the first and last third to the front and down, forming a U *(2-11)*.

2. Begin with a knot ¼″ in from the starting raw edge (point **a**). Running-stitch the outside edge of the U, curving the stitch line in to finish ¼″ inside the finishing raw edge, at point **b** *(2-11)*. Note: Left handers begin at **b** and finish at **a**.

3. Pull the thread to gather. This forms the three front petals. Flip the large center petal to the front.

4. Pull the bottom wire out of the 5″ ribbon length, then crease-mark the ribbon's mid-point. Beginning with a knot at point **a** (¼″ in from the raw edge), stitch a crescent moon curve from the center to ¼″ from the other end *(2-12)*. (Left handers begin at **b** and end at **a**.)

5. Pull the thread to gather. This forms the two back petals.

6. Stitch the front petal unit on top of the back petal unit *(2-13)*.

7. Lightly tack (use the pointillist stitch) the pansy to a 1″ diameter circle of AidaPlus. Fill the center with French knots of 4mm Mokuba Heirloom Sylk ribbon.

Embellishment

Because this method leaves a hole at the pansy's center, you can fill it with a ⅝″ x 5″ (sz3 x 8SQs) length of yellow shaded wired ribbon tied at the center with an overhand knot, then pushed up through the pansy center and stitched in place. If, as suggested, you fasten the incomplete pansy to a circular backing, you can embellish its center with beads or French knots stitched in embroidery floss. In photo 2-5, the pansy's streaks of jet have been embroidered in fine black silk thread.

A Simple Bud

1. From the center, fold the right side of the bud ribbon length to the back *(2-14, Step 1)*. Fold the left side forward *(2-14, Step 2)*. Roll the bud from right to left, into a tight wrap *(2-14, Step 3)*.

Twist the ribbon tails together into one, to hold the bud shape and form a stem.

2. Cuff the green calyx ribbon by folding a ³⁄₁₆″ cuff away from yourself at the top ribbon edge. Wrap the calyx, right side over left, tightly around the bud. Stitch to hold.

Rounded Leaves, U-Turn Gathered

1. U-turn gather the light-colored edge of the leaf ribbon unit *(2-15A)*.

2. Fold the ribbon right side over left *(2-15B)*. Running-stitch the two light side selvages together, beginning with a tuck, (point **a**), to form the leaf tip. End by securing stitches at point **b**.

3. Finger-press a central point for the leaf tip *(2-15C)*. Next, fingernail-pleat the leaf's outer edge into a pansy leaf's roundly irregular margin *(2-15D)*. Fingernail pleating is done by pinching the wired edge—½″ at a time— between the thumbnails and forefingers of both hands and pushing it out into a tiny peak ¼″ or so deep. The thumbnails define the shape. Tweezers or hemostats also work

FIGURES 11–13 SHOW HOW TO MAKE A FIVE PETALED PANSY AND BUD

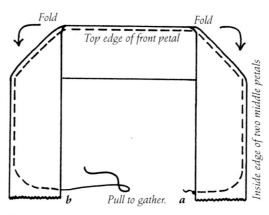

2-11. FRONT PETALS

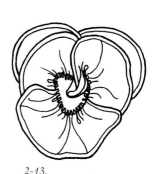

2-13.

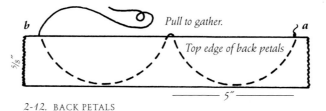

2-12. BACK PETALS

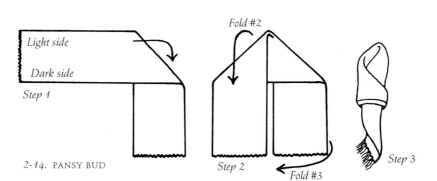

2-14. PANSY BUD

2-16. PANSY BARRETTE OR PIN
CENTERED WITH FRENCH KNOTS

2-17. PANSY CENTERED WITH AN
OVERHAND KNOT

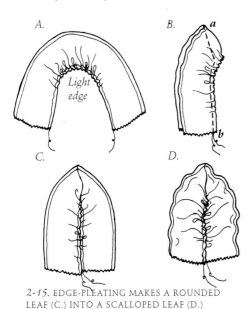

2-6. *Pansy and echo leaf corsage fashioned by the author from techniques in Lesson Two.*

A.

Light edge

B.

a

b

C.

D.

2-15. EDGE-PLEATING MAKES A ROUNDED
LEAF (C.) INTO A SCALLOPED LEAF (D.)

well to hold and pleat the ribbon.

Hybrid: The Echo Leaf

The echo leaf shown in photo 2-6 is made like the rounded leaf (2-15C). To create an echo, simply cut a 2SQs longer length of a second, different color ribbon. On the pansy corsage pictured, an antique gold metallic ribbon from Offray outlines the rounded leaf which has been laid over it and stitched on to it.

Hybrid: The Pressed Flower Pansy

This hybrid must be done with imported French wired ribbon. Once the pansy's basic structure is made, wet and crush it for the antique look described in *Getting Started*. Photo 2-5 and figure 2-16 picture this pansy looking as though your great great-grandmother had pressed it into Flora's Album generations ago.

Hybrid Center: Knotted Pansy Center

Pleat the ends of a $7/8''$ x $3''$ (sz5x 3½SQs) shaded yellow wired ribbon and tie an overhand knot in it (2-16B). Press the knot into a triangular shape. Thread the ribbon tails through the pansy's open center (2-17), positioning the knot with the narrow side pointing towards the front petal. At the back, clip off the longer tail and tack down the remaining free ends. This is a great center for a perky freshly made pansy.

To my taste, figure 2-16 shows an exquisite pansy in need of a center less robust, more demure. The pansy brooch (photo 2-5), on the other hand, has an adamantly pressed-in-the-trunk look. I played up its vintage charm by centering the pansy with a delicate combination of seed beads and silk stitchery, then antiqued the leaves and sprinkled them with tiny beaded sparkles.

ASSEMBLY

1. Arrange the bud and pansy blossoms over the pair of leaves. Glue or stitch together.

2. Trace the outline of this ornament onto the wrong side of AidaPlus. Cutting the backing to shape strengthens the piece, supporting even small protrusions like leaf and bud tips.

3. After cutting the backing shape out, spread its wrong side with white glue and press the flower to it (2-16). To complete the project, glue a barrette finding to its back.

To Stem or Not to Stem?

No stems show in any of the projects taught so far! Even the more complex of these first Ribbon Appliqués, the primrose necklace, the miniature basket of blooms and the pansy barrette reveal no stems. Some Ribbon Appliqués with more foundation exposed still avoid stems by grouping leaves and flowers over background foliage or over layered ribbons.

Certain Ribbon Appliqués, though, require a stem or stems. Lesson Four introduces two such Ribbon Appliqué patterns calling for stems. Lesson Five ties Ribbon Appliqué firmly into classic American quiltmaking. It pictures Baltimore Album blocks with speedily stitched silk ribbon embroidered stems. Whether for personal ornament or appliquéd embellishment, some happy solutions to the stem question follow.

Stitched Stems

1. Embroider stems in cotton, silk or rayon floss (rayon is the shiniest of these flosses) or in wool embroidery yarn. Various thread weights will give different effects. You may choose to stitch the stems in 2mm to 7mm Mokuba Heirloom Sylk or silk embroidery ribbon. Models in *Romancing Ribbons* show several embroidery stitches, including those pictured here.

2. The impression of stems can be achieved by incorporating artificial stemmed foliage into your piece. The stem on store-bought craft leaves serves as a well-defined stem. It is quick, easy and visually effective. In addition, green-wrapped wired stems for floral art are sometimes the ideal touch. They can be bent to the appropriate shape, and then couched down.

Tendrils

To make tendrils, use the copper wire pulled from French ribbon and the green-wrapped stem wires from small scale artificial flora. Coil the wire around a crochet hook, a knitting needle or a drinking straw to make fine tendrils and add another texture to your ribbonry. To protect them, press the coils flat and couch them down.

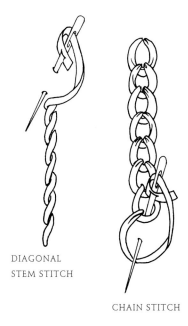

DIAGONAL
STEM STITCH

CHAIN STITCH

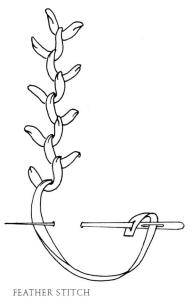

FEATHER STITCH

THE SUGAR SCOOP GATHERING PATTERN

LILIUM

Once in a rare winter, I splurge on three stems of Rubrum Lilies, each wearing at her throat rubies on gold. From ancient stock and Oriental climes (their ancestors brought from Egypt, Greece, Japan, and China by explorers like Marco Polo) these three thousand year old cultivars breath romance. Though I enter the room distracted, their Eden-scent snares me—intoxicating— even before my eyes are forced to pay these stately beauties homage. Shouldn't we stitch so regal a flower into our needleart?

Unlike nature's six-petaled lilies, photo 2-7 shows artistic license in a five-petaled lilium. The sugar scoop gathering pattern shown in figure *2-18A* is running-stitched, then gathered to give each petal its basic structure. As befits so large a floral dynasty, you can vary that stitched path a bit, and experiment with ribbon widths and lengths.

For petal A
Cut a 1½″ x 4½″ (sz9 x 3SQs) length of French wired ribbon.

For petal B
Cut a ⅞″ x 4″ (sz5 x 4½SQs) length of French wired ribbon.

For petal C
Cut a ⅞″ x 3″ (sz5 x 3½SQs) length of French wired ribbon.

1. With a strong matching thread, knotted, stitch from point *a* to point *b* (2-18A). When the sugar scoop is stitched, pull the thread to gather, but do not yet secure it. Hybridize: in *Petal A,* the tightest gathers cluster toward the petal's base. In *Petals B* and *C,* the bowl of the scoop has been elongated and the gathers spread evenly between *a* and *b.* Secure the stitches to hold your chosen petal shape.

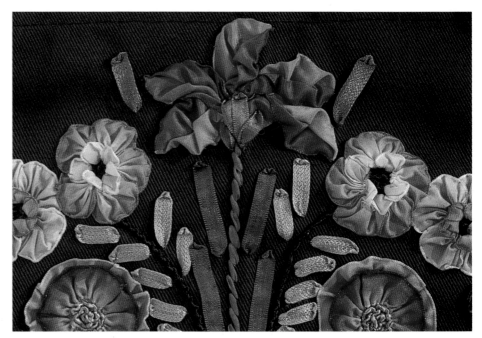

2-7. *Lily made by Lesson Two's sugar scoop gathering technique by the author. Detail from* Everlastings, *Project 7, Lesson Three*

FIGURES 18, 19, AND 22 SHOW HOW EFFECTIVELY THE SUGAR SCOOP GATHERING PATTERN MAKES BOTH LEAVES AND PETALS

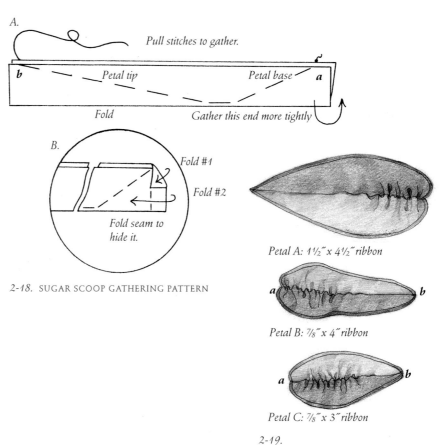

2-18. SUGAR SCOOP GATHERING PATTERN

Petal A: 1½″ x 4½″ ribbon

Petal B: ⅞″ x 4″ ribbon

Petal C: ⅞″ x 3″ ribbon

2-19.

2-20. HARLEQUIN LILY

2. Fold the seam under, so that it is hidden at the petal's base and tip *(2-18B)*. For a sharp point, trim back the seam below **a** at the tip, and seal the cut edge with clear nail polish.

3. Tack-stitch the lily petals to the background. From some angles as few as four petals may show. In figures *2-20* and *2-21* the trumpeted Madonna Lily and the hanging Harlequin Lily entice you with the exotic Lilium's potential. A prominent pistil and stamens characterize lilium. Use artificial purchased stamens or embroider your own.

☆ *Miniature Memo*

The lilium can be miniaturized by using the above proportions in a narrower ribbon. You can also use the same sugar scoop gathering and radically different ribbon lengths to make other flora. For example:

1. Figure *2-22*, ⅝″ x 1½″ (sz3 x 2½SQs), shapes a petal either round or pointed, depending on which end you attach to the flower's center.

2. Figure *2-23*, 2″ x 3″ (sz16 x 1½SQs), is full of surprises. The ribbon is folded in half, raw edge to raw edge, then stitched in a modified sugar scoop, from point **a** to **b**. After the thread is gathered and secured, the seam is trimmed to a scant ¼″ and sealed. Turn the blossom right-side out. The folded side forms a hood when you push it back and down. The resulting shape resembles a foxglove or similar flower *(2-24)*. Ink its throat for a foxglove, or fill its center with a ½″ ribbon circle, edge-gathered and stuffed into a puff for something more like a lady's slipper *(2-25)*.

3. Miniature Calla Lily: For petal *2-26A* cut the ribbon 1½″ x 4″ (sz9 x 2¾ SQs). Fold the ribbon length in half, selvage over selvage. Next, between the seam allowances, trace the bottom half of a 1¾″ circle. Running-stitch the deep

2-21. MADONNA LILY

FIGURES 23–25 SHOW HOW A MODIFIED SUGAR SCOOP GATHERING PATTERN MAKES TWO HOODED BLOOMS

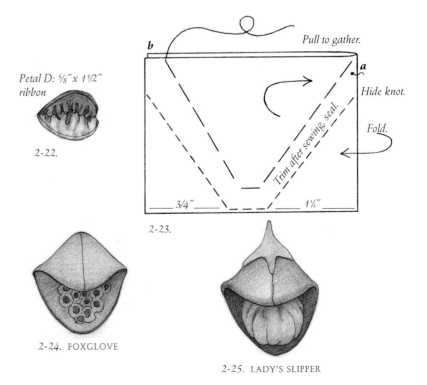

Petal D: ⅝″ x 1½″ ribbon

2-22.

2-23.

2-24. FOXGLOVE

2-25. LADY'S SLIPPER

saucer shape from point *a* to point *b*. Pull the thread to gather. Secure the stitches; then finish the flower as in step 2 above.

For the Pistil and Stamens:

Fold a ⅝″ x 2″ (sz3 x 3¼SQs) green to pink wired ribbon in half *(2-26B)*. Fringe the raw edges down ¼″ by pulling out a thread. Roll the ribbon into a tight cylinder ¼″ in diameter by 1″ tall. Pull the wire out of the ribbon and wrap it around the base of the cylinder *(2-26C)*. Stitch the cylinder fringed end up, into the center of the lily *(2-26D)*.

The Calla Lily's saucer-shaped gathering is a harbinger of Lesson Three. The lily (photo 2-7) modeling this lesson's sugar scoop gathering pattern gets planted in Lesson Three on Project 7, *Everlastings*. There begins a series of larger Ribbon Appliqué projects which tie last century's ribbonart to twentieth century quiltmaking, and on to heirlooms of the twenty-first century! Though the millennial prospect is grand, Lessons Three and Four also continue teaching easy flowers made by patterned-gathering. To transit from Ribbon Appliqué for personal adornment to Ribbon Appliqué for quilts and other home decor, introduce yourself to the ribbon embroidery which—with silken streamers—binds these needleart eras and this lesson to the next. Then, as befits ladies entering a new epoch, our lessons will conclude, in Lesson Six, with an ornamental embroidery scissors-sheath to wear while doing fancywork, and, for the weekend, opera pearls bearing a georgette rose!

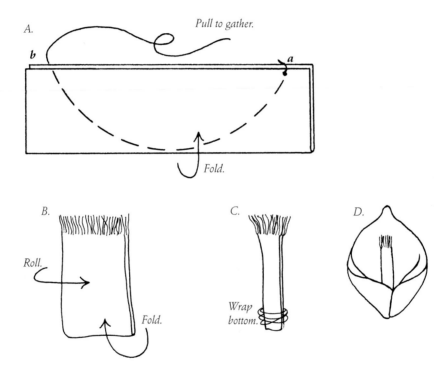

2-26. THE CALLA LILY WITH A FRINGED CENTER
While the Calla Lily is unique, its simple fringed center suits many different flowers.

2-8. *An original Album block design by Wendy Grande from her quilt,* Ribbon Appliqué. *With wondrous innovation, Wendy combines broad Ribbon Appliqué and Lesson Two's silk ribbon embroidery!*

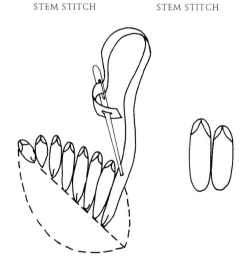

DIAGONAL
STEM STITCH

VERTICAL
STEM STITCH

PIERCED LEAF STITCH

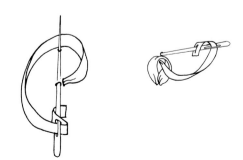

LAZY DAISY STITCH

Elegant, Easy Silk Ribbon Embroidery

Almost all we ever needed to learn about ribbon embroidery we absorbed long ago. As children we were taught embroidery. As young adults we did crewel work. Silk ribbon embroidery's stitches are those same basic stitches of your earliest embroidery: satin stitch, stem or outline stitch, French knots, and all the familiar flat and looped stitches.

While any standard embroidery book will refresh your embroidery vocabulary, the unique pierced leaf stitch is my favorite stitch for textured appliqué. More controlled than its sister satin stitch, its pointed tip evokes a rose leaf's serrations or a rose stem's thorns. To season classic appliqué to *haute cuisine*, a dozen stitches are taught here.

THE 12 BASIC RIBBON FLOWER STITCHES

1. Diagonal stem stitch

2. Vertical stem stitch

3. Pierced leaf stitch

4. Veined leaf stitch

5. Leafed stem stitch

Sew the leaf's length from stem base to leaf tip in Madeira rayon floss, three strands. (Madeira silk or cotton floss can also be used.) Complete the broad leaf in 7mm silk ribbon; or 7mm Mokuba Luminous Ribbon or organdy ribbon.

6. Straight stitch

The straight stitch can reduce the amount of thread wasted on the underside. By re-entering next to your last stitch rather than across from it, you leave a minimum amount of ribbon on the underside of the piece.

7. Satin stitch

8. Back stitch

9. Feather stitch

10. Lazy daisy stitch

11. French knot

Increase the size of this knot as you take one, two, three, or more twists around the needle before pulling the knot through.

12. Couching

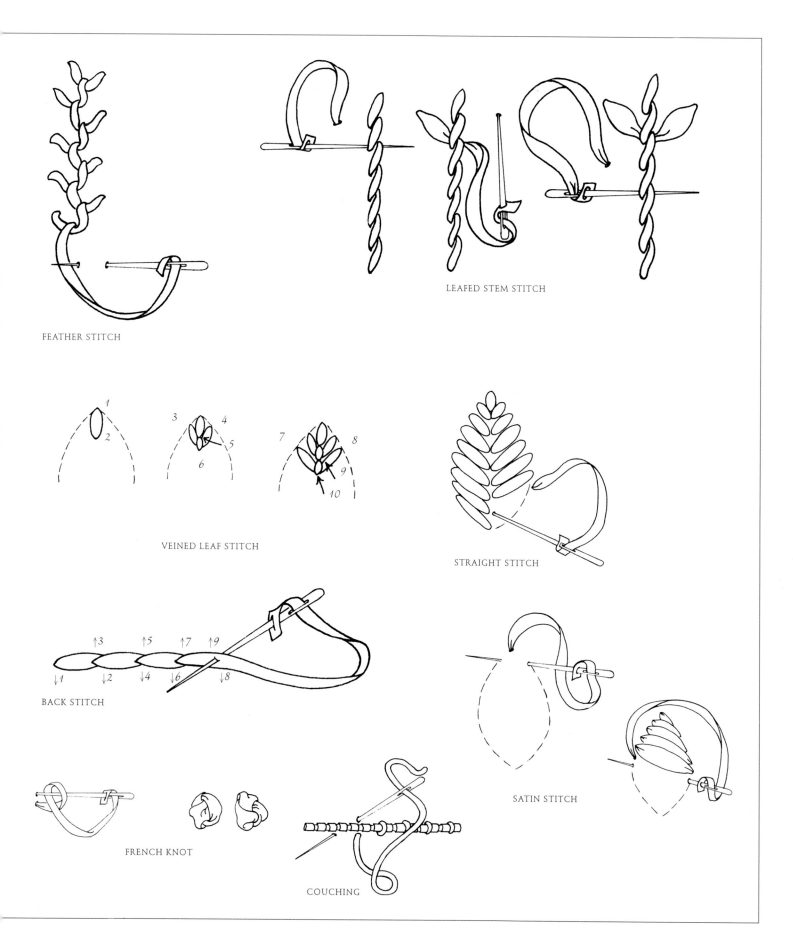

FEATHER STITCH

LEAFED STEM STITCH

VEINED LEAF STITCH

STRAIGHT STITCH

BACK STITCH

SATIN STITCH

FRENCH KNOT

COUCHING

A.

B.

C.

THREADING AND KNOTTING SILK RIBBON

THREADING, STITCHING, AND FINISHING TIPS

1. Threading a Chenille Needle

Use a Chenille needle #26 for 2-4mm wide silk ribbon floss, and lower numbers (larger needles) for wider floss. The Chenille needle, which has a large eye and a sharp point, is good for embroidering quilt-weight cloth. Cut a 12″ to 18″ length of embroidery ribbon on the diagonal. Thread this through the needle *(A)*. Occasionally, for mysterious reasons, the ribbon won't pass through the eye of the needle. When this occurs, cut the diagonal afresh, then seal it to razor sharpness with a touch of clear nail polish. Only its priciness requires that we not leave silk ribbon hanging languidly through the needle's eye. Ribbon embroiderers opt for a shorter ribbon length (ideally 12″) and pass the threaded needle right back into and through the ribbon's neck *(A)*, thus economically capturing the needle until the ribbon's length has been consumed by stitches.

2. Knotting Embroidery Ribbon

Aim the tail end and the needle's point toward each other. Take an in-and-out stitch at the ribbon's end *(B)*. Pull the needle through completely *(C)* to form a knot in the tail. Pull gently, for a knot tied too tightly will not hold.

3. Stitch Secrets

Use a small hoop to do silk ribbon embroidery. To embroider a shape marked for appliqué, stitch up on one side of the shape and down on the other. We who come to ribbon embroidery from floss or yarn embroidery are wont to pull the twisted thread down firmly, but ribbon's breadth requires a looser tension. Pulling the ribbon through tightly narrows the ribbon, giving the work a tense and messy look. Ideally, the ribbon lies flat, gathering tightly only where it exits or enters the cloth. Pull the ribbon completely through as you exit the underside. Loose loops of ribbon on the back are wasteful and get in the way of subsequent stitches. Avoid back loops by feeling (with the hand beneath your base cloth) the ribbon loop diminish as it enters the cloth. If in doubt, peek at the underside!

For most stitches the ribbon should not twist between its entry and its exit. (The brilliant exception is photo 2-9's chrysanthemums, where Wendy Grande twisted silk ribbon around and around before she re-entered the cloth!) When flatness is the goal, you can avoid twisting by thumb-pressing the ribbon down lightly after it exits the cloth. If it winds around before re-entry, slide the needle's shank under the ribbon. Pushing upward, pull the ribbon taut, then pass the needle back and forth under it. This will straighten the ribbon so it re-enters straight. Even adept embroiderers inadvertently pull the ribbon just a tad too tightly once in a while. A milliner's needle threaded with invisible thread can save the day. Smooth out the ribbon with the needle's shank and tack-stitch it down into broad flatness. It's likely you'll need this mending in multiple places, so leave it until the embroidery is finished. Conversely, you'll know instantly if a ribbon stitch is hopelessly tight. Then and there, take a relaxed stitch directly over the wretchedly small one before passing serenely on to your next stitch.

4. Finishing off an embroidery ribbon

Yes, of course it's easier to finish off with a longer tail end! When you have a tail of 3″ or more, you can end with a tailor tack on the underside (D). Clip after tying the tailor-tack knot. However, in this imperfect world our ribbon tails are often very short. Then, from the back, simply weave it through the underside of a previous stitch. Your embroidery should command such respect that it will be protected from rough handling and the shorn-tail finish will hold just fine.

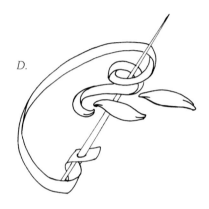

D.

TAILOR TACK KNOT

2-9. *Detail from the quilt* Ribbon Appliqué *by Wendy Grande. The chrysanthemums are made by a twisted silk ribbon stitch described on page 64.*

Detail From Rosa Rugosa—Victorian Beach Rose

LESSON THREE

Flowers Gathered on the Curve

*F*lowers gathered on the curve include crescent moon curves, steep-sided saucers and sliced orange rounds.

Lesson Three teaches separate petals and separate leaves as well. These flowers can be made with their petals gathered all in a row from a single cut of ribbon, or with separate petals from shorter cuts. With five rounded petals, these blooms look like members of the *Rosaceae* or Rose family. This large horticultural family includes everything from roses to plum and raspberry blossoms.

Review *Getting Started*.

RIBBON TYPES

Raw-edged bias cut silk, wired ribbon, single or double-faced satin, grosgrain, velvet, rayon, silk, acetate, moiré and georgette.

RIBBON SIZES

From 8mm up to 2″ wide (size 1H up to size 16).

PROJECTS

Lesson Three's projects lay plots for Ribbon Appliqué gardens on a large scale. They teach an embellishment style based on antique ribbonart, yet one so modern and appealing that it will usher us into the new century with needlework in our hands and smiles on our faces!

Project 7: Everlastings, A Ribbon Appliqué, Pattern 1, included in this lesson.
Project 8: Pennsylvania Dutch Nouveau, A Ribbon Appliqué, Pattern 2, included in this lesson.

RIBBON FLOWER TECHNIQUES

Lesson Three's techniques make impressionistic flora and flowers reminiscent of their natural sisters: California Poppy, Cherry Blossom, Cherry Blossom Bud, Cone Flower, Daffodil, Delphinium, Double Primrose, Foxglove, Harlequin Lily, Hibiscus, Hollyhock, Johnny Jump-Up, Madonna Lily, Moss Rose Bud, Narcissus, Poinsettia, Rubrum Lily, Simplest Pansy, Snapdragon, Tiger Lily and Tulip.

RIBBON LEAF TECHNIQUES

Echo leaf and split leaf.

3-1. *A classic butcher apron and a toaster cover both display Lesson Three Ribbon Appliqué patterns fashioned by the author.*

3-1. EVERLASTINGS: A VICTORIAN THROW

Project Seven

EVERLASTINGS: A RIBBON APPLIQUÉ MOTIF

Our shops abound with accouterments inviting ribbon embellishment by busy women of the 'nineties. Today's fashions feature simple shapes, with table coverings and throw pillows which are quick to ornament. I purchased a tempting apron and a toaster cover and show the results here. So elegant is the finished apron in photo 3-1 that I confess I wish I'd embellished something less humble. Yet the Ribbon Appliqué took only a day or so. By comparison to other fancy work, ribbon embroidery and Ribbon Appliqué are not only facile but fast.

Project 7 teaches how to stitch a Ribbon Appliqué design. If you yearn for an heirloom treasure, stitch the design onto a throw quilt (3-1) to be draped as the Victorians did, over a sofa or chair. I envision it on wool or velveteen, pulled up against the evening draft —a warmth for hands and heart. As a pillow or a Christmas tree skirt, it would surely be a family treasure. Or perhaps, like me, you'll wear it as a hostess apron, but only after the dinner is fully prepared!

3-2. Everlastings, *Project 7, Lesson Three Ribbon Appliqué fashioned by the author.*

The *Everlastings* motif is crowned by a lily made with Lesson Two's sugar-scoop gathering pattern. Primrose or narcissus-like flowers sprout beside the lily. Romantically, they are rendered by crescent-moon gathering.

SUPPLIES

This Ribbon Appliqué motif can be made in multiple ribbon sizes and colors. The following supplies are used to make Project 7, *Everlastings*, as pictured in photo 3-2.

Ready-made base

Any suitable finished item like the apron pictured in photo 3-1 or a 12½″ square (includes seam allowance) of quiltweight cotton cloth. If off-white, use a tone-on-tone print with a bit of weight to it. "Scroll", my Baltimore Beauties® background fabric, is the sort of neutral print which balances Ribbon Appliqué well (see *Resources*). For a heavier cloth, use wool flannel, fine corduroy or cotton velveteen.

Make one Flower A, Tiger Lily

Cut five 1½″ x 3″ (sz9 x 2SQs) pieces of wired ribbon per flower.

Make four Flower B, Double Primrose

Cut four ⅝″ x 13½″ (sz3 x 21½SQs) pieces of Elégance wired ribbon, shaded yellow to lavender, per flower.

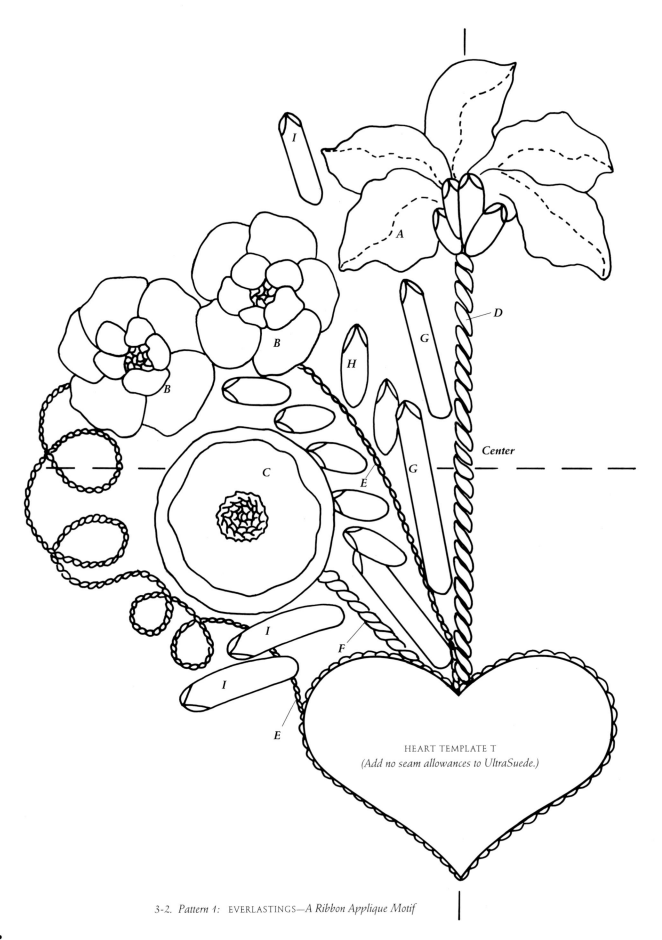

I

A

D

B

B

B

G

H

Center

E

C

G

I

F

I

E

HEART TEMPLATE T
(Add no seam allowances to UltraSuede.)

3-2. Pattern 1: EVERLASTINGS—A Ribbon Applique Motif

Make two Flower C, Cone Flowers

Cut one ⅝″ x 10½″ (sz3 x 17SQs) piece of Offray's shaded Cedar color wired ribbon, for each of two bottom petal wreaths, and gather on the dark edge.

Cut one ⅝″ x 7″ (sz3 x11¼SQs) piece of the same Offray Cedar ribbon for each of two upper petal wreaths, and gather on the light edge.

Make the decorative tendrils, four Flower B centers, two of Stem E, and outline the heart

Mokuba No. 0962 Rayon Cord color #36, 3 yards.

Make two Flower C centers

Mokuba No. 0962 Rayon Cord, color #14 (old gold), ½ yard total.

Stem D

Use 4mm Mokuba Heirloom Sylk embroidery ribbon in green shade #366, and use the diagonal stem stitch.

Stem F

Use 4mm Mokuba Heirloom Sylk embroidery ribbon in green shade #379, 1 yard total.

Leaves G

Use 7mm Mokuba No.4599 Luminous Ribbon, color #7, 1 yard total.

Leaves H

Use 7mm Mokuba No. 1512, color #48, 1 yard total.

Leaves I

Use Mokuba No. 1512, color #18, 1 yard total.

Heart

2½″ x 4″ rectangle of red UltraSuede.

Basic sewing kit and ribbon tools, including embroidery hoop, chenille needles #24 and #26, milliners #10 and glue-stick.

PROCEDURE

1. *Make a master pattern, then mark Pattern 1 (3-2) onto your base.* Trace the pattern out of the book. Use a lightbox to trace the mirror image to complete both sides of the master pattern. Next, mark the pattern onto the background. See *Appendix 2: Pattern Transfer.*

2. *Embroider the stems and leaves.* Using a hoop and a chenille needle #24, embroider Stems D and F. Couch stem E. Use the pierced leaf stitch to embroider the leaves. (See basic ribbon flower embroidery stitches in Lesson Two.)

3. *Make Flower A, Tiger Lily.* Shape each of five petals with the sugar scoop gathering pattern as shown on page 58. Adjust the petals' length to the particular petal on the pattern. Appliqué the petals to the background in the shape of a lily. At the lily's base, embroider stem-colored sepals in leaf stitch.

4. *Make four of Flower B, Double Primrose.* Follow the directions on page 79. Gather two of the ribbon pieces so the inside petals are on the dark side of the ribbon. Gather the other two ribbon pieces with the inner petals to the light side of the ribbon. Appliqué the finished flowers to the base. Couch a piece of Mokuba rayon cord using as much as needed to fill each center.

5. *Make two of Flower C, Cone Flowers.* Using the ribbon cuts specified under materials, follow the directions for a single primrose in Lesson One. Tack-stitch the lower petals to the background. Appliqué an upper petal wreath over the lower petal wreath, allowing about ¼″ of the lower petals to show. Coil and couch Mokuba rayon cord, to form each center.

6. *Make the decorative tendrils* by couching Mokuba's dark green twist cord along the marked pattern line. Seal the cord's starting and finishing ends with clear nail polish. Tuck the starting end under the appliquéd heart and the finishing end under adjacent cord.

7. *Cut the Heart Template T (3-2)* from UltraSuede, adding no seam allowance. Pin or glue (with gluestick) it in place. Appliqué the heart using the tack stitch. As you appliqué, couch the green rayon cord around the heart, outlining it. Tuck the cord's cut end under the heart.

ASSEMBLY

If the Ribbon Appliqué has been done on a ready-made wearable like the apron, finish the piece by backing the embroidery. Iron fusible web to the wrong side of quiltweight cotton. From this fabric, cut a round-cornered square which covers the underside of the embroidery. Iron, keeping the embroidery face down on a towel to heat-bond this backing, to seal in the needlework's thread ends. If you've ornamented a ready-made pillow slipcover, the work's underside should not require further backing. If you've been more ambitious and stitched your Ribbon Appliqué on a quilt block or other item, basic sewing or quilting skills will be required to finish it.

Project 8

PENNSYLVANIA DUTCH NOUVEAU

*T*his Ribbon Appliqué pattern takes only a day to complete, a reasonable day including a bit of home-making. I used that day to upgrade a store-bought toaster cover to informal elegance. More valuable than the finished needlework is the happy memory of planting these flowers in this charming design. Perhaps you would prefer to work this wonder on a tea cozy, a pillow,

3-3. PENNSYLVANIA DUTCH NOUVEAU TABARD

a quilt square, or a wearable as in figures 3-3, 3-4, and 3-5. Watch for the perfect site, then gather up the supplies and enjoy your day in the garden!

SUPPLIES

This Ribbon Appliqué motif can be made in multiple ribbon sizes and colors. The following supplies were used to make Project 8, *Pennsylvania Dutch Nouveau,* as pictured in photo 3-3. The embroidery stitches used to execute this motif are also listed here.

Ready-made base

Any suitable work in progress or ready-made cloth item.

Make one of Flower A, Tulip

Cut three 1½″ x 3½″ (sz9 x 2⅓SQs) pieces of Elégance wired organza ribbon shaded pink to red. This is made by a familiar ribbon bud method, but the shaded wired organza ribbon is critical. It imitates a tulip petal's soft curves in a way that other ribbons cannot.

Make two of Flower B, California Poppy

Cut a ⅝″ x 4″ (sz3 x 6½SQs) length of shaded yellow to lavender wired ribbon for each flower. (See Lesson One, page 38 for directions to make this flower.)

Make two of Flower C, Delphinium, Foxglove or Hollyhocks

Cut a ⅞″ x 10″ (sz5 x 11½SQs) length of overdyed, shaded French wired ribbon per flower. See page 59 for directions to make this flower.

Make two of Flower D, Daffodils

Wreath of petals: Cut five ⅝″ x 3″ (sz3 x 5SQs) of French yellow to lavender shaded wired ribbon per flower.

Flower's trumpet or cup

Cut one ⅝″ x 4″ (sz3 x 6½SQs) French yellow to lavender shaded wired ribbon per flower. Note that in photo 3-3, one flower cup faces light edge up, the other faces dark edge up.

Diagonal-stem stitch the three stems E

Use two shades of 4mm green em-broidery silk ribbon (Mokuba Heirloom Sylk colors #374 and #366 are suggested).

Pierced leaf-stitch the tulip sepals F

Use 7mm wide Mokuba No. 4599 Luminous Ribbon in color #7.

Feather-stitch the two stems G

Use Mokuba No. 1512 (100% rayon, one size only) in color #48.

Couch the two stems H, their tendrils, the heart outline, and the motif outline

Use 3 to 5 yds. of Mokuba Metallic Bead Cord No. 0140, color #3 (black).

Lazy daisy stitch leaves I

Use 7mm wide Mokuba No. 4599 Luminous Ribbon in color #7.

Pierced Leaf stitch leaves J

Use 7mm wide Mokuba No. 4599 Luminous Ribbon in color #5.

Make a paper template of heart K

Cut one heart out of dusty rose UltraSuede, adding no seam allowances. Alternatively, turn the seams under on a

3-4. PENNSYLVANIA DUTCH NOUVEAU PILLOW

3-5. PENNSYLVANIA DUTCH NOUVEAU QUILT

3-3. Pennsylvania Dutch Nouveau, *Project 8, Lesson Three Ribbon Appliqué fashioned by the author.*

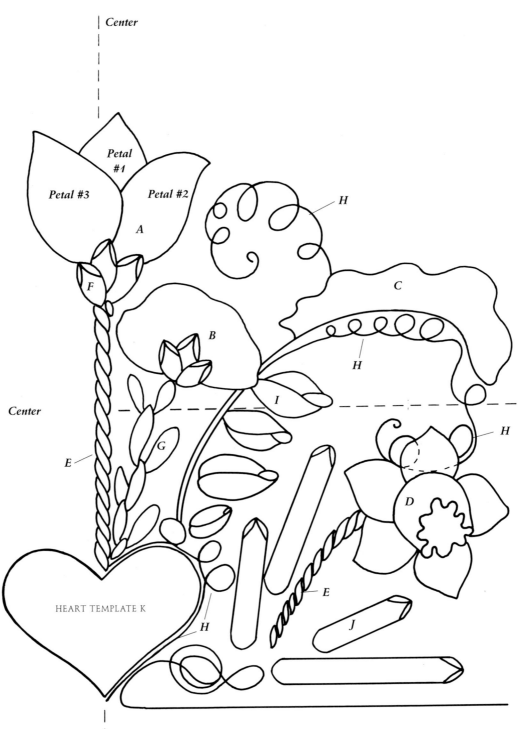

Center

Petal #1

Petal #3   Petal #2

A

F

H

C

B

H

Center

I

H

E

G

H

D

E

HEART TEMPLATE K

H

J

3-6. Pattern 2: *PENNSYLVANIA DUTCH NOUVEAU—A Ribbon Applique Motif*
NOTE: *When you transfer this pattern, use minimal lines. Mark a single line for each leaf and stem. Mark ¼" inside of the heart and flowers so the drawn lines are covered by the needlework.*

heart appliqué in cotton or crepe de Chine.

Basic sewing kit and ribbon tools, including threads to match the heart, bead cord, and flower; embroidery hoop, chenille needles #22 (for leaves and sepals) and #26 (for stems), milliners #10, and (optional) gluestick for basting the flower petals and the heart to the background.

PROCEDURE

1. *Mark Pattern 2 (3-6) onto your base.* Trace the pattern out of the book. Using a lightbox, trace the pattern's mirror image to complete both sides of a master pattern. Transfer the pattern to the background. (See *Appendix 2: Pattern Transfer.*)

2. *Appliqué the heart.* Baste, pin, or glue (with gluestick) the heart to the background, then appliqué using the tack stitch.

3. *Embroider the stems, leaves, and tendrils.* Use a hoop and the ribbon, needle, and stitches specified to embroider the stems, leaves, and tendrils. (To review how to do a certain stitch, see *Elegant, Easy Silk Ribbon Embroidery* in Lesson Two).

4. *Make Flower A,* a three-petaled tulip. To repeat the model's shading, make petals #2 and #3 *(3-7)* by folding *(#1)* the right side down diagonally (from the top, darker edge) to the left. Then (from the same point on the top edge) fold *(#2)* the left side down over it to the right. Running-stitch from point *a* to *b* *(3-8)*. Pull thread to gather to a ⅝″ width. Trim the excess to ¼″ below the stitch-line.

Make petal #1 with the light edge of the ribbon at the top. Fold the right side down to the left, then from the same point on the top edge fold the left side down over it to the right.

Pin the three petals to fit the marked background. Gather-stitch the layered petal bases to ¾″ width across the tulip. Appliqué the flower, including both sides of each petal. Leaf-stitch the three sepals to cover the tulip's raw-edged base *(3-9)*.

5. *Make two of Flower B and two of Flower C.* The showy but simple Flower B poppy and the cascading bell-like Flower C are taught in Lesson One.

6. *Make two of Flower D, Daffodil.* Although daffodils are all straight-line sewn, they are taught as part of this project. The softly cupped center is the one pictured on the left of Pattern 2 in photo 3-3. The pleated trumpet is on the right.

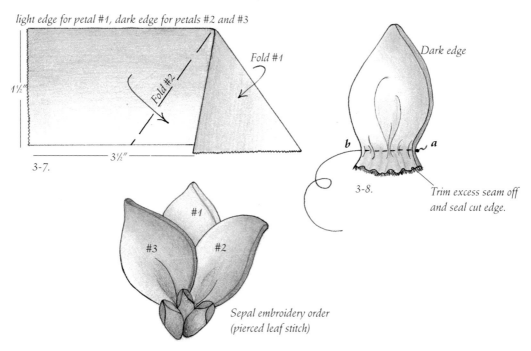

light edge for petal #1, dark edge for petals #2 and #3

Fold #1

Fold #2

1½″

3½″

3-7.

Dark edge

b   a

3-8.

Trim excess seam off and seal cut edge.

#1

#3   #2

Sepal embroidery order (pierced leaf stitch)

3-9. FLOWER A, *Petal applique order*

Daffodils and Narcissus have six petals. In the model, the flower on the right has five petals, while that on the left has six. Your choice!

Daffodils

1. Cut six ⅝″ x 2¼″ (sz3 x 3½SQs) lengths of yellow to lavender shaded wired ribbon for the petals. Cut a ⅝″ x 3″ (sz3 x 4¾SQs) ribbon length of the same ribbon for the daffodil's center.

2. To make one petal, follow steps A through D of figure 3-10. To make a five-petaled wreath follow steps E and F of figure 3-10.

3. *Softly cupped center:* Cut a ⅝″ x 3″ (sz3 x 4¾SQs) length of shaded wired ribbon. Seam and gather as in figure 3-11 If you push the front lip of the trumpet down below the back edge, then the wire-edged base automatically cups as in figure 3-12. This cupped center can then be appliquéd to the petal base. Or you can make one of the following two alternate centers.

4. *Frilly center:* Pin-pleat the top selvage by threading a long quilter's pin in and out every ⅛″. Use one pin for the front edge of the cup, one for the back, and a third for the bottom edge which you can pin through two layers. (It will look as though you took running stitches with the straight pins.) Push the stitches firmly toward the pin head. The ribbon will fall into pleats. Soak it with hair spray and allow a few minutes for drying. With your fingertip, open the cup's lips, and push its base into a rounded shape (3-13). Then appliqué this frilly-edged trumpet to the daffodil petal-wreath.

5. *Stuffed cushion center:* Put a tuft of fiberfil into the cupped center. Whip-stitch the top selvage, full circle, then pull the thread to gather (3-14). Pull as tightly as needed for the look you want. Low, flat on the top and gently sloped? Or saucily round and stand-uppish? Secure the thread when you're satisfied. Now is the time to add embellishment. My favorites are seed beads, or French knots embroidered with shiny Madeira 100% rayon embroidery floss (3-15).

ASSEMBLY

See the Assembly directions for Project 7. They also lead you to completion of Project 8: *Pennsylvania Dutch Nouveau.*

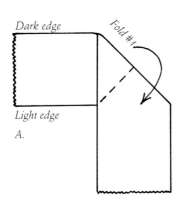

A.

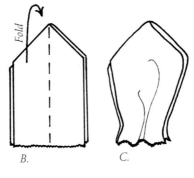

B.   C.

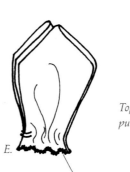

D.

Stitch to secure.

E.

From the wrong side, whip-stitch one petal to the next, right sides and top sides together.

3-10. DAFFODIL PETALS

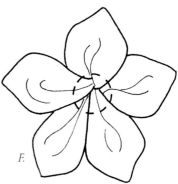

F.

Topside view: wreath of 5 petals, the seams pushed under to the wrong side.

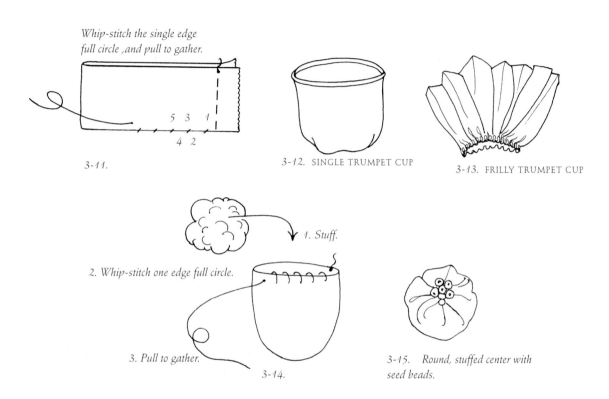

*Whip-stitch the single edge
full circle ,and pull to gather.*

5 3 1

4 2

3-11.

3-12. SINGLE TRUMPET CUP

3-13. FRILLY TRUMPET CUP

1. Stuff.

2. Whip-stitch one edge full circle.

3. Pull to gather.

3-14.

3-15. *Round, stuffed center with
seed beads.*

3-16. DAFFODIL WITH FRILLY TRUMPET

3-17. PUFF-CENTERED BLOOM

Three Clever Curves

Lesson Three's pattern-gathered flowers can be made on one long ribbon cut, with their petals gathered in a row. They can also be made with separate petals—or even separate flowers—each gathered on a shorter cut.

1. The curved line for gathers can be stitched repeatedly along the full ribbon's length.

2. The curved line for gathers can be sewn once, from seam to seam for a single petal's ribbon length.

THE CRESCENT MOON CURVE

This is a shallow, continuous curve, a sliver of the whole, a crescent of a moon. Like that celestial orb, this line has wondrous properties!

3-4. *Kathy Rabun interprets* Willanna's Basket *(pattern from* Dimensional Appliqué*) in Lesson Three's Ribbon Appliqué techniques. Her exuberant interpretation of this Album Quilt block incorporates silk flowers!*

A.

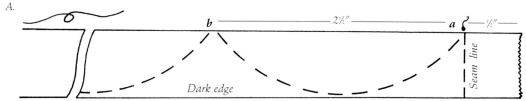

The dark edge on this side makes a rim of dark inner petals.

B.

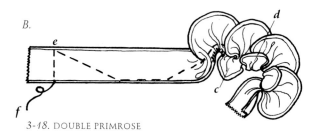

3-18. DOUBLE PRIMROSE

3-19.

To make a Double Primrose:

Cut a ribbon ⅝″ x 13½″ (sz3 x 21½SQs).

1. Mark the curve units *(3-18A)* with a fine mechanical pencil. Figure 3-18A is full size. Use a plastic circle template for drawing its curve onto the ribbon, or make your own template. Leave ½″ seam allowance at either end. This will be trimmed down to ¼″ after the stitching is completed. Leave in both edge wires.

2. With a strong matching thread, running-stitch from one tip *a* to the next tip *b*, repeating this pattern along the ribbon length. At the top of each curve, pass the thread over the edge and begin the next stitch on the opposite side (topside or underside) of the ribbon.

3. After three or four crescent moons have been sewn, pull the thread to gather *(3-18B)*. Magic! You've stitched larger petals around the outside, and a second row of petite petals becomes the flower's center. Take each tiny petal *c* and press it back over the larger petal *d*.

4. Continue the running stitches to *e*. Gather the string of petals to fit the pattern. Secure the stitches; but do not cut the thread. *Note:* When you are looking at both rows of petals, you are looking at the top side (or right side) of the ribbon.

5. Fold the string of petals in half (right sides together) so the raw edges lie on top of each other. Use the same threaded needle to sew a ½″ seam from *e* to point *f*. Secure the stitches. Trim the seam to ¼″ and seal the edges with clear nail polish.

6. Appliqué the finished flower to the background. Four of these flowers are planted on Pattern 1. Note that in the model, two of them are dark petal-centered; two are light petal-centered *(3-19)*. Their middles should be filled with a spiral of twist cord, couched down.

THE STEEP-SIDED SAUCER CURVE

Before gathering, this curve is flat, like the bottom of a saucer, then resumes its curve. Its name recalls a kitten bent over a saucer's edge, curling up milk with her tongue, catching it in droplets on her whiskers, then shaking them quickly off and licking her lips.

To make a Cherry Blossom

1. For a single petal, cut a ribbon ⅝″ x 3¼″ (sz3 x 5¼SQs). Pull out the bottom wire. For a five-petaled cherry blossom, cut five of these lengths.

2. Mark the curve units *(3-20A)* with a fine mechanical pencil. Figure A is full size. Use a plastic circle template for drawing its curve onto the ribbon, or make your own template. Leave ¼″ seam allowance at both ends.

3. With a strong matching thread, running-stitch from **a** to point **b**.

4. Pull the thread tightly to gather into a petal *(3-20B)*.

5. Sew five petals together, each one overlapping the other *(3-20C)*. Cover the raw-edged center with French knots made with sewing thread, or fine seed beads.

Hybrids: Shorten the ribbon to 3″, and change the length of the gathering unit to 2½″, in order to make a less puffy flower *(3-21)*. Cuff the sides of this petal, bring them to touch in the front, and you have a blossom bud *(3-22)*.

★ *Speed Tip:* To make the cherry blossom more quickly, sew five adjacent steep-sided saucer curves on a ribbon length which includes the ¼″ seam allowances. When sewn repeatedly, the inside rim will have a slight flare between each petal. It is not big enough to be decorative, so just push it to the wrong side of the ribbon before seaming the petal wreath's raw edges together.

3-21. HYBRID I

3-22. BLOSSOM BUD

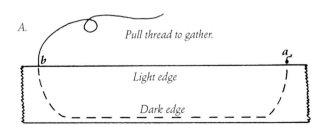

A.

Pull thread to gather.

b   a

Light edge

Dark edge

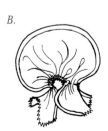

B.

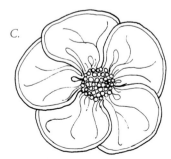

C.

3-20. CHERRY BLOSSOM

To make a Simple Pansy

Though pansies were taught in Lesson Two, those pansies were never this simple!

1. For a single petal, cut a shaded wired ribbon 2″ x 3½″ (sz16 x 1¾SQs). Leave both wires in. Fold in half so the light edge is in the front.

2. Mark the curve unit *(3-23A)* with a fine mechanical pencil.

3. Running-stitch from *a* to *b*.

4. Pull to gather the ribbon to 1⅛″ wide. Secure the stitches.

5. Sculpt the pansy by concentrating most of the gathers in the center and tacking them with a ¼″ stitch taken several times on top of itself.

6. Shape the wired edge to look pansy-like *(3-23B)*. Stitch the pansy's face, or ink it with a Pigma Micron .01 pen.

☆ *Miniature Memo:* When the ribbon is ⅝″ x 1¼″, and stitch-gathered into a steep-sided saucer *(3-24A)*, it becomes a tiny Johnny Jump-Up, shown in figure *3-24B*.

A.
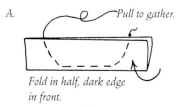
Pull to gather.

Fold in half, dark edge in front.

B.

3-24. JOHNNY JUMP-UP

A.
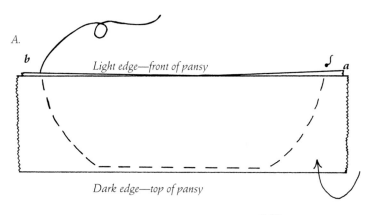

b

Light edge—front of pansy

a

Dark edge—top of pansy

3-23. SIMPLE PANSY

B.
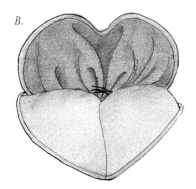

THE SLICED ORANGE ROUND

This curve circles from one side of the ribbon to the other. The line it makes could draw a Florida orange, freshly cut in two. So fresh is the blossom this pattern stitches, that it is ready to burst into bloom!

To make a Victorian Moss Rose Bud

1. For a single petal, cut a ribbon 2″ x 2½″ (sz16 x 1¼SQs). Leave both wires in. Fold in half so the light edge is in front.

2. Mark the curve unit. It is shown full size in figure 3-25A.

3. With a strong matching thread, running-stitch from *a* to point *b*.

4. Pull to gather the half circle. Push most of the gathers to the bottom. Then push the lower edge to the underside, behind the bud. This excess ribbon will round out the bud's base. Shape the top into a soft point.

5. Using the calyx template *(3-25C)*, cut a calyx from moss green UltraSuede and appliqué it over the bud. Embroider the moss around it, using silk sewing thread and the blanket stitch.

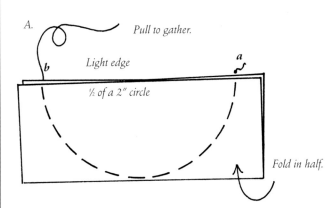

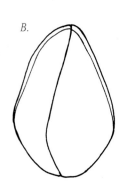

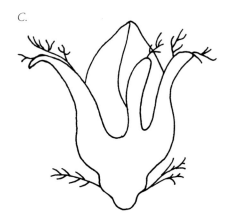

3-25. VICTORIAN MOSS ROSE BUD

3-5. *The quilt* Ribbon Appliqué *was designed and stitched by Wendy Grande.*
This masterpiece's wealth of flora, fauna, and ribbonry techniques is cradled by bright yet soft color and a peaceful repetition of design elements.

Ribbon Flower Techniques

HIBISCUS

1. Cut five 2″ x 3″ (sz16 x 1½SQs) lengths of rose to peach shaded wired ribbon for the petals.

2. Fold the ribbon's top edge forward on the diagonal *(3-26A)* until its edges meet in the middle at *a*.

3. Stitch from *a* to *b*, using the glove (or leather) stitch so that the edges are brought together, but do not overlap. Secure the stitches at *b*.

4. Draw the crescent moon gathering line from cut edge to cut edge *(3-26A, again)*.

5. U-turn gather both top edge wires *d* and twist them together to secure. Gathered, point *a* pulls forward and down as in figure *3-26B*.

6. Running-stitch down and up around the crescent moon curve. Pull the stitches to gather until a petal *(3-26B)* is formed. Secure the stitches. Fingerpress the curved-under edges to hold the petal shape. (If need be, wet, fingerpress and allow to dry.)

7. Repeat steps 2 through 6 until five petals are completed.

8. Overlap the lower right side of one petal and appliqué it for an inch or so, on top of the left edge of the next petal. Sew a fan of three petals together, each over-

lapping the next. Insert the stamens and pistil (directions for making it follow), tacking ½″ of its base to the flower's underside. Appliqué it in a graceful curve as in figure 3-29. Then complete the round of petals.

HIBISCUS STAMEN

1. Cut a 1½″ x 2″ (sz9 x 1⅓SQs) length of rose to pink shaded wired ribbon. Cut a 1½″ x 3″ (sz9 x 2SQs) length of orange to yellow shaded wired ribbon.

2. Cut off the selvage edges (with the wires) and round the top as in figure 3-27A and B. Fringe the sides and top of both ribbon cuts by pulling out threads to a ¼″ depth.

3. Roll the stamen center from left to right (3-27A) into a tube. Baste to hold the shape. Roll the stamen on the diagonal (3-27B) to wrap around the center. Baste to look like figure 3-27C.

HIBISCUS LEAF

1. Cut two ⅞″ x 3″ (sz5 x 3½SQs) ribbon lengths. Cut one of Mokuba No. 4480 Bright Velvet Ribbon in color #16. (This is a flat, shiny 100% rayon pile ribbon in a rich, mossy green.) Cut the second length of moss green shaded wired ribbon.

2. Overlap the velvet selvage over the wired ribbon (3-28) and glove-stitch the two together.

3. Trace a leaf shape from figure 3-28, cutting out the shape just inside the drawn stitch line. Use this tracing to make a leaf template.

4. Using two straight pins for stability, pin the template to the underside of the ribbon lengths. Leave the template in place while you stitch around it.

5. Running-stitch the leaf's curves. Stitch from **b** to **c** (3-28) and from **d** to **e**. Trim the excess to a ¼″ seam and seal with clear nail polish. Pull the threads to gather. When tight, secure the stitches. Dampen the edge and crease it over the template. Remove the template. Appliqué the leaf, bud and hibiscus blossom to a base.

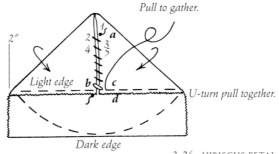

A.

Pull to gather.

2″

Light edge

Dark edge

U-turn pull together.

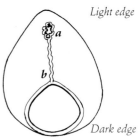

B. Underside of finished petal

Light edge

Dark edge

3-26. HIBISCUS PETAL

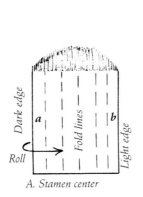

Dark edge

Roll

a

Fold lines

b

Light edge

A. Stamen center

Dark edge

Fold lines

Roll

Light edge

B. Stamen outside

C. Finished stamen

3-27. HIBISCUS STAMEN

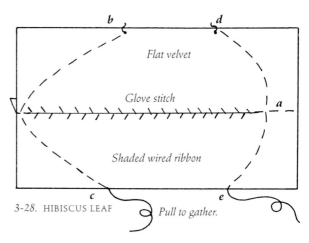

b   *d*

Flat velvet

Glove stitch   *a*

Shaded wired ribbon

c   *e*

3-28. HIBISCUS LEAF   Pull to gather.

HIBISCUS BUD

1. Cut two 1½″ x 1½″ (sz9 x 1SQs) lengths of rose shaded to peach wired ribbon for the bud petals. Cut two ⅞″ x 1½″ (sz5 x 1½SQs) lengths of moss green shaded wired ribbon for the bud calyx.

2. Make the petals following the method illustrated by 3-30A. Make the calyx by the method illustrated in 3-30B.

3. Appliqué the leaf, bud and hibiscus blossom to a base.

3-29. HIBISCUS

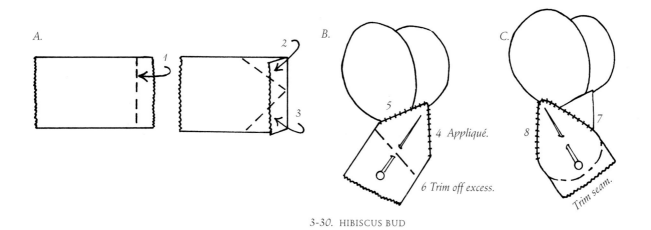

A.

B.

C.

1

2

3

5

4 *Appliqué.*

6 *Trim off excess.*

8

7

Trim seam.

3-30. HIBISCUS BUD

MORE ROSACEAE

As befits the large Rosaceae family, there are still more ways to ruche (pattern-gather) a rose. As a flower sculpting technique, pattern-gathering is power-packed. Lesson Two introduced the method with several unique gathering routes. While Lesson Three explored curved-line gathering, the next lesson focuses on angular gathering. Unless the differences are played up, a five-petaled bloom made by rake ruching closely resembles a five-petaled bloom made by crescent moon gathering. Yet joy in small differences delights—if not defines—the ribbon flower connoisseur. Beyond the delicate ruffle of inner petals, crescent moon gathered flowers lie flatter than do rake-ruched flowers. Because the gathering line ascends steeply and straight, Lesson Four's rake-ruched petals are puffier and fuller.

This brings us to the mid-point in our lessons, or what would be summer in a ribbon gardener's year. As though warmed by that season, let's pause from our labors, sit back, and enjoy a naturalist's poetic affection for the wild rose:

Most of the wild roses are single and five petalled. They have all the delicacy and charm of a host of butterflies alighting in their thousands along every arching branch of the shrub. ...Their singleness often reveals beautiful crowns of golden stamens, sometimes of amber, apricot or ruby...They carry their wildness in their scent...diffusing on the air and made more sweet by rain.

— Judyth A. McLeod, *Our Heritage of Old Roses*

Old roses are popular once more, as this century turns to the next. Cuttings are collected from such romantic spots as antique graveyards, where a century and more ago, roses—before prolonged blooming was bred in and their intoxicating scent bred out—were planted in fond remembrance. Venerable wild roses have enhanced country roadsides all of our lives and, in appreciation, have been heirloom-stitched into our next project, Lesson Four.

3-6. Spring Blossoms, Summer Cherries *by Wendy Grande, from her quilt,* Ribbon Appliqué.
Exquisitely, Wendy combines ribbon appliqué and silk ribbon embroidery.

Victorian Beach Roses, *the Project 9, Lesson Four Ribbon Appliqué designed and stitched by the author. The ribbon is Elégance wired ribbon and the fabric is from the Baltimore Beauties collection.*

Rake Ruching and Mountain/Valley Ruching

*F*lowers gathered in the sparsely spiked outline of an old iron garden rake, silhouetted at dusk...flowers gathered in mountain/valley triangles forming the zig zag "rail fence" pattern of West Virginian farm fields...and of Victorian ruching.

These two gathering patterns—the rake and the mountain/valley ruching—are simple ribbon flower techniques with spectacular results. This lesson's project provides an alluring site for a rake-ruched flower, then suggests an optional pattern and a whole quilt genre inviting mountain/valley ruched roses.

Review *Getting Started*.

RIBBON TYPES

Wired ribbon (shaded, solid, and luminous), organza, raw-edged bias-cut silk, single or double-faced satin, grosgrain, velvet, rayon, silk ribbon floss, acetate, moiré, georgette and Mokuba Heirloom Sylk embroidery ribbon.

RIBBON SIZES

From 9mm up to 2″ wide.

PROJECTS

Project 9: Rosa Rugosa—Victorian Beach Rose quilt block, Pattern 3, given in this lesson.

Optional Project 1: Friendship Wreath with a Showy Rose.

Pictured, no pattern given.

RIBBON FLOWER TECHNIQUES

Lesson Four's techniques make both impressionistic flora and flora reminiscent of their natural sisters: African Violet, Ageratum, Alyssum, Anemone, Azalea, Bachelor's Button, Carnation, Chrysanthemum, Crocus, Daffodil, Dahlia, Fruit Blossom, Hyacinth, Indian Paint Brush, Lilac, Oriental Poppy, Peony, Pink, Plumaria, Ranunculus, Rhododendron, Rosa Rugosa—the Wild Rose, Sailor's Britches, Showy Rose, Snowdrop, Sweet Alyssum, Tulip and Velvet Pansy.

Project 9

ROSA RUGOSA— VICTORIAN BEACH ROSE

O no man noes
through what wild centuries
roves the rose.
—Anonymous Old English verse

*R*osa Rugosa is the Latin name for this most ancient rose. Because wild roses carpet Cape Cod and color my memory of the place, this papercut block names the flower in both a dead and a living tongue. Victorian papercut blocks often have an unexpected tang. It is as though the paper pattern was cut twice. Once folded into an obvious eight-repeat approach, it is then folded a second time, with one quarter of the pattern cut apart and re-arranged, spontaneously—like jazz. That vintage "nothing is as simple as it appears" aesthetic still appeals!

Asymmetry adds zest to this antique block. The first-cut pattern's symmetrical rose stem must have been clipped free from the wreath, pruned, and then repositioned on the diagonal. Tradition's rhythm was restored by repeating that quadrant four times, clockwise around the square. That last century prototype has the beloved look of unembellished appliqués in Turkey red and Victoria green. Photo 4-1 shows my Ribbon Appliqué interpretation of the antique, while photo 4-2 displays Ruth Meyer's dramatic rendition of pattern 3 as a wall quilt. Both take Rosa Rugosa to the brink of another century.

SUPPLIES AND PREPARATION

Like most quilt blocks, pattern 3 can be interpreted in many fabrics and by multiple methods. It is an ideal block to make by hand, using the cutaway appliqué method or by hand-finished fused appliqué. While the latter is taught here, this pattern also suits machine appliqué using the blanket or satin stitch.

Make a Master Pattern

1. Fold a 12½″ square of freezer paper into quarters, then open flat.

2. In bold black pen, trace Pattern 3,

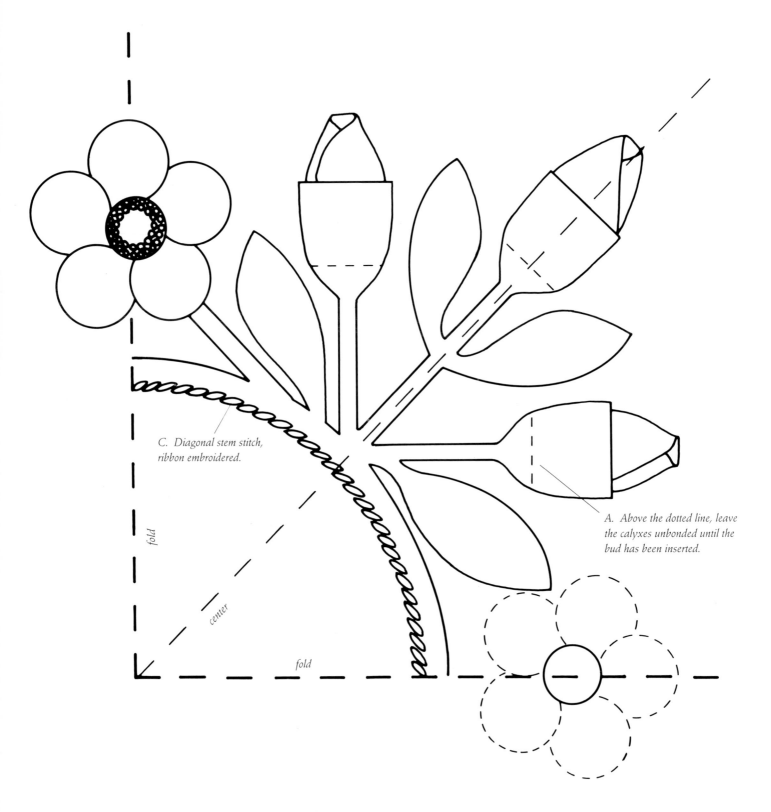

C. Diagonal stem stitch,
ribbon embroidered.

A. Above the dotted line, leave
the calyxes unbonded until the
bud has been inserted.

fold

center

fold

4-1. Pattern 3: *ROSA RUGOSA*–VICTORIAN BEACH ROSES

Rosa Rugosa (4-1) onto each quadrant of the square, progressing clockwise around the block. Keep the paper from shifting by securing it over the book with repositionable tape.

☆ *Speed Tip:* Paste four photocopies of Pattern 3 onto the 12½″ freezer paper square. Position them counterclockwise around the block. (You may need to accommodate a slight distortion.) The photocopy lines can usually be traced through the fusible or pale background cloth without the aid of a light box.

For leaves and stems, fused and blanket-stitched

1. Cut a 12″ square of regular weight iron-on fusible web such as Aileene's®, Heat'n'Bond® or WonderUnder®. Trace Pattern 3 onto the fusible web's protective paper side, not its rough side. Omit the flowers and buds from this tracing.

2. Cut a 16″ square of leaf/stem green cotton cloth. Following the bonding web's package directions, iron the marked fusible square to the wrong side of the green cloth.

3. Cut a 16″ square of a subtle tone-on-tone print in off-white. Crease the vertical and horizontal centers into the cloth. Use these as registration lines to orient your appliqué placement.

4. Use decorative wool, cotton, or synthetic embroidery floss in a variegated green, or a green that matches the leaf/stem fabric. Use one strand of heavier thread, or two strands of finer thread for outlining the leaves and stems in a blanket stitch.

5. Use a variegated tubular nylon ribbon embroidery floss or 7mm Mokuba Heirloom Sylk variegated silk ribbon embroidery floss to stem-stitch the pattern's center circle.

6. Use a betweens #10 needle for doing the blanket stitch in embroidery floss and a chenille #24 for the tubular nylon embroidery or the 7mm ribbon embroidery.

7. Use your basic sewing kit and ribbon tools, including a small embroidery hoop.

For the Beach Roses

For each of four flowers, cut a ⅞″ x 13″ (sz5 x 15SQs) length of red (some solid, some shaded) wired ribbon for the petals and a ⅞″ x 1¼″ (sz5 x 1½SQs) length of yellow to gold shaded wired ribbon for the center.

For each of eight buds, cut a ⅞″ x 2½″ (sz5 x 3SQs) length of red wired ribbon.

Use gold and amber colored seed beads, beige Nymo thread, and a milliner's needle for beading the outer rim of each flower center.

PROCEDURE

Wreath, Stems and Leaves

1. From the fused green fabric, cut out the leaf/stem unit on the drawn line, adding no seam allowances. Cut a line across the paper backing at the base of the bud calyxes *(4-1A)*.

2. Remove the paper backing everywhere except behind the eight bud calyxes. (These, too, will be ironed down, but only after the buds have been inserted.)

3. Position the background block over the master pattern, matching the cloth's crease lines with the center lines on the pattern. (You should be able to see the pattern through the cloth. If not, use a light box.) Put the leaf/stem cut-out in place and pin sparsely to hold.

4. Bond the fused leaf/stem appliqué to the background block. Caution: remove the pins just before each quadrant is ironed, so the appliqué lies absolutely flat. Follow the time and temperature directions on the packaging.

5. Blanket-stitch the leaves' and stems' raw edges except for the bud calyxes. You'll stitch-finish the calyxes after the buds have been inserted *(4-2D)*.

6. Embroider the inner circle with a decorative wreath of stem stitch, using silk ribbon or tubular nylon ribbon floss *(4-1C)*. The stem stitch is illustrated in the stitch guide, *Elegant, Easy Silk Ribbon Embroidery,* on page 62.

Beach Roses (make four)

Follow the directions for *Rosa Rugosa* in the Angular Ruching directions beginning on page 94.

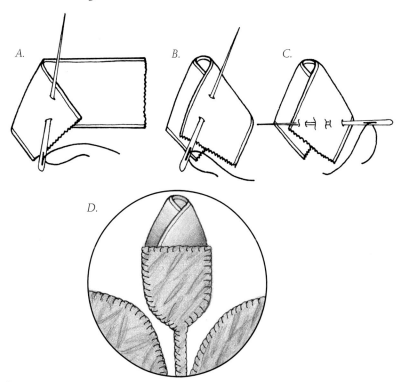

4-2. *ROSA RUGOSA* BUDS

Buds (make eight)

1. The bud is made the same way as the bud leaf. Pull the wire out from both edges. Fold the ⁷⁄₈˝ x 2¼˝ (sz5 x 2½SQs) ribbon length left side over right as shown in figure *4-2A* and *B*. Running-stitch from fold to fold. Pull to gather until the distance between the folds is roughly ³⁄₄˝. Secure the stitches *(4-2C)*.

2. Pin the bud in place under the calyx. Remove the protective paper from the calyx and, with an iron, bond the calyx over the bud.

3. With one strand of green or varie-gated green floss, blanket-stitch the raw calyx edges *(4-2D)*. Tack the top of the bud down with the pointillist stitch.

Wreath Center

This wide-open wreath center invites embellishment! Consider making an exquisite silk ribbon embroidered motif like those Ruth Meyers has created. My favorite is to pen heirloom inkwork in the centers, commemorating an event, shar-ing a favorite passage from literature, or portraying a loved one. While this is not the place to present ready-to-trace cal-ligraphed sentiments or to instruct in writ-ing on cloth in Copperplate script, nor for transferring engravings to quilt blocks by photocopies, this information is given on pages 21-23 in the author's *Baltimore Beauties and Beyond, Studies in Classic Album Appliqué, Volume II* (see *Resources*).

4-1. Detail, Victorian Beach Roses

4-2. *The quilt,* Rosa Rugosa—Victorian Beach Roses, *was designed using Project 9, Pattern 3, and fashioned by Ruth Meyers.*
It dances with Ruth's Mokuba ribbon flowers and her unique Mokuba Heirloom Sylk ribbon embroideries.
The fabric is from the author's Baltimore Beauties collection. Machine appliquéd and hand quilted.

Angular Ruching

SHELL RUCHING

Centuries old, ruching (pronounced "roo' shing") is a resilient needle-work technique. The word probably derives from the German word for ruf-fling (pronounced "rue' sha"), for the words are close and ruching ruffles cloth magnificently. As with any method that sparks creativity, the concept —that of gathering in a repeated pattern— has spawned multiple off-spring. The most familiar of these was called "shell" ruching by the Victorians, and we can understand why. Working so closely with last century's needleart, one cannot help but feel a spiritual connection to the women whose threads we follow. The era inculcated romance. It also reflected a deep reverence for nature, for there one read the Great Architect's penciled plans.

The running stitch is taken in broad-based triangles which string together like mountains in a folk art painting. When the gathering thread is pulled, scal-lop-like shells appear. As Victorian sentiment becomes more familiar to us, we can guess why our sisters of yore called repeat-triangle gathering shell ruch-ing. The Victorian era was dubbed "The Heyday of Natural History" and to stitch observations of nature into needleart was lauded as a rational pursuit.

MOUNTAIN/VALLEY RUCHING

As needleworkers, we pass the culture—the designs, the symbols, the methodology, and where known, the nomenclature—on. Some of us are faithful reproductionists. Others blend tradition with the stuff of their own lives. Sometimes you can spot a unique needleart thread and trace it from ancient to modern. As my own shell ruching progressed, I folded shaded rib-bon 1/8″ off-center *(4-3a)* creating a contrasting border which outlines each ruched petal.

Because we are more literal today, I call this triangular gathering

Ribbon folded 1/8″ off-center to create a decorative edge.

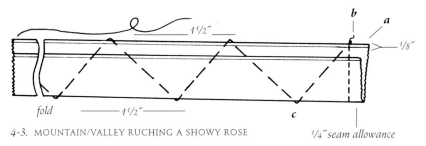

4-3. MOUNTAIN/VALLEY RUCHING A SHOWY ROSE

Mountain/Valley ruching. This geographic metaphor makes instructions easy to communicate.

At the starting end, insert your needle in at the back face of the mountain peak, (*b*). *When you come to the bottom of the valley, pass the thread over the fold* (*c*) *to begin climbing the next mountain.*

RUCHING A SHOWY ROSE

This showy rose differs from the triangular ruching taught in my previous books. Mountain/Valley ruching makes it a hybrid with double-edged petals. Even its final assembly from the underside, rather than appliquéing from the topside, is original. Victorian ruching is stitched down flat, while mountain/valley ruching leaves the petal tips free and more dimensional. Because of their wired edges, you can cup each petal's two layers separately, arranging them to perfection!

1. Fold the 1½˝ x 41˝ (sz9 x 27⅓SQs) length of shaded wired ribbon lengthwise, ⅛˝ off-center (*4-3*). This makes a flower approximately 3½˝ in diameter. The wires are left in both edges of the ribbon.

2. Mark the ribbon for gathering. Across the top selvage, begin ¼˝ in from the raw edge and mark off every 1½˝. Along the folded (bottom) edge, begin marking 1˝ in from the raw edges.

☆ *Marking tips:* Mountain/Valley ruching (sz9 x 1SQ) should be one ribbon square wide (1½˝) across each triangle's base and 1½˝ apart from peak to peak. Mark the sewing line by creasing 45° angles (*4-4*). Fold the ribbon into a prairie point and then fingerpress the folds tightly to get a sharp sewing line. The ribbon will hold the crease just one prairie point ahead of where you are stitching. I pin-mark the first few triangles, using a 1½˝ x 2˝ 3M Post-It® (*4-5*) which is the perfect size and sticks to the ribbon just long enough to mark the spacing. On a long length of ribbon I prefer to crease-mark the ribbon, which brings me to the stitching faster.

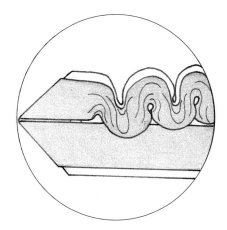

4-4. CREASING 45° ANGLES

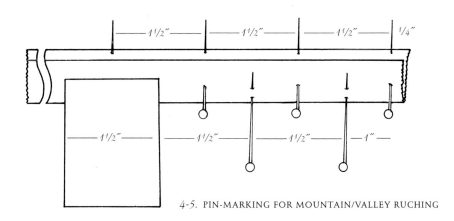

4-5. PIN-MARKING FOR MOUNTAIN/VALLEY RUCHING

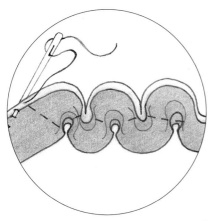

4-6. *Mountain/Valley stitches pulled into puffs, front view*

4-7. *Back view*

4-8. *Front view*

3. Match a strong 18″ thread, knotted, to the color of the ribbon on the front of the fold. (The color behind the fold may be different.) Begin ¼″ in from the right edge, allowing for a seam *(4-3)*.

4. Pull to gather *(4-6)* after stitching three full mountains. Repeat this stitching and pulling until the ribbon's end.

5. Before securing the stitches, size each puff. The ribbon should just outline your thumb when pressed over the petal. Beyond its colorful double edge, the showiness of this flower comes from its large, even-sized petals. When you're satisfied with their uniformity, secure the stitches. If the first thread runs out before the ruching is completed, finish with a second thread.

6. Thread (18″, knotted) another needle to shape the rose. Since colored thread will show a bit, invisible thread is handy. Begin stitching at the underside of the ribbon *(4-7)*.

7. At the starting end, tuck the seam allowance behind the first petal *(4-7)*. Take one running stitch through the folded edged of the first five petals.

8. Pull to gather these into a five-petaled flower *(4-8)*. Stitch the right side of this petal wreath to hold its shape.

9. From the underside again *(4-9)*, running-stitch the bottom of each petal to the gather line of the previous row of petals. This fashions a bold round bloom *(4-11)* which looks you straight in the eye.

10. Sew in a snail-like spiral, until the ribbon runs out. At that point, tuck the tail under, behind the adjacent petal, just as you did when you began *(4-7)*.

☆ *Art Note*: As you sew, estimate the blossom's finished size. If it appears too big, shrink the petals in towards the center a bit as you stitch. You can adjust the winding of the petals to have the rose glance over its shoulder as in *4-10*.

4-9. *Back view*

4-10. SHOWY ROSE VIEWED IN PERSPECTIVE

In fact, this beauty is full of choices! If you make it from an even wider ribbon length, the distance from the center to the first outer row of petals will be longer. If you fold the ribbon length exactly in half, and then mountain/valley ruche, your flower will resemble a carnation, chrysanthemum or dahlia. If you shorten the cut and crinkle the ribbon in your palm, the ruched flower will look like sailor's britches, bachelor's buttons, pinks, alyssum or Indian paint brush.

The rose's center (4-10) can be left unembellished. For our *Friendship Wreath* model (photo 4-5), Marge Walthers folded a 1½″ x 4″ (sz9 x 2¾SQs) ribbon in half lengthwise, then seamed its raw edges together (4-12) to make a central ruff. She running-stitched its selvages full-circle, gathered them, then thread-wrapped them several times (4-12) before fastening the thread. Figure 4-11 shows this stitched to the showy rose's center. Your own sewing basket is rich with beads and floss for French knots and other floral-center possibilities! Even some of the buds on this rose are showy. These buds are made like those taught for Project 9, *Rosa Rugosa*. The fancy one at the right (4-11) has a cuff, folded back before the bud is made.

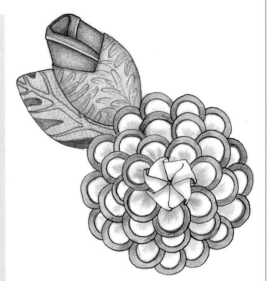

4-11. SHOWY ROSE VIEWED HEAD-ON

RAKE RUCHING

In geometry, Victorians saw a metaphor for morality, so they took angles seriously. A person of sketchy integrity was called "a corner cutter". By measurable contrast an honorable person followed "the right angle". Their message echoes in our modern lingo. If each one chipped off his "rough edges", Victorians hypothesized, he would become a "perfect square" and a new moral world order could be built. Rake ruching is actually my own term and I've seen no vintage prototype for the method. Nonetheless, it conforms to Victorian standards. Rake ruching has a wide angle which can be varied to taste, but its corner must never be cut!

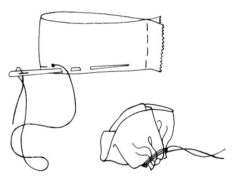

4-12. MAKING FIGURE 11'S ROSE CENTER.

*One Wild Beach Rose—**Rosa Rugosa—Rake Ruched***

1. For each flower, cut a ⅞″ x 13½″ (sz5 x 15½SQs) length of red wired ribbon. Remove the bottom edge wire.

2. Along the top edge, pin-mark the ribbon between the seam allowances into five 2½″ petal units (4-13). To allow for seam allowances, begin marking ¼″ in from the raw edge and finish ¼″ in from the end.

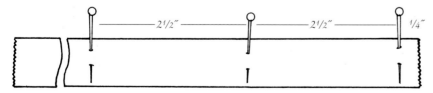

4-13. *ROSA RUGOSA—RAKE RUCHED*

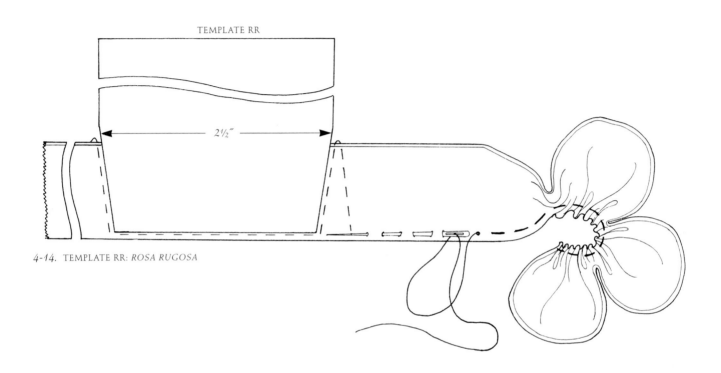

TEMPLATE RR

2½"

4-14. TEMPLATE RR: *ROSA RUGOSA*

4-15. *ROSA RUGOSA* PINNED TO PROJECT 9

☆ *Marking Tip*: Use Template RR *(4-14)* to mark the angle of the rake tines with a Pigma Micron pen. Make the template out of a file card, or out of a 3″ Post-It cut to size.

3. Knot an 18″ length of strong color-matched thread. As in mountain/valley ruching, pass the thread over to the opposite side when you cross the ribbon's upper edge, but never stitch over the lower edge *(4-14)*.

4. Running-stitch Template RR's garden rake pattern. After three tines of the rake have been stitched, pull the thread tightly to gather the ribbon into petals *(4-14)*. Continue until five petals are ruched.

5. Upon completion, gather the thread just tightly enough to leave a ½″ opening for the flower's stamen center. Secure the stitches, and without cutting the thread, sew the two raw-edged tails together along a ¼″ seam line. Tuck these tails in one direction, pushing them out of sight under an adjacent petal.

6. Yellow center: baste the ⅞″ x 1″ (sz5 x 1SQs) length of yellow ribbon to the background where the rose will be placed. Baste it with an X through the center.

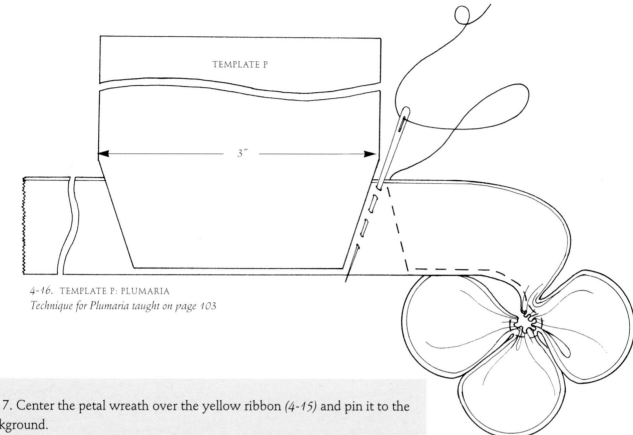

4-16. TEMPLATE P: PLUMARIA
Technique for Plumaria taught on page 103

7. Center the petal wreath over the yellow ribbon *(4-15)* and pin it to the background.

8. Tack-stitch the outer wire edge of each ribbon petal. Tip: to make perfectly round petals, mark Pattern 3's flower very lightly onto the background with a fine mechanical pencil. Stitch in and out of the drawn line, then up and over the wire edge, pulling the two into alignment.

9. Embroider the center's edge with two close rows of seed beads.

Rosa Rugosa —Victorian Beach Roses showcases this bloom, and instructions are close at hand in Project 9. You'll find this rose, and indeed the whole block, refreshingly quick and straight-forward. Ah, but while its sewing is simple, what possibilities for romance its name bespeaks!

Note : 4-16 demonstrates that by widening the distance between the points of the tines to 3˝, and widening the angle at their base, a fuller-petaled flower is made. You can also change the nature of the flower by sculpting the petal tips into soft points or plump rounds. Template RR can be used to fashion not only a wild rose but also an anemone, azalea, rhododendron, sweet alyssum, snowdrop, or any number of familiar fruit blossoms. Similarly sculpted, Template P, also bursts with potential!

Lorraine Ryuku Fukuwa,
Flower Fabricatrice

4-3. *A pansy barette made from overdyed velvet ribbons, using mountain/valley ruching from Lesson Four, by Lorraine Fukuwa.*

*M*idnight-purple pansies recall plush velvet. Following that fancy, Lorraine Fukuwa fashions velvet pansies by a simple technique. Recently, she wrote, "My love of feminine details, especially from the Victorian era, contributes to my vintage velvet hand-dyed flower pieces." Her festive jewelry's upbeat elegance recalls fairy wonderlands.

In the two short years since Lorraine made her first ribbon flower, she has honed a unique style into a flourishing sideline business. Her pieces are embellished by beads, glitter, antique buttons and laces, old dotted hat netting, miniature blooms, jewelry fragments, wired bead flowers, sprays of pearls and lush remnants from bridal departments. Sometimes she sets a petite plush animal or a miniature perfume bottle into a floral still life. By profession a technical translator (English/Japanese), interpreting instructor and writer, Ms. Fukuwa notes that "Ribbonart is a relaxing hobby, which fulfills creative urges."

Trips into Los Angeles's fabled garment district net supplies and ideas. The shockingly high $150 wholesale price tag on a ribbonart/vintage ornament pin inspired her to "try making something like it." She buys the critical natural fiber ribbon—100% rayon or silk— from Dawn's Discount Laces (see *Resources*), focusing on size 5 (⅞″ wide) and size 6 (1″) ribbon. Lorraine recommends Dawn's Discount Laces' pre-color-stripped 100% rayon velvet, ready for over-dyeing into any color. She also uses light-colored 100% rayon velvet (darker colors can be stripped) by Le Roi, "Taffeta-Back Velvet Woven Fast Edge." Silk velvet is excellent but expensive. Lorraine warns that if a ribbon's pile is thin, it will lack shine. Polyester will not dye. The pansy's upper two petals she fashions of synthetic or silk organza, explaining that it gives a delicate look. Because it is sheer, the underlying embellishments show through softly, adding a touch of poetry while integrating the piece.

DYEING 100% RAYON VELVET OR 100% SILK RIBBON
Lorraine uses Dr. Ph. Martin's® Radiant Concentrated Watercolor Dyes and Luma® Brilliant Concentrated Watercolor Dyes, available at comprehensive art and craft stores (see *Resources*). These dyes are liquid cold water dyes which can be mixed or diluted for softer effects. As with any new process, read the accompanying directions carefully. Lorraine emphasizes that the

words "brilliant" or "radiant" should be in the dye title; otherwise the end-product's color will be dull. She also notes that there are two ways to dye ribbon.

1. Lay the dry ribbon on wax paper, and apply the dye with a paintbrush. Using a paper towel as a press cloth, iron the ribbon dry. However, color thus applied can be too unvariegated and has a stark, unpainterly quality.

2. Lorraine prefers to wet the ribbon, squeeze the water out, and leave it damp. Then she runs an eyedropper full of dye along one or both selvages so that the color bleeds in towards the center. (Colors can also be brush-painted on wet ribbon for a mixed-shade look.) To dry the ribbon quickly, she microwaves it on high for 2.25 minutes. Because the dye is water soluble, the dry ribbon must be sprayed with an art fixative like Krylon® clear spray fixative. Do not spray stamens or anything you want shiny (or wipe it off those areas), for fixative gives them a milky finish. Let it dry fully, until it loses its odor.

4-4. *A whimsical pin fashioned by Lorraine Fukuwa, using mountain/valley ruching from Lesson Four.*

LORRAINE'S VELVET PANSIES

Lorraine's pansy-ruching technique is similar to that taught in *Dimensional Appliqué*, but Lorraine's petals are fuller than mine and require three squares of ribbon each.

1. *Three front petals*: Cut 7/8″ x 8½″ (sz5 x 9½ SQs) of 100% rayon velvet, overdyed. Leaving ¼″ at each raw edge, running-stitch a "W" of three equal triangles. Begin at the top of a mountain, ¼″ in from the starting seam allowance. End at the top of a mountain ¼″ short of the seam. This leaves bookends of facing right-angle triangles at the right and left raw edges. These ends get tucked out of the way, under the bottom petal.

2. *Two back petals*: Cut 7/8″ x 5¼″ (sz5 x 6SQs) of metallic-edged organza. Leaving ¼″ at each raw edge, stitch an "m" a bit loosely so you can position the folds easily when stitching the front petals over the back petals.

3. On both petal sets, pull the thread to gather, then secure the stitches (4-17).

4. *Embellishing*: Gluing the flower to a backing, Lorraine builds her jewelry collages using ribbon leaves and any combination of her favorite embellishments. She mixes fine powdered iridescent and metallic glitter with regular size metallic glitter. On wax paper, using her fingertips or a paper pusher, she builds a glitter shape—a string or a pompom—by sprinkling glitter over dribbled household glue. When dry, she lifts the shape and glues it onto her ribbonart. Alternatively, she dips the piece in the powdery glitter, taps off the excess, then uses hair spray as a fixative.

4-17. LORRAINE'S VELVET AND ORGANZA PANSY

4-5. *An Album Quilt block,* Friendship Wreath, *sports the Showy Rose fashioned from mountain/valley ruching.*
This quilt block, Optional Project 1, was stitched by Marge Walthers using the author's Wreath of Folded Roses *pattern from Baltimore Album Quilts.*

Ribbon Flower Techniques

Thumb through the pages of a comprehensive flower book, looking at the large five-petaled *Rosaceae* or Rose family. All of its members are candidates for rake ruching in ribbon. Consider as well these other exotics.

4-18. PLUMARIA, RAKE-RUCHED

PLUMARIA

The heavy-scented plumaria is beloved of Hawaiian lei-makers. Yellow to lavender shaded French wired ribbon is ideal for portraying this waxy, sculptured flower.

1. Cut a ⁷/₈″ x 16½″ (sz5 x 18¼SQs) length of the ribbon. Remove the wire from the lavender side.

2. Beginning ¼″ in from the raw edge, mark off every 2½″ on the yellow (light) side, using Template P (4-16, on page 99).

3. Run the horizontal gather along the lavender (dark) side, with the tines peaking at the yellow edge. Follow the directions for rake-ruching a Rosa Rugosa.

4. When the flower's inner center has been gathered as tightly as possible, and the raw edges' ¼″ seamed together, gather the inner edge a second time, using a strong matching thread and a whipstitch. Close the center by pulling tightly. Secure the stitches. Leave the center plain (4-18) or embellish with seed beads. Aloha!

☆*Miniature Memo:* When narrower rayon or silk ribbon is used, these closed-centered, five-petaled flowers make exquisite miniatures. For an African violet (4-19), use sz3 x 18SQs and make as the plumaria, but point the petals slightly and embroider French knots in the center.

ORIENTAL POPPY I

Brilliantly colored, yet fragile-looking, oriental poppies are relatively rare in the northeast, which is my home. They are cherished, for they bridge the hiatus between spring's parade of snowdrops, crocuses, tulips, hyacinths and daffodils, and the lilacs and peonies which herald summer.

1. Cut 1½″ x 27⅓″ (sz9 x 18¼SQs) of poppy-colored wired ribbon. Antique it (as taught in *Getting Started*) for the papery look characteristic of this flower.

4-19. AFRICAN VIOLET

A. Pin-pleating the petal's edges

4-20. ORIENTAL POPPY I

2. Follow the directions for the plumaria until the flower resembles figure 4-20.

3. *Crimping a poppy's petals:* after the five-petal wreath is made, crimp the defining pleated edge (4-21B). Do this by threading a long straight pin in and out every ⅛″ across the petal's tip. Pleat the ribbon by pushing it back tightly on the pin (4-21A). Pleat all five petals, then spray with hair spray and allow to dry. When you open it, round the petals, leaving their tips pleated (4-21B).

4. *Make the poppy's center.* Second to color, a poppy's greatest distinction is its bold black center. Any of the following centers can supply the appropriate color accent: French knots in floss or embroidery ribbon; jet bugle beads tipped with seed beads; or black glass beads up to ⅛″ diameter.

B. The pleated petal

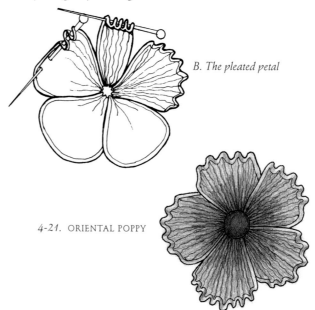

4-21. ORIENTAL POPPY

RANUNCULUS

1. Fold the 2″ x 15½″ (sz16 x 7¾SQs) length of hand-dyed raw-edged bias silk ribbon in half, lengthwise. Beginning ¼″ in from the right end, mark off every 3″ across the fold. Stitch from pin to pin, approaching the pin at an angle, so the stitch pattern looks like a wide-tined garden rake.

2. Pull the thread to gather.

3. Join the two ends with a ¼″ seam. Re-sew the flower center with a whipped gathering stitch taken over the edge. Pull tightly and secure the thread.

4. Cut a ½″ circle of yellow silk. Running-stitch ⅛″ inside the raw edge, full circle. Place a pinch of polyester filling on the wrong side, in the center. Pull the thread tightly to gather the circle's edges, forming a puff. Secure the stitches, then continue stitching up to the puff center, to the middle of the petal wreath *(4-22)*.

The dyed silk augments the simple beauty of this flower. That same simplicity invites embellishment by embroidery or beading. If it intrigues you, find a good flower book and discover how many blooms this can be, just with a refinement of its center.

4-22. RANUNCULUS

Optional Project One

FRIENDSHIP WITH A SHOWY ROSE

Inspired by the crossed stems—the crowns—of roses in Baltimore's antebellum Album Quilts, I drafted a simple quilt block whose showy rose is taught in full here. *Friendship with a Showy Rose* (photo 4-5) is Marge Walther's interpretation of that introductory Album block. The original pattern, Wreath of Folded Roses, is Pattern 3 in *Dimensional Appliqué,* and other suitable Baltimore Album block patterns abound (see *Resources*). For us this lesson's message is: if you can make a block like Project 9's *Rosa Rugosa*, then you can make a classic Baltimore style Album Quilt. Baltimores are albums (collections) of different appliquéd blocks, most botanical and therefore inviting ribbon flowers. If quilts are where you want to plant your ribbon garden, this is the style for you! Lesson Five teaches a more complex Baltimore Album block, showing how easily it can be rendered in Ribbon Appliqué.

Detail from Rosa Rugosa—Victorian Beach Rose

PHOTO 5-1 Rose Without Thorns, *a pillow or quilt square, Project 10.*
This Victorian-inspired Ribbon Appliqué was fashioned by the author.

Ribbon Appliqué and Roses

A new millennium needlework style is evolving, right here and now! Rooted in Baltimore Album appliqué and Victorian ribbonwork, it remains compellingly fresh. This Ribbon Appliqué interprets both European folk needlework and classic Baltimore quilt block patterns, all with an elegant flair. Ribbon Appliqué's combination of techniques is so innovative that it inspires a unique turn of the twentieth century style. The inclusion of ribbon roses into revivalist Baltimore Album blocks led me to Ribbon Appliqué and so this lesson teaches that ribbonwork style—and pays homage to the rose.

Review *Getting Started.*

RIBBON TYPES

Wired ribbon, velvet, rayon, silk, organza and georgette.

RIBBON SIZES

Embroidery ribbon from 2mm up to 12mm, and broader ribbon from 5/8″ to 2″ wide (sz3 to sz16).

PROJECTS

Project 10: Rose Without Thorns
Ribbon Appliqué a pillow or quilt square, Pattern 4 given in this lesson.
Optional Project 2: Basket of Flowers
Ribbon Appliqué a classic Album block. Pictured, no pattern given.

RIBBON APPLIQUÉ AND FLOWER TECHNIQUES

Silk ribbon embroidered stems and leaves, full-blown flower, silk ribbon fern, Trumpet Flower, Petunia, Rose, Rosebud, traditional reverse appliquéd basket, UltraSuede appliqué, wired ribbon flowers made on a marked background, and beads—jewels in the crown.

RIBBON LEAF TECHNIQUES

Traditionally appliquéd cotton leaves, velvet ribbon leaves, the boat leaf and split boat leaf, a center-shaded boat leaf, folded leaves, and veined leaves in the pierced leaf stitch.

Project 10

ROSE WITHOUT THORNS: A PILLOW OR QUILT SQUARE

Seeking to bloom anew, a century old rose stole from a book and into my soul. That picture's ruby *bas relief* so intrigued me that I had to make it my own. The pattern, which blossoms on a parlor pillow, is shared in photo 5-1. The pillow front is a day's project, even for a novice, a fact that ranks it high on a list of elegant but easy gifts. Romanced by a different ribbon gardener, this rose motif could happily grow into a quilt as suggested by figure 5-1. Project 10's rose pattern reinforces three elements of Ribbon Appliqué: fused appliqué, decorative stitching and ribbon flora. The name comes from an aphorism, "The only rose without thorns is Friendship". A charming, though anonymous, thought!

SUPPLIES

This pillow front can be made from many ribbon types, sizes and colors. The following supplies were used to make one *Rose Without Thorns* medallion pillow center as pictured in photo 5-1.

One 9″ background square

"Scroll" in off-white from the author's designer collection is pictured. Look for the ombré prints of medium scale to balance this *bas relief* style.

One 9″ green foliage square

"Vermiculate" in Victoria green from the author's designer fabric is pictured in the model. A small to medium scale green print is needed.

One 9″ square fusible bonding

Trace Pattern 4 onto the smooth side of a fusible bonding web like Wonder Under®, regular weight. Following the package directions, iron the fusible web to the wrong side of the green print.

Ribbon for rose and bud

7/8″ x 1 yd. (sz5 x 41SQs) of shaded French wired ribbon.

Metallic ribbon for the decorative knot

Cut a 1/3″ x 18″ (sz1H x 54½SQs) length of Offray's "Firefly" gold metallic ribbon.

Gold metallic thread

Kanagawa® fine metallic thread in gold (Quilter's Resource order #4210) and a #10 crewel needle were used to blanket-stitch the leaves and the bud calyx.

Green thread

DMC moss green variegated machine embroidery thread and a milliner's #10 needle were used to blanket-stitch the stems.

Seed beads

For dewdrops, stitch a few pearled seed-beads onto the rose and bud.

Basic sewing kit and ribbon tools

Supplies to finish the medallion center into a pillow cover (optional)

Two 18″ squares (includes ½″ seam allowance) of decorator fabric background for pillow cover front and back. Ribbon medallion frame: cut generously 7/8″ x 45″ (sz5 x 51½SQs) of Mokuba striped velvet laid over 5/8″ x 45″ (sz3 x 72SQs) of Offray's metallic gold woven with black. Miter ribbon corners by folding. Hem the ending raw edge over the beginning raw edge. Use a 16″ square pillow form.

PROCEDURE

Foliage

1. Cut the stemmed foliage shape — all in one piece—out of the fused green fabric (5-2). Along the pattern's dotted line **a**, cut just the protective paper. Leave the paper backing on the upper calyx, but remove it (below the line) from the rest of the appliqué shape. The protective paper will keep the bud calyx from being bonded until the bud has been slipped beneath it.

2. With an iron, heat-bond the green foliage fabric to the right side of the off-white background square. To protect

5-1. ROSE MOTIF QUILT MADE FROM PATTERN 4

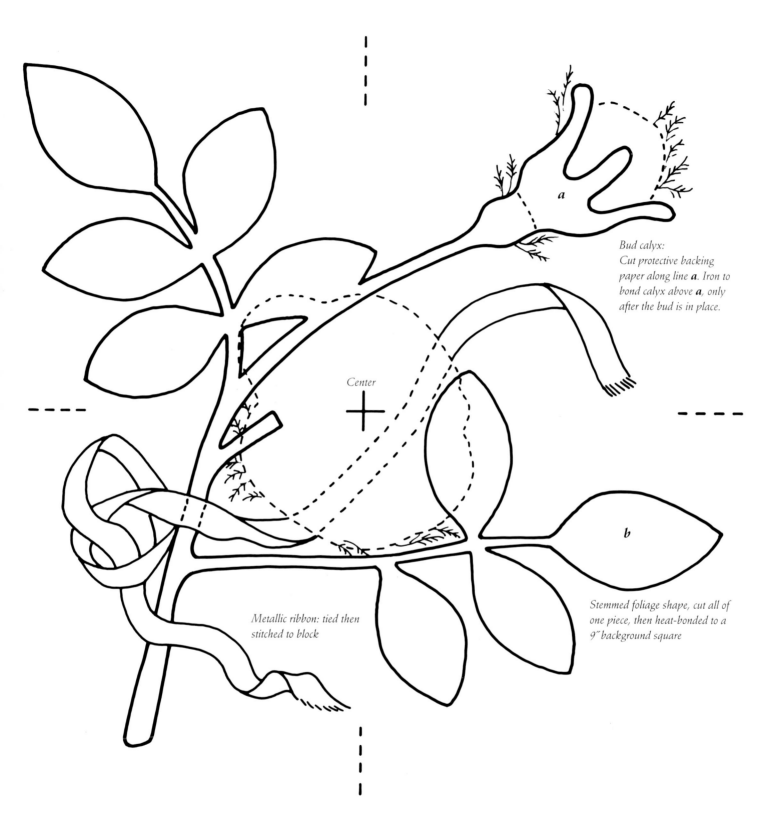

Bud calyx:
Cut protective backing
*paper along line **a**. Iron to*
*bond calyx above **a**, only*
after the bud is in place.

a

Center

b

Metallic ribbon: tied then
stitched to block

Stemmed foliage shape, cut all of
one piece, then heat-bonded to a
9˝ background square

5-2. Pattern 4: ROSE WITHOUT THORNS—*A Ribbon Appliqué Quilt Block*

5-3. Stem blanket-stitched in green thread, legs pointing in towards the stem center.

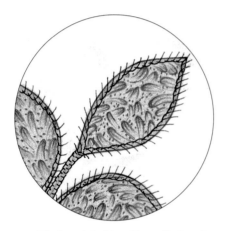

5-4. Blanket-stitched in gold metallic thread. The legs are pointing out and slant towards the top of the leaf.

5-5. The rose moss is actually two rows of blanket-stitch, back-to-back.

your background from iron smudges, use a thin presscloth.

3. Blanket-stitch the stems in green thread. Gauge your stitches to border each side of the stem attractively *(5-3)*. Because the bonding holds the edge, the stitches can be about ⅟₁₆″ long, and ⅟₁₆″ apart. They do not need to be closer.

4. Blanket-stitch the leaves with gold, stitching from beyond the appliqué back toward it, so the leg is over the off-white fabric and slants toward the leaf's tip *(5-4)*. To imitate the serrated rose leaf edge, take these stitches ⅛″ long and ⅛″ apart.

5. *Embellishments:* after the rose and bud are in place, surround them with a softening corona of moss, blanket-stitched in variegated green and gold thread *(5-5)*.

Rosebud

1. Cut a 1½″ x 6″ (sz9 x 4SQs) strip of rose-making ribbon. Take Fold #1 from bottom to top *(5-6)*. Edge-seal both ends with clear nail polish. Bud construction quickly consumes the ribbon's length. Sealing prevents any loss due to fraying.

2. Fold the left and right hand ends down at an angle as in figure *5-7*.

3. Begin at the right hand end to roll the bud from right to left as in *5-8*. Judge from the drawing how tightly to roll.

4. Pause for a minute and, with tweezers, twist the bud center into a tight whorl. Push the ribbon down at **a** to reveal the bud center more clearly. The sculpting of our bud has become more art than craft!

5. Continue rolling and folding the

FIGURES 6–9 ILLUSTRATE HOW TO MAKE PROJECT 10'S ROSE

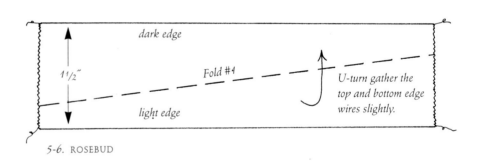

5-6. ROSEBUD

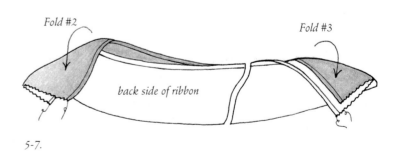

5-7.

bud by following figures *5-8* and *5-9*. Running-stitch the base and pull to gather gently as in *5-9*.

6. When the bud is fully formed, tuck it in place under the calyx. Use two fine pins to hold it.

7. From the calyx's wrong side, remove the protective paper backing. By ironing, heat-bond the calyx over the bud and to the background. With invisible thread, tack-stitch the bud in place. Blanket-stitch the calyx's raw edges *(5-10)* with green thread and some of the rose moss with either green or gold *(5-11)*.

Rose

Use the remaining 30˝ ribbon length and follow the directions for the Cabbage Rose in Lesson One. To fit Pattern 4, the rose must be sculpted to shape and brought to scale. The wired edge in the ribbon makes this easy to do. Add seed bead dewdrops just before finishing the block.

The Ribbon Knot

Tie a loose overhand knot just above the ribbon's lower third and flatten it gently *(5-3)*. Arrange the ribbon by eye, luxuriating in the wire's capacity for holding sensuous curves. Pin the ribbon down, then running-stitch just inside the edge to hold it in place.

Optional Project 2

RIBBON APPLIQUÉ ON A BALTIMORE ALBUM SQUARE

While Ribbon Appliqué can ornament a multitude of objects, a particularly rewarding path applies this needlework style to mid-nineteenth century Baltimore-style block designs. Hundreds of these classic quilt squares are patterned, full-scale, in the *Baltimore Beauties and Beyond* series (see *Resources*). Rather than present yet more patterns here, let's learn to recognize which squares most graciously invite interpretation in Ribbon Appliqué.

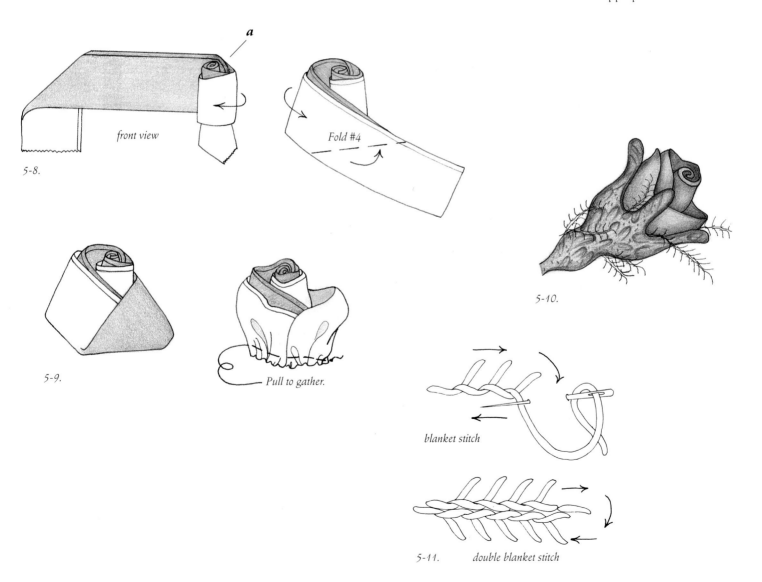

a

front view

5-8.

Fold #4

5-9.

Pull to gather.

5-10.

blanket stitch

5-11. *double blanket stitch*

5-2. Basket of Flowers, *a Ribbon Appliqué interpretation by the author of a classic Baltimore Album block from* Spoken Without a Word, *Optional Project 2.*

We'll walk through one classic Baltimore Album square, *Basket of Flowers* (photo 5-2) step-by-step. Familiarity thus gained, plus notes on other blocks pictured here in *Romancing Ribbons,* will give your needleart the wings to soar in this style! Ask the following questions to assess the extent to which a printed pattern is suitable for Ribbon Appliqué.

1. Does the pattern's scale suit Ribbon Appliqué?

My Ribbon Appliqué style developed on blocks whose leaves are 1¾˝ long or less. These fine scale leaves are ideal for the veined leaves, using the pierced leaf stitch in 2mm to 4mm wide silk embroidery ribbon. The beauty of this ribbon/leaf stitch combination would be lost on leaves of a larger scale. On the other hand, Wendy Grande's approach enhances larger leaves, for she embroiders with wider silk ribbon (7mm to 12mm) made appropriately delicate by a secondary stitching of Madeira silk floss-embroidered veins over the ribbon.

2. Do specific pattern motifs invite your favorite ribbon embroidery stitches?

Wendy delights in twisting lengths of silk ribbon into the textured grace of a swallow tail (photo page 20), or in twining it, wiry and irregular, into a wild vine wreath (photo page 20). I love the tidy sculptural quality of the pierced leaf stitch, whether used for leaves or to echo the textural look of rose stems.

3. Will the pattern's layout allow inclusion of silk ribbon fern?

Traditional appliqué inadequately portrays the airiness of fern. To include silk ribbon embroidery fern, look for a floral arrangement loose and spacious enough to welcome the inclusion of a pair or more of fronds.

4. Does the pattern have small tedious shapes more easily done in UltraSuede?

Little design elements with tight curves and tiny points are more easily tack-stitched with UltraSuede than by hemmed appliqué. Not only does this save time, but it also adds texture to your piece.

5. Does the pattern include flowers which could be interpreted in ribbon?

If the answer to one or more of the preceding questions is yes, then the pattern you are considering is a candidate for this lesson. Because the basics of Ribbon Appliqué are easily grasped, and because they cordially invite inclusion of this book's ribbon flowers, the pertinent techniques are taught here. You can apply Ribbon Appliqué's procedures to any printed pattern that suits your style and strikes your fancy.

SUPPLIES

This Album block can be made with many printed fabrics, ribbon types, sizes, and colors. The following supplies were used to make the *Basket of Flowers* as pictured in photo 5-2. If you can't find these specific materials, choose your own. You can take the full-size pattern from *Spoken Without a Word* (see *Resources*) or make your own from the graphics included in this lesson.

One 16˝ background square

"Scroll" from the the author's designer collection is pictured.

One 6˝ x 8˝ rectangle of basket print

"Ombré Stripe" in brown from the author's designer collection is pictured.

Green scraps for leaves

"Maze" in green and "Scroll" in teal from the author's designer collection are the cotton cloth leaves shown. All unlettered leaves in the Needleart Key *(5-12)* are appliquéd from quilt-weight cotton.

UltraSuede scraps for acorns and calyxes

Green UltraSuede is used for the calyxes, gold for the acorns and brown for the acorn caps.

5-3. *Detail,* Spring Blossoms, Summer Cherries, *by Wendy Grande from her quilt,* Ribbon Appliqué. *Exquisitely, Wendy combines ribbon appliqué with silk ribbon embroidery.*

Silk embroidery ribbon for the stems, ferns, and leaves

Use 4mm silk or Mokuba Heirloom Sylk embroidery ribbon, in variegated greens for the ferns and leaves, and solid gold color for the stems. All the ribbon embroidery uses the pierced leaf stitch.

Green velvet ribbon for leaves A

Cut four ⅛″ x 2″ (sz3 x 3¼SQs) lengths of 100% rayon moss green velvet ribbon. (I used vintage velvet ribbon.) To replicate antique ribbon, steam-iron the rayon ribbon in different directions, to crush its pile.

For each of three Flowers A (Full-Blown Flowers)

Cut a ⅝″ x 12″ (sz3 x 19¼SQs) length of Elégance yellow to lavender shaded wired ribbon for the scalloped outer petal wreath.

Cut a ⅝″ x 6″ (sz3 x 9½SQs) length of the same ribbon for the inner petal wreath.

Cut a ⅞″ x 1¼″ (sz5 x 1½SQs) rectangle of yellow to bronze shaded wired ribbon for the flower's center. Baste it to the background, covering the center. Further directions are given under Procedure, which follows.

☆ *Cautionary Note:* With clear nail polish, edge-seal the wired ribbon's raw edges for Ribbon Appliqué.

For each of two Flowers B (Trumpet Flowers)

Cut a 1½″ x 2″ (sz9 x 1⅓SQs) length of luminescent wine-red wired ribbon for the trumpet. Fold the raw edges in to form the triangular base and appliqué it to the marked background (5-13).

Cut a ⅞″ x 3½″ (sz5 x 4SQs) length of Vaban light to dark wine-red shaded wired ribbon for the top petal wreath. U-turn gather both edges' wires. (Coil them around a pin, then remove it. The coil acts as a knot. See 5-14.)

Gather this rectangle along its center (5-14) to a 2″ length. Fold the dark side ¼″ shorter than the light side. Fold under the outer corners (5-15).

Pin, then appliqué this wreath of outer petals over the trumpet base (5-16). Add beads to the center.

For two Buds A

Cut a 1½″ x 3″ (sz9 x 2SQs) length of wine red to pink shaded wired ribbon.

Fold it in half lengthwise so that the dark side lies ¹⁄₁₆″ below the light side (5-17). Use Folds #2 and #3 to form the bud.

Stitch-gather the bud base as in figure 5-17. Trim off the excess seam allowance.

Sculpt the bud center with hemostats. I've made the buds swirl in opposite directions (5-18A). Finish as in 5-18B.

For two Buds B

Cut a ⅝″ x 2″ (sz3 x 3¼SQs) length of yellow to lavender shaded wired ribbon. U-turn gather the edges on both wires. Coil the wire ends to secure. Appliqué the upper edge (the darker, lavender side) to the bud's upper edge (marked on the background). Cut the calyx out of UltraSuede, adding no seam alowance. Appliqué the calyx over the bud, always stitching into the marked lines (5-19).

Seed bead centers

Bronze seed beads (called antique) are clustered at the centers of Flowers A and B.

Basic sewing kit and ribbon tools

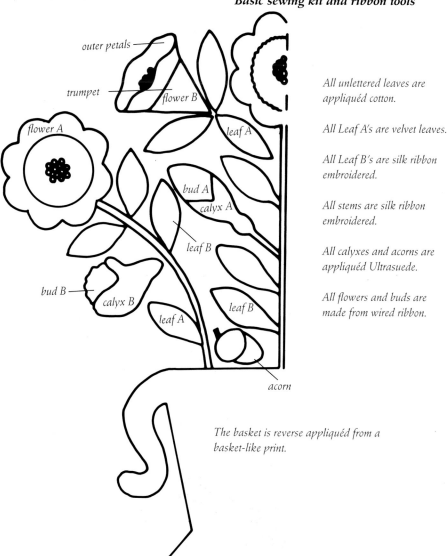

All unlettered leaves are appliquéd cotton.

All Leaf A's are velvet leaves.

All Leaf B's are silk ribbon embroidered.

All stems are silk ribbon embroidered.

All calyxes and acorns are appliquéd Ultrasuede.

All flowers and buds are made from wired ribbon.

The basket is reverse appliquéd from a basket-like print.

5-12. BASKET OF FLOWERS—*Needlework Key*

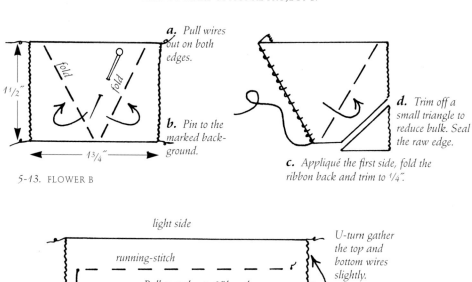

a. *Pull wires out on both edges.*

b. *Pin to the marked background.*

fold

fold

1 1/2″

1 3/4″

5-13. FLOWER B

d. *Trim off a small triangle to reduce bulk. Seal the raw edge.*

c. *Appliqué the first side, fold the ribbon back and trim to 1/4″.*

light side

running-stitch

Pull to gather to 2″ length.

U-turn gather the top and bottom wires slightly.

5-14.

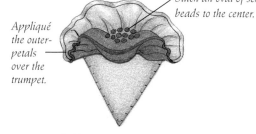

fold   *fold*

5-15.

Stitch an oval of seed beads to the center.

Appliqué the outer petals over the trumpet.

5-16.

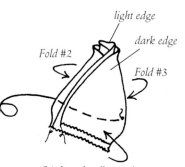

light edge

dark edge

Fold #2

Fold #3

Stitch and pull to gather to 1/2″ diameter.

5-17. BUD A

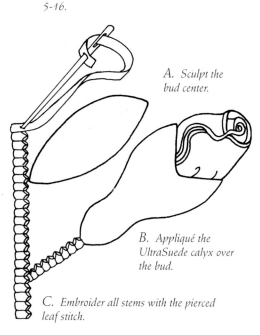

A. Sculpt the bud center.

B. Appliqué the UltraSuede calyx over the bud.

C. Embroider all stems with the pierced leaf stitch.

5-18.

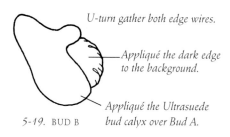

U-turn gather both edge wires.

Appliqué the dark edge to the background.

Appliqué the Ultrasuede bud calyx over Bud A.

5-19. BUD B

PROCEDURE

Optional Pattern

Adapt these procedures to any suitable Baltimore Album block pattern. Alternatively, use the pattern *Basket of Flowers* from *Spoken Without a Word* (see *Resources*). Using a Pigma Micron .01 brown pen, trace the pattern lines onto the right (top) side of a 16″ Album background square. For a marked block in progress, see *Rose Amphora*, photo 5-4. On *Basket of Flowers*, trace leaves, flowers, stems, acorns, and just the outline of the basket, not its interior.

Traditional Reverse Appliquéd Basket

1. Baste a 5″ x 8″ piece of basket-type cloth (1/2″ outside the drawn basket line). The basket print rectangle should be right side up against the wrong side of the background.

2. Using off-white thread, reverse appliqué the background cloth to the basket print, cutting the 1/4″ seam just 2″ or so at a time, ahead of where you're sewing.

3. Upon completion of the reverse appliqué, trim the basket print from the underside, so the 3/16″ seam is hidden under the 1/4″ background cloth seam. This prevents the basket's shadow from showing on the top of the block.

Silk Ribbon Embroidered Stems

Silk ribbon embroider the stems, using a chenille needle #26, 4mm ribbon floss, and the pierced leaf stitch. Bring the needle up through the drawn line on the side of the stem. Insert it into the cloth directly opposite, piercing the flattened ribbon, and through the line marking the other side of the stem *(5-18C)*.

You'll be thrilled at how quickly these stems work up in silk ribbon embroidery compared to appliqué! The leaf stitch is controlled and has the tactile look of a rose twig or tree branch.

Leaves

Six Lovely Leaves on page 118 teaches how to make leaves for this block by cotton appliqué, Ribbon Appliqué, and silk ribbon embroidery.

UltraSuede Appliqué

UltraSuede is a synthetic leather which hand-needles exquisitely. Like real suede, the cut edges will not ravel, so there's no need for seam allowances. For this project, both bud calyxes and the acorns are UltraSuede appliqués. Attach the calyxes over the sewn buds with a dab of gluestick. Add an 1/8″ seam to the top of the UltraSuede acorns so that the acorn's cap overlaps that seam. With a matching thread color, tack-stitch the UltraSuede appliqués to the background.

☆ *Design Note:* In photo 5-4, *Rose Amphora* (Pattern #72 from *Papercuts and Plenty*) shows a square in progress. The pen-drawn lines to which the UltraSuede and other appliqués are stitched are visible in the unfinished portion.

Ribbon Appliqué Three Flowers A

1. Fold in half, raw edge to raw edge, the 12″ ribbon cut for the outer petals and the 6″ ribbon cut for the inner petals (5-20). Take a 1/8″ seam across the cut ends.

2. Gather each strip tightly on the dark side's wire.

3. Appliqué the outside edge of the larger wreath to the scalloped flower pattern drawn on the background cloth (5-21). Appliqué the inner petal wreath over the outer one.

4. Edge the center with seed beads, or fill the center as in *5-22*.

Silk Ribbon Embroidered Fern

Dotting with a Pigma pen .01 in brown, lightly mark the fern stem's arch (5-23). Using 4mm overdyed silk ribbon, leaf-stitch at the outer tip, then continue taking the leaf stitch down the stem, from the right side to the left. Rather than being symmetrical, fern frond leaves are off-set from left to right. Taper the leaves so that they are widest at the bottom of the stem. A fiddlehead fern in my unfinished piece, *Fern-Wreathed Heart* (photo 5-6), is stitched the same way.

Beads—Jewels in the Crown

Seed and bugle beads add sparkle to Ribbon Appliqué. In *Basket of Flowers* (photo 5-2) the yellow centers are edged by seed beads. For bead appliqué, use a sharps or milliner's needle and Nymo thread.

5-21.

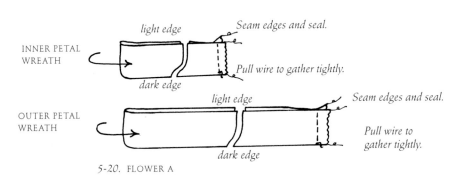

INNER PETAL WREATH — light edge — Seam edges and seal. — dark edge — Pull wire to gather tightly.

OUTER PETAL WREATH — light edge — Seam edges and seal. — dark edge — Pull wire to gather tightly.

5-20. FLOWER A

Appliqué the ribbon to the background, easing the fullness to fit.

Appliqué the inner wreath over the outer wreath.

Stitch seed beads in the center.

5-22. FLOWER A

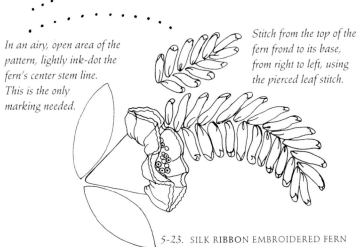

In an airy, open area of the pattern, lightly ink-dot the fern's center stem line. This is the only marking needed.

Stitch from the top of the fern frond to its base, from right to left, using the pierced leaf stitch.

5-23. SILK RIBBON EMBROIDERED FERN

5-4. Rose Amphora, *a Ribbon Appliqué Album block in progress, from* Papercuts and Plenty, *by the author. Lesson Five teaches Ribbon Appliqué, begun by marking the pattern onto the background cloth. These are the same roses taught in Project 10.*

Six Lovely Leaves!

Variety makes Ribbon Appliqué sing. The variety is found both in texture and technique. Half a dozen effective leaves are taught here, and shown in photos 5-2, 5-4, and 5-6. Remember that like flowers, leaves can be made in multiple sizes. Just use a wider or narrower ribbon, but keep the repeats of ribbon width the same as the number of squares (SQs) in the formulas below.

TRADITIONAL APPLIQUÉD COTTON LEAVES

Strike a balance between embroidery, Ribbon Appliqué, and traditional cloth appliqué. To retain the Baltimore style, for example, a fair portion of the block must be cotton appliqués. Needleturn appliqué with a scored turnline, a nineteenth century appliqué technique, follows.

1. Work on cardboard rather than on a harder surface.

2. Pin Leaf Template A (made of plastic) to the underside of the appliqué cloth.

3. With an awl (or head of a darning needle), outline the template *(5-24A)* with a crease in the cloth.

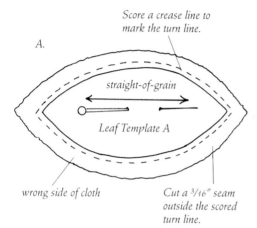

A.

Score a crease line to mark the turn line.

straight-of-grain

Leaf Template A

wrong side of cloth

Cut a 3/16" seam outside the scored turn line.

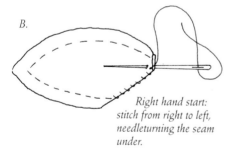

B.

Right hand start: stitch from right to left, needleturning the seam under.

C.

Appliquéd leaves from the Basket of Flowers project.

5-24. TRADITIONAL APPLIQUED LEAF

5-5 Rose Without Thorns, *Pattern 4, reduced, and stitched into a simple papercut appliqué frame by the author. The rose is the Turncoat Tea Rose from Lesson One.*

A.

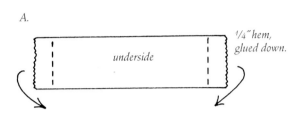

1/4″ hem, glued down.

underside

B.

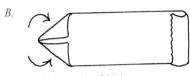

Add more glue, fold the corners to meet at the middle.

C.

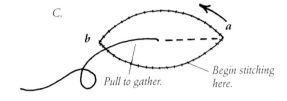

b
a

Pull to gather.

Begin stitching here.

D. Appliquéd velvet leaf from the Basket of Flowers

d
c

E.

F. Hawaiian Tack Stitch

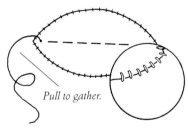

Pull to gather.

1. *Bring the needle up from underneath, through the drawn pattern line.*
2. *Put the needle down into the velvet.*
3. *Come up through the drawn pattern line.*

5-25. VELVET RIBBON LEAF

4. Trim a 3/16″ seam beyond the creased turn line and pin the appliqué right side up to the background.

5. Match the thread color to the leaf. Needleturn the seam under, using the tack or blind stitch *(5-24B and C)*.

THE VELVET RIBBON LEAF

1. Use rayon velvet, which crushes for an antique look. Cut ribbon 5/8″ x 2¼″ (sz3 x 3½SQs). Finger-crush or iron the ribbon to create eddies of light.

2. With the ribbon wrong side up, dab glue (from a gluestick) on both ends. Next, turn the raw edges under ¼″, hemming them inwards *(5-25A)*. The seams can be ironed to dry the glue.

3. Place more glue on the hem, then press the left and right corners down to meet in the middle *(5-25B)*. This forms the leaf tip.

4. Matching tips at *a*, appliqué the ribbon leaf to the marked background. Ease the bound edge to fit the drawn line, matching the tips at *b*, then stitching back up to *a*. *(5-25C)*

5. Running-stitch (through the ribbon, not the background) down the center vein from point *c* to *d (5-25D)*. Pull thread to gather and then secure the stitches. The leaf will be full and sculptured *(5-25E)*.

6. The Hawaiian Tack Stitch holds velvet down well. Figure *(5-25F)* shows how to do it and shows a slightly larger velvet ribbon leaf as well. This stitch successfully forces a larger appliqué into a smaller shape drawn on the background.

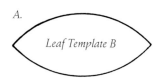

A.

Leaf Template B

B.

5-26. BOAT LEAF

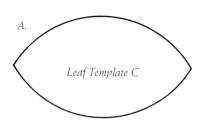

A.

Leaf Template C

B.

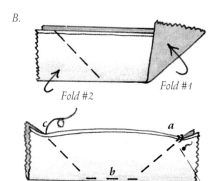

Fold #2   Fold #1

Pull to gather   Sink the
here.   starting knot.

Secure stitches (at a, b, and c)

C.

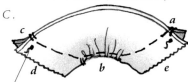

d   *b*   *e*

Hide the finishing thread.

5-27 SPLIT BOAT LEAF

THE BOAT LEAF AND SPLIT BOAT LEAF

Lesson One taught the single-tipped boat prow leaf. By contrast, the full boat leaf is ovate, with a tip at both ends. Free-standing, it is particularly useful for Ribbon Appliquéd Baltimore blocks. Sherry Cook, a fellow Album teacher, showed me this leaf's versatility.

1. To make a Template B size solid color boat leaf, cut a $^7/8''$ x $2^1/2''$ (sz5 x 3SQs) satin or luminous ribbon. These ribbons catch the light intriguingly and make appealing leaves *(5-26B)*. Stitch this like the split boat leaf which follows.

2. To make a Template C size split boat leaf, cut a $1^1/2''$ x $2''$ (sz9 x 1 $^1/3$SQs) shaded wired ribbon. Fold it in half, laying the light selvage over the dark *(5-27B)*.

3. Fold the bottom corners up so the raw edges extend $^1/4''$ above the selvage line *(5-27B)*.

4. Following the creases, sew *a* to *c*. At *b*, pull the thread to gather the leaf down to fit the template *(5-27C)*. Secure the stitches; then continue stitching to *c*.

5. Trim the excess seam at *d* and *e*. Open the leaf, fold the seam points down and hide the seam behind the points. The center seam gives the impression of two distinct shades of ribbon sewn together *(5-27D)*. One side of the leaf is light, the other dark.

6. To make a split boat leaf to fit the *Basket of Flowers* Ribbon Appliqué, cut a $^5/8''$ x $2''$ (sz3 x $3^1/4$SQs) ribbon and follow steps A—D *(5-27)*.

THE CENTER-SHADED BOAT LEAF

1. Cut a $^5/8''$ x $6''$ (sz3 x $9^1/2$SQs) length of shaded wired ribbon. Fold the ribbon in half at Fold #1 *(5-28A)*, laying one cut end over the other. The top (dark) edge of the ribbon forms the outside of the leaf.

2. Press the Fold #2 corner up to lie on the dark-edge selvage *(5-28A)*. Press the Fold #3 corner to lay $^1/4''$ above the dark selvage. This $^1/4''$ gives the seam allowance.

3. Stitch a boat shape as in *(5-28B)*. Pull the running stitches to gather. Secure the stitches.

4. Taking advantage of the wire in the ribbon, shape the leaf's margins *(5-28C)*. To make a light-edged leaf with a dark center, begin at step #1 with the light edge on top *(5-28D)*.

D.

*Dab glue to hold the
seam under at the points.*

E.

THE FOLDED LEAF

Lesson One taught the simplest of leaves, a bud leaf, where the ribbon was folded in half on the diagonal, left over right.

1. The folded leaf is made the same way, but from a longer $^5/_8"$ x $6^1/_2"$ (sz3 x $10^1/_2$SQs) ribbon. This makes a lily-like leaf. *(5-29A)*.

2. The leaf's base can be pinned until a flower is appliquéd over it, or stitched, or twisted to hold the shape.

3. The underside of this leaf can be used to add variety *(5-29B)*.

4. Yet another variation is to fold the left half forward and the right half backward*(5-29C)*.

THE VEINED LEAF IN THE PIERCED LEAF STITCH

A pierced leaf stitch is taught in Lesson Two. There, first one side of the leaf is stitched, then the other. This allows for a split leaf: one side sewn in one color, the opposite side in another. A second version of the pierced leaf stitch is sewn alternating a stitch to the right, then one to the left. This one is ideal for overdyed silk ribbon which has its own variegation built in. To make a leaf sized to the *Basket of Flowers*:

1. Onto the background marked for Ribbon Appliqué, add the center vein line of the leaves to be silk ribbon embroidered.

2. Begin embroidering at the top of the leaf as in figure *(5-30)*. Bring the needle up on the vein line *a* and insert it through the ribbon and into the drawn margin line *b*.

3. Stitch from the vein to the right (*c* to *d*), then from the vein to the left. The stitches alternate and overlap just a touch, creating a center vein line. This works well when stitching the leaf all in one color ribbon, whether solid or variegated. If you want a split leaf, work the right side (from top to bottom) in one color. Then work the left side (from bottom to top) in a second color.

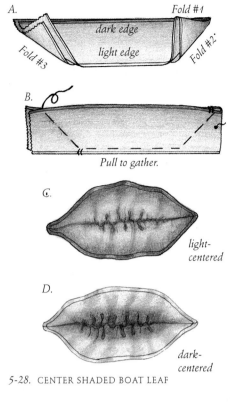

5-28. CENTER SHADED BOAT LEAF

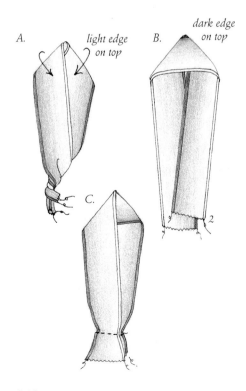

5-29. FOLDED LEAVES

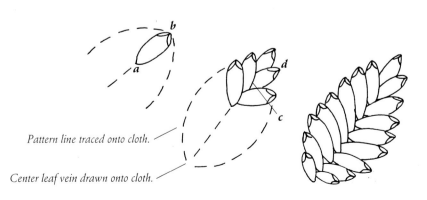

5-30. VEINED LEAVES IN PIERCED LEAF STITCH

WHITHER RIBBON APPLIQUÉ?

The world's bazaar—beads, ribbons, cloth, threads—is as close as the morning mail. This variety tempts the collector in us and, like our Victorian sisters, inspires our needlework. Small botanicals cut from leather-like Ultra-Suede, embroidered silk ribbon, ribbons stitched as though cut from cloth or twined into flowers—Ribbon Appliqué has it all. The result is a sensual texture, romantic and mysterious.

The stitcher knows secrets. How was that bud fashioned (photo 5-1)? How do the leaves convey such dimension? How can silken thread so evoke the rough bark of a rose branch (photo 5-1)?

While most fancy flowers are sculpted right in hand, then arranged, full-blown, Ribbon Appliqué suits a more formal style. As we have seen, the style rides on a fully drawn pattern traced onto a background square. You'll find that delightful and more creative than it sounds! With Ribbon Appliqué, you'll quickly develop a style all your own.

5-6. Fern-Wreathed Heart, *a velveteen quilt block in progress by the author. The fiddlehead fern uses the pierced leaf stitch fern technique, and the organza pleated flowers use Lisa McCulley's technique.*

5-7 Meadow Larks *by Wendy Grande from her quilt* Ribbon Appliqué. *Wendy used mountain/valley ruching for the flower, and exquisite fabric interpretation to transform an antebellum Baltimore block from* Papercuts and Plenty *into a modern masterpiece!*

Basket of Fruit, *from the original album quilt,* Ribbon Appliqué, *designed and stitched by Wendy Grande.*

Flowers From Other Ribbon Techniques

*K*notted, looped, folded, pleated and rolled—thus are made more of ribbonart's easiest blooms. They take little time, little ribbon, little effort —and for this small investment, they reward you with delight!

These simple techniques make everything from petite baby's breath type blossoms to spider mums to all the pointed petal flowers of the composite family. Members of this large plant family *(Compositae or Asteraceae)* comprise the most highly developed plants, including the daisy, aster, dandelion and marigold, and are called, in botany, complex flowers. Happily, in ribbonwork, they are not complex at all!

Of all this lesson's methods, folding makes such diverse flowers that it leads us seamlessly into roses, the flower of love and the diva of romantic ribbonry.

Review *Getting Started*.

RIBBON TYPES

Wired ribbon, wired organza, luminous ribbon, rayon, bias-cut silk, silk embroidery ribbon, Mokuba Heirloom Sylk embroidery ribbon, double-faced satin, grosgrain, velvet, acetate, moiré and georgette are all possibilities.

RIBBON SIZES

From 9mm up to 2˝ wide.

PROJECTS

Project 11: Sophisticated Sunflower— a dramatic pin.
Project 12: Sophisticated Sunflower— a showy necklace.
Project 13: Sophisticated Sunflower— a half-glasses case.
Project 14: Lisa McCulley's Blossoming Scissors-Sheath.
Project 15: A Tailored Rose and Opera Pearl Jewel.

RIBBON FLOWER TECHNIQUES

Lesson Six's techniques make both impressionistic flora and flora reminiscent of their natural sisters: Dahlia, Folded Chrysanthemum, Folded Flower, Folded and Rolled Rose, Sunflower, Tailored or "Gallica" Rose, Oriental Poppy, Lisa McCulley's Pleated Flower, Knotted Chrysanthemum, Lisa McCulley's Cosmos with a Pleated Center, Suzanne Charleston's Puffed and Stuffed Buds, Suzanne Charleston's Baby's Breath, Lisa McCulley's Baby's Breath, Star Flower, and the *Centifolia* Rose "Fantin Latour".

RIBBON LEAF TECHNIQUES

Kimono folded leaves and double-ended kimono folded leaves with knotted leaf overlay.

Project 11

SOPHISTICATED SUNFLOWER PIN: AN INFORMAL BUT DRAMATIC BROOCH

*S*unflowers are in vogue. I cannot see a sunflower without thinking of my sister Erica. Years ago, as a military wife, she lived on the economy in Japan and felt forever foreign. She was, her letter said, "the giant mother at the nursery school". Of all the mothers, she towered highest as parents and children danced in a circle. "Even the 'zinnia' seeds I planted around our little house turned into looming sunflowers! Everything about us is too big." Despite this experience, Erica's New Jersey home is filled with fond mementos of Japan and she now favors sunflowers.

Affectionately, folk-art stylizes sunflowers from every angle. Sunflowers in buckets brighten city flower stalls, and sunflowers in gardens are the most eye-catching of all the flowers. Sunflowers quickly become a bit disheveled, but they are stately—even when they have dried *in situ* and offer their plump seeds to passing birds. Project 11 pleases me, for the center is fecund with seed beads and the wired ribbon petals bend up and twist a bit, like those of a head-strong flower of the field.

My outdoors-woman daughter, Katya, pins a sunflower to her backpack (photo 6-1) while I wear mine on jasper beads (photo 6-2). Perhaps you can fashion this lesson's sunflower into something as practical as Project 13's floreate case for ubiquitous half-glasses. Instructions for fashioning the sunflower pin follow.

SUPPLIES AND PREPARATION

This pin or necklace medallion can be made in more than one ribbon type, size and color. The following supplies were used to make one sunflower pendant.

Sunflower petals

Three layers of petals mix three colors of ribbon and surround the center. The number and color of petals are up to you. I designed my model from the following, not quite using all the petals.

From 1 yd. of wired ribbon shaded orange to brown, cut 12 petal pieces $\frac{7}{8}$″

6-1. *Katya sports Elly's sunflowers from Lesson Six on a backpack.*

x 3″ (sz5 x 3½SQs). Make the top edge brown.

From 1 yd. of the same type ribbon, shaded orange to yellow, cut 12 petal pieces $\frac{7}{8}$″ x 3″ (sz5 x 3½SQs). Make the top edge yellow.

From ½ yd. of wired ribbon shaded beige to brown, cut six petal pieces $\frac{7}{8}$″ x 3″ (sz5 x 3½SQs). Make the top edge beige.

From ¼ yd. of Elégance wired organza ribbon shaded yellow to orange, cut six $\frac{7}{8}$″ x 3″ (sz5 x 3½SQs) petal pieces. Make the top edge orange.

The stuffed and beaded Sunflower center

Foundation for the flower center: draw Template S *(6-1A)* onto AidaPlus or a file card. Cut on the drawn line. In addition, cut Template S out of thin quilt batting, then trim $\frac{1}{8}$″ off all around *(6-1B)*. Cut a second layer of batting, ½″ smaller all around than Template S.

Optional: cut a third layer of batting 1″ smaller all around than Template S. Mound these over the foundation, like a beehive; adhere the layers with gluestick.

FIGURE 1, A–E ILLUSTRATES A SUNFLOWER FROM START TO FINISH

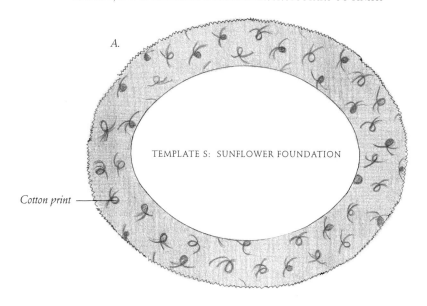

A.

TEMPLATE S: SUNFLOWER FOUNDATION

Cotton print

B. *Padding the center foundation*

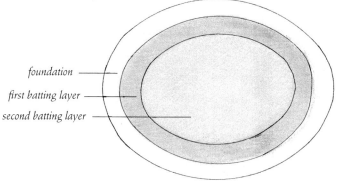

foundation

first batting layer

second batting layer

6-1. A SUNFLOWER CENTER

Cloth cover for the flower center

Draw Template S on the top (right) side of a small dark brown and black calico or similar cotton print. Cut this shape out, adding a ³/₄″ seam allowance *(6-1A)*.

Seed beads for center

Clear amethyst color in size 6 (or larger) for beading an oval about half the diameter of the flower's center. Use black, dark green, or clear chartreuse accent beads (sizes 9, 10, and 11) for the outer half of the flower center.

Make two boat prow leaves

Cut two ⁵/₈″ x 6″ (sz3 x 9½SQs) pieces of green shaded wired ribbon for one flower. Use the light edge on the inside of the leaf. Follow Lesson One's directions for boat prow leaves and embellish with green seed and bugle beads.

Backing for pin or necklace

4″ x 8″ of UltraSuede; two gold-headed hat pins.

Basic sewing kit and ribbon tools

C. Attaching the center's fabric cover

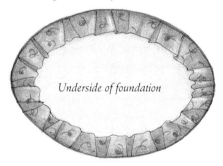

Underside of foundation

D. Making a petal

Pull to gather to ³/₄″ width.

PROCEDURE

1. *Flower center:* with gluestick, attach the batting layers (the smallest on top) to the center's foundation *(6-1B)*.

2. Cover the front (batting) side with the calico. Center the cloth, right side up, over the batting. Use a dab of gluestick to secure the cloth.

3. Rim the foundation's underside with a ½″ wide outline of gluestick. Pull the cloth over the foundation snugly, but not so tightly as to flatten the center front. Press the calico's ³/₄″ seam allowance into the glue *(6-1C)*. Secure the seam. Iron the glue dry. Crisscross the center with stitches catching the cloth's edge, or tape the edges down.

4. *Make the petals:* fold the ribbon petal pieces from the top center, right over left *(6-1D)*. Stitch-gather across the base of the folds, pulling the petal to a ³/₄″ width. Do not cut off the excess. Instead, spread more gluestick over the foundation's seam *(6-1C)* and press the petals' seams to it.

5. *Arrange the petals:* outline the flower's stuffed center with 9-10 orange to brown shaded petals *(6-1E)*. Arrange a second row of 13-14 petals peeking out from behind. Make this second row predominantly brown to beige petals with accent petals in orange to yellow organza. Place a dozen or so yellow to orange petals around the outside. Omit this last layer where the leaves are placed.

E. Bead-embroidering the Sunflower center

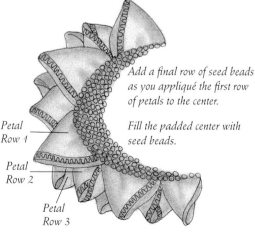

Add a final row of seed beads as you appliqué the first row of petals to the center.

Fill the padded center with seed beads.

Petal Row 1

Petal Row 2

Petal Row 3

6. *Add the leaves* to the left and right of the flower. With gluestick, glue them to the flower back. For the pin, just two boat prow leaves are needed.

7. *Bead the center* concentrically, using a milliner's #10 or #11 needle and black Nymo or polyester thread. Stitch through all the layers. You'll need a thimble!

8. *Face the back of the flower with UltraSuede.* For the pin, place the assembled flower on the wrong side of the synthetic leather, trace around it with a black Pigma Micron .01 pen, and cut the backing shape out on this line. Spread white Gem Tac glue thinly across the cloth's wrong side and press it to the back of the flower.

9. *To wear the finished flower as a pin:* I prefer two gold hat pins to pin it to clothing. The brooch seems too long for a ready-made pin-back—and hat pins are a happy reminder of flowers pinned on formals in my youth!

Project 12

SOPHISTICATED SUNFLOWER NECKLACE

SUPPLIES

Use the same supplies as for Project 11 except for the pin-back. In addition, for the necklace:

Armature for necklace

Cut a plastic drinking straw to a 6″ length, the length of the leaf/flower unit when it has been assembled. Reinforce the straw by wrapping it with a layer of duct tape or masking tape.

Two green velvet leaves, approximately 2½″ long by 1³/₄″ wide (from Lacis, see *Resources*). Alternatively, two larger boat prow leaves, ⁷/₈″ x 7″ (sz5 x 8SQs), can be substituted for the velvet leaves. Add a 30″ string of glass or semi-precious stone beads, available at bead stores.

6-2. *This showy necklace fashioned by the author is the Sophisticated Sunflower, Project 12.*

PROCEDURE

1. Follow steps 1 through 7 for Project 11.

2. To the top left and right sides of the sunflower, I appliquéd a velvet leaf to curve the bloom upward. If you prefer, make two additional boat leaves for these positions.

3. Attach the armature for the necklace. Place the straw to fit lengthwise from leaf tip to leaf tip. Use Gem Tac to glue it in place. The armature forms a tunnel. I threaded heavy monofilament through the beads and through the flower via the straw armature. I did not unstring the purchased beads, but simply ran a second monofilament through them and hid the knot within the straw. This could also have been done with beading wire. Consult your bead store proprietor for which wire weight works best. My necklace is long. Adjust the length to your own taste.

4. Back the flower/leaf assemblage with UltraSuede, as in Project 11 in step 8. The finished necklace blossoms in photo 6-2.

Project 13

SOPHISTICATED SUNFLOWER HALF-GLASSES CASE

SUPPLIES

Use the same supplies as for Project 11. For the half-glasses case, cut two 4″ x 8″ rectangles of UltraSuede. This material will show a bit, around the leaves and to the left and right top edge above the flower.

PROCEDURE

1. Follow steps 1 through 3 for Project 12.

2. Trace Template SC *(6-2)* onto UltraSuede. Cut two of this shape, the front and the back, on the drawn line.

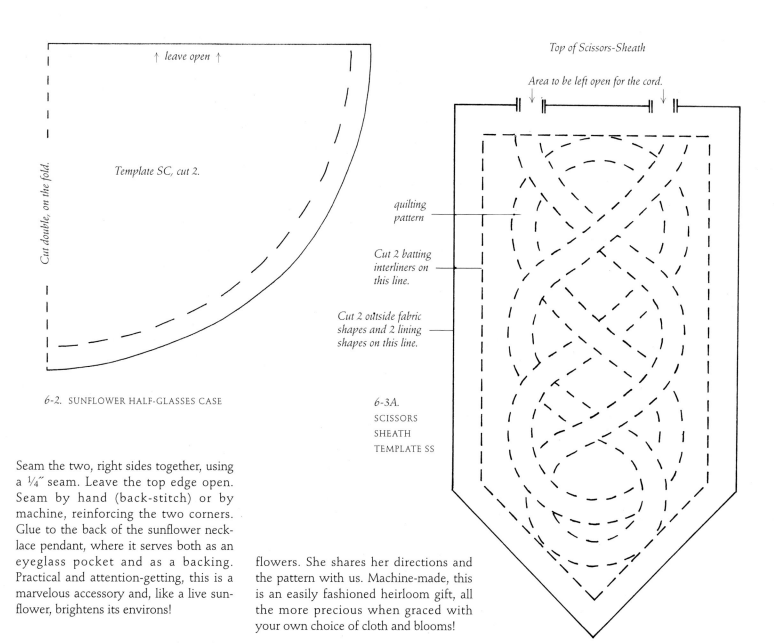

↑ *leave open* ↑

Template SC, cut 2.

Cut double, on the fold.

6-2. SUNFLOWER HALF-GLASSES CASE

Top of Scissors-Sheath

Area to be left open for the cord.

quilting pattern

Cut 2 batting interliners on this line.

Cut 2 outside fabric shapes and 2 lining shapes on this line.

6-3A.
SCISSORS
SHEATH
TEMPLATE SS

Seam the two, right sides together, using a ¼″ seam. Leave the top edge open. Seam by hand (back-stitch) or by machine, reinforcing the two corners. Glue to the back of the sunflower necklace pendant, where it serves both as an eyeglass pocket and as a backing. Practical and attention-getting, this is a marvelous accessory and, like a live sunflower, brightens its environs!

Project 14

LISA MCCULLEY'S BLOSSOMING SCISSORS-SHEATH

*I*nspired by a design from Janice Love's *Hardanger Stitcher's Treasures,* Lisa McCulley fashioned an elegant embroidery scissors case (photo 6-3). Her specialty is art needlework by machine, so her scissors-sheath is ornamented by machine quilting and pleated ribbon flowers. She shares her directions and the pattern with us. Machine-made, this is an easily fashioned heirloom gift, all the more precious when graced with your own choice of cloth and blooms!

SUPPLIES AND PREPARATION

Sheath cover
Cut two 3″ x 5½″ rectangles of heavy raw silk.

Sheath lining
Cut two 3″ x 5½″ rectangles of crepe de Chine or cotton.

Sheath batting
Cut two 3″ x 5½″ rectangles of low-loft batting.

Neck cord
1 yd. of purchased cord.

Two of Lisa McCulley's Pleated Flowers
Directions in this lesson, and four bud leaves (from Lesson One).

PROCEDURE

1. Make a sturdy template from Template SS (6-3A). Template SS already includes the sheath's ¼″ seam allowance. Trace around it onto the cloth. On the marked line, cut a front and a back of this shape in the case's outside fabric, and two of the lining cloth.

2. Make a second template on the Template SS line marked for the batting interliners. Cut two of this shape out of low loft batting *(6-3A, again)*.

3. Sew the sheath's front cover to the back, right sides together, along seam *A*. Leave the seam open for the cord, between the two pairs of marking lines *(6-3B)*. Back-stitch to reinforce both sides of each of these openings.

4. Stitch the two lining pieces together, stitching just ½″ into the seam at either side *(seam B)*. Backstitch at the beginning and end of this opening. (This opening is for turning the case right side out after the outer fabric and lining are stitched around the side and bottom edges.)

5. Press seams *A* and *B* open on both of the fabric pieces.

6. Lay the batting pieces on the wrong side of the lining and baste very near the edge of the batting.

7. Lay the lining on the fabric, right

6-3. Blossoming Scissors-Sheath, *designed and fashioned by Lisa McCulley, Project 14.*

FIGURE 3, A–C SHOWS THE BLOSSOMING SCISSORS SHEATH, PROJECT 14, FROM START TO FINISH

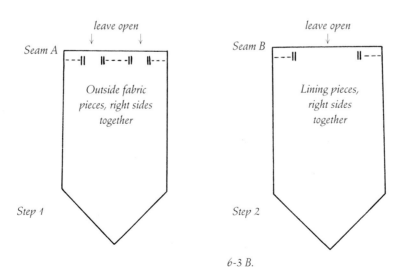

leave open

Seam A

Outside fabric pieces, right sides together

Step 1

leave open

Seam B

Lining pieces, right sides together

Step 2

6-3 B.

sides together (batting out). Stitch a ¼″ seam (seam C) all the way around the case.

8. Clip the points and trim the seam allowance if necessary.

9. Turn right sides out and pull/push each corner into a sharper point. Press.

10. Mark the quilting design (6-3A) and quilt by hand or by machine.

11. Add bud leaves (from Lesson One) and ribbon flowers. (Lisa's Pleated Flowers follow in this lesson.)

12. Thread a twisted cord through the openings in the fold. Seal the ends with clear nail polish and tie an overhand knot in each.

13. Thread the ends of the cord through the embroidery scissors' handles and tie in an overhand knot. When not in use, retract the scissors into the case.

14. Fold in half and, by hand, whip-stitch or buttonhole-stitch seams *D* and *E* (6-3C). Wear your fancywork scissors - sheath with pleasure!

6-4. Petunia Scissors-Sheath *inspired by Lisa McCulley's Scissors-Sheath, fashioned by the author.*

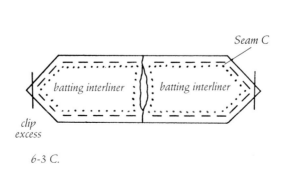

6-3 C.

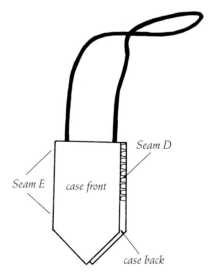

6-5. The Tailored Rose on Opera Pearls *fashioned by the author, Project 15.*

A.

B. Backing the rose to wear on beads

On the underside, overlap
raw ends and glue. ↓

Fold #1

Fold #2

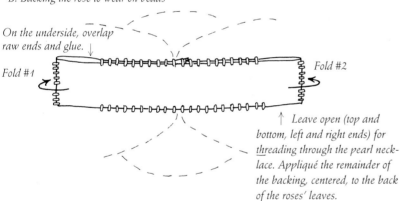

↑ *Leave open (top and*
bottom, left and right ends) for
threading through the pearl neck-
lace. Appliqué the remainder of
the backing, centered, to the back
of the roses' leaves.

C.

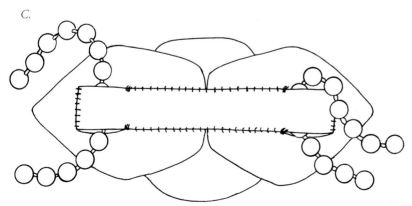

Thread the pearls through the backing after it has been attached to the rose leaves.

6-4. GALLICA ROSE

A TAILORED ROSE AND AN OPERA PEARL JEWEL

SUPPLIES

Gallica Rose

Cut a 1½″ (38 mm) x 1 yd. length (sz9 x 24SQs) of Mokuba No. 4546 Crepe Georgette Ribbon, color #12.

Double-Ended Kimono Fold Leaves

Cut a 1½″ (38 mm) x 10″ length (sz9 x 6½SQs) of Mokuba No. 4546 Crepe Georgette Ribbon, color #17.

Knotted Leaf Overlay

Cut a ⅝″ (15mm) x 11″ (sz3 x 17 ½SQs) length of Mokuba's No. 4586 Luminous Ribbon in color #17.

Backing

Cut a ⅝″ (15mm) x 8″ (sz3 x 13SQs) length of Mokuba No. 4586 Luminous Ribbon in color #17.

Beads

This pendant rose can be worn on the necklace of your choice. I wear mine hanging on a 30″ strand of pearls, doubled.

PROCEDURE

1. *The Rose:* from the length of white georgette ribbon above, make a Gallica or Tailored Rose from this lesson.

2. *The Leaves:* from the length of green georgette ribbon above, make the double-ended kimono fold leaves with knotted leaf overlay from this lesson.

ASSEMBLY

1. Appliqué the Gallica Rose to the double-ended kimono fold leaves with knotted overlay (see photo 6-5). Use the pointillist stitch sparingly, so the rose stays plump and dimensional *(6-4A)*.

2. Make the backing, following the steps in *6-4B*.

3. Undo the clasp and thread the necklace through each loop of the backing, as in *6-4C*.

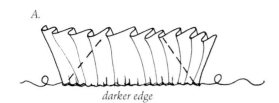

A.

darker edge

B.

C.

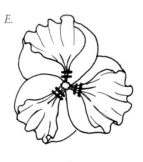

Fold and gather each petal.

D.

E.

5 petals

3 petals

F.

8 petals (5 petals + 3 petals = 8 petals)
Layer the petals. Finish the center with seed beads covering
the ¹/₂″ diameter circle of black UltraSuede.

6-5. ORIENTAL POPPY II

PLEATED FLOWERS

ORIENTAL POPPY II

Lesson Four taught a poppy made from a single length of ribbon. By contrast, this one *(6-5F)* is layered with eight separately crimp-pleated, folded and gathered petals.

1. Cut eight 1½″ x 5¼″ (sz9 x 3 ½SQs) lengths of wired ribbon for the petals. U-turn gather the bottom edge wire to add fullness.

2. Pin-pleat the ribbon's upper edge *(6-5A)*. Also called crimp-pleating, this is taught in Lesson Four (page 103). Pin-pleat the ribbon in ⅛″ deep pleats until the pin holds the ribbon's full length. Fingerpress. The pleats hold better if you wet them with hairspray, then blow or air-dry.

3. Fold the left and right corners forward and down at an angle until the raw edges meet the bottom bound edge *(6-5B)*.

4. Running-stitch across the bottom edge and pull tightly to gather *(6-5C)*. Secure the stitches. Repeat this process for eight petals.

5. Assemble a five-petal unit and a three-petal unit as in figure *6-5, D* and *E*.

6. Pointillist-stitch the smaller petal wreath onto the larger.

7. Finish with a ½″ circle of Ultra-Suede glued (with gluestick) to the center, then covered with black seed beads *(6-5F)*.

Hybrids

Center options include an antique button, French knots, bugle and seed beads, or a stuffed center from Lesson One. A stuffed circle center can be embellished with seed beads or French knots. A real poppy's center crown is a regal display. Look at a fresh poppy, a fine silk flower imposter, or a clear close-up photo for inspiration!

LISA MCCULLEY'S PLEATED FLOWER

1. Begin with a ⅝″ x 25″ (sz3 x 40SQs) length of shaded wired ribbon.

2. Roll the starting end's edge into a tight roll, wrapping towards the ribbon's length. Roll the ribbon so the selvages lay on top of each other, all at an even level *(6-6A **a**)*.

3. Make a ¼″ pleat to the right at **b** *(6-6A)*.

4. Make another pleat to the left, coming up at **c** about as far as the first pleat.

5. Make the next pleat to the right, to **d,** about half-way to the first pleat.

6. Continue in this manner *(e–f)* until all the ribbon has been pleated.

7. Whip-stitch along the bottom edge.

8. Begin rolling the pleated ribbon from starting end to finishing end. Whip-stitch the layers together as you roll. Do not offset the layers. Keep the entire selvage at one level.

9. Fold the finishing raw edge down at a 45° angle and bring it under the rolled ribbon. Stitch in place.

10. Lift and separate the pleated petals *(6-6B)*, shaping them into a perky stand-up flower like those on photo 6-3.

Hybrid I

Fold a 1½″ x 30″ (sz9 x 20SQs) length of shaded wired ribbon lengthwise, folding the dark edge to ¼″ below the light edge *(6-7A)*. After step 7 above, roll the pleated length so the top selvage just covers the bottom selvage *(6-7B)*. The result will be a flatter flower, spiraled like a chambered nautilus.

Hybrid II

Pleat a 1½″ x 30″ (sz9 x 20SQs) length of organza shaded wired ribbon. Pleat and roll as in steps 1 through 7 above, but do not whip-stitch the layers together. Instead, shape it into an evocative side view against the background *(6-8)* and appliqué it down.

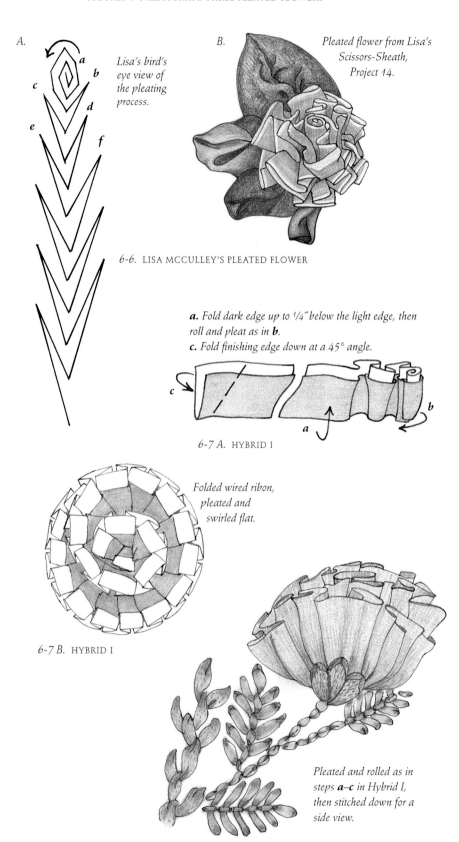

A.

Lisa's bird's eye view of the pleating process.

B.

Pleated flower from Lisa's Scissors-Sheath, Project 14.

6-6. LISA MCCULLEY'S PLEATED FLOWER

a. *Fold dark edge up to ¼″ below the light edge, then roll and pleat as in **b**.*
c. *Fold finishing edge down at a 45° angle.*

6-7 A. HYBRID I

Folded wired ribon, pleated and swirled flat.

6-7 B. HYBRID I

*Pleated and rolled as in steps **a–c** in Hybrid I, then stitched down for a side view.*

6-8. HYBRID II

6-6. *The author fashioned this badge to wear fastened onto a fringed velvet shawl by a vintage hat-pin. Wired ribbon forms Lesson Six's folded and rolled rose, while a lush variety of Mokuba ribbon provides an enviable setting.*

KNOTTED FLOWERS

KNOTTED CHRYSANTHEMUM

*T*his is a favorite flower in turn of the century ribbonwork manuals, a *pièce de résistance*. Formulas for this showy bloom call for ribbon from ½″ wide up to ⅝″ wide and for lengths as long as 9¼ yards cited for one 72 petal flower! At that full-blown state, making many of these mums would be expensive as well as time-consuming. I've chosen a moderate bloom formula—one that teaches the construction and makes this flower's acquaintance. The basic recipe follows.

1. Cut 12mm x 4 yards (sz2 x 306SQs) of Mokuba's No. 4882 Gradation Ribbon (100% rayon) in color #4, rusty red/brown/taupe. Substitute other rayon ribbon, satin, soft grosgrain, or 12mm ribbon embroidery silk.

2. With a pencil, mark off every 5″, beginning 5″ in from the starting end.

3. Tie an overhand knot in the ribbon at every mark along the length *(6-9A)*. This leaves 3″ of flat ribbon remaining between each knot. Pulling these knots tightly changes the style dramatically. I prefer a soft, almost loose knot and take a pointillist stitch to hold it tied.

4. Running-stitch the valley between each knot, sewing one loop to the next *(6-9B)*. Pull the thread to gather.

5. Roll this length of knotted loops in a spiral, from the starting end to the finishing end. Do not off-set. Keep all the valleys on one level, stitching one row to the next. If your resulting flower looks a bit different than figure *6-9C*, you've simply imitated Mother Nature!

Hybrids

Some ribbonwork manuals suggest winding the ribbon length repeatedly around a 2½″ x 6″ rectangle of cardboard. The bottom fold of each wrap is then cut, leaving a bunch of equal-length ribbon pieces to be tied in a knot, then stitch-gathered back together. It would take a particular personality to prefer this method instead of keeping the ribbons together. While I fail that test, it is a useful technique to note, especially since the separate petals can be machine-gathered in a string. Use a heavier, wider ribbon like size 3 grosgrain for machine sewing.

LISA MCCULLEY'S COSMOS WITH KNOTTED CENTER

This delightful flower reverses the chrysanthemum's loop. The fold becomes the top of each petal; the knots cluster at the center. So quick, so easy, so pretty!

1. Use a $^5/_8$″ x 36″ (sz3 x 57½SQs) length of rayon ribbon. (Lisa notes that she bought her skein of overdyed rayon ribbon from a knitting shop.)

2. Mark off every 5″, beginning 5″ from the starting end.

3. Center an overhand knot at each 5″ mark.

4. Loop the ribbon so the knot is at the base of a flower petal *(6-10A)*.

5. Tack the petals together sequentially, forming a wreath of seven petals with a knotted cluster at the center *(6-10B)*.

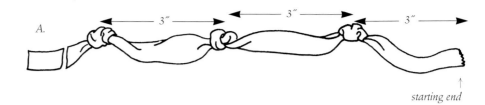

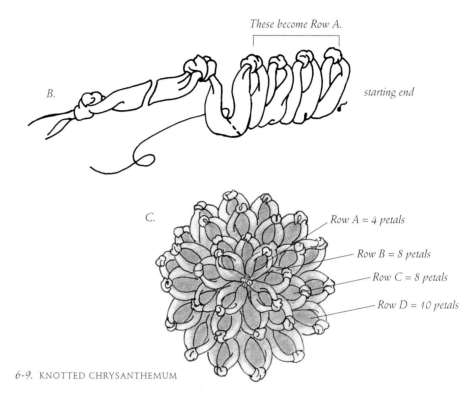

6-9. KNOTTED CHRYSANTHEMUM

Row A = 4 petals
Row B = 8 petals
Row C = 8 petals
Row D = 10 petals

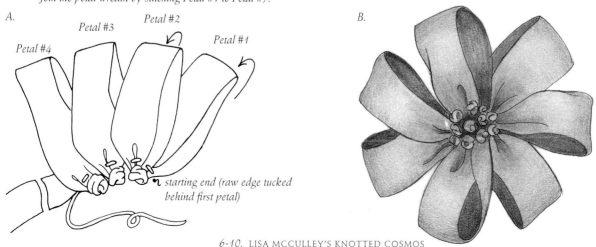

Stitch all seven petals, then pull to gather the knots into a center.
Join the petal wreath by stitching Petal #1 to Petal #7.

6-10. LISA MCCULLEY'S KNOTTED COSMOS

Focus on Filler Flowers

What a wonder is a good florist! In Washington, D.C., my home town, I love to visit Johnson's Florists in winter. In summer, multiple double-doors welcome the season, propped open by flats of bedding plants which overflow, winking and blinking bright, onto the city's sidewalk. In winter, the doors are shut against the cold, the high racks at the parking lot entrance hold garden pottery in tidy rows, and rhododendron, pine and mountain laurel, brown string-tied and neatly stacked, tempt the house-bound with their evergreen. However, it is the air that stuns the senses first when, all winter-wrapped, one enters Johnson's. That first inhalation is tropic-moist, perfume-heavy, and super-oxygenated. Liven up! Colors dance before your eyes—not stern colors like headlights and traffic signals, but inviting hues from friendly blossoms.

Flowers in winter are costly. The showy ones are priced per stem; smaller bunches of blooms stand in water, rubber band-bound. When you check out, the red-jerseyed clerk wraps your bundle in green waxed paper, tucking in maidenhair fern and foil-packaged flower food. A low galvanized bucket of baby's breath stands next to the register, the contents priced to sell. "Let me take this, too," you tell him, for the baby's breath and fern are filler flowers, modest botanicals to fill out your chosen bouquet. Did you know ribbon also has filler flowers? These cloth botanicals are at most a small investment of your time, but they people the floral landscape and show their more elaborate big sisters off to best advantage. Leaves are the quintessential botanical fillers, but less expected fillers follow. All such candidates are quick and easy to make —the very qualities that define the filler flower.

SUZANNE CHARLESTON'S PUFFED AND STUFFED BUDS

1. Cut a 1″ x 1½″ (sz6 x 1½ SQs) length of ribbon. If wired, remove the wires.

2. Draw a circle from bound edge to bound edge.

3. Running-stitch a gather line just inside of the drawn circle, but don't pull it yet.

4. Take a pinch of fiberfil the size of a robin's egg. Roll it between your palms until it is firm and round.

5. Center an 8″ beading wire over it, twist the wired ends tightly beneath it, and pat the filler into renewed roundness.

6. Cap the ribbon over the wired bud and pull the gathering thread.

Wrap the thread end tightly around the wires and secure it with stitches taken one on top of the other.

7. Beginning right under the bud, wrap green florist tape taut so it pulls the excess ribbon in tightly, forming a calyx. Then continue it down the twined wires to effect a stem.

Hybrids: To vary the Puffed and Stuffed Buds' sizes, use 1½SQs of ⅝″ and 1½″ ribbon.

SUZANNE CHARLESTON'S BABY'S BREATH

Baby's Breath—what romanticist named this flower? Consider! He must so have loved the tender beauties of this earth to personify the ethereal and tie it to a flower.

1. Cut seven (or more) 6″ lengths of beige 7mm or 9mm silk ribbon.

2. Use the chrysanthemum knotting technique. Tie a soft overhand knot at the center of one 6″ length. Take several tiny stitches to secure the base of the knot so the ribbon lengths (the "stems") lay one on top of the other, and the beige knotted flower stays tied.

3. With a fine brush, put a dab of resist at the base of the tied and sewn knot. Then, with Dekka® silk dye paints or SetaColor®, paint the flat ribbon a mossy green to look like stems. Do this for all seven flowers.

4. Stitch the stem bases together, one flat on top of the other, but offset. Tuck these into a ribbon flower arrangement.

LISA MCCULLEY'S BABY'S BREATH

Again the chrysanthemum knotting technique is used.

1. Cut a 4mm x 35″ length of white/off-white silk embroidery ribbon.

2. Mark a pencil point 2½″ from each raw-edged end and every 5″ between. There will be a total of seven pencil points.

3. At each point, loosely tie an overhand knot to form the flower.

4. Loop the ribbon so the seven knots top each loop. Take a stitch at the base of each knot to have it sit up as a bud.

5. Stitch the bottom loops together. Cluster them so just the knotted buds and a bit of their stems show behind the ribbon flower arrangement's larger botanicals.

Hybrids: Try using soft greens for fern fronds, or floral colors for anonymous small blossoms. Vary the width of the ribbon, and even the type. Organza, for example, brings to mind autumn wildflowers blowing gossamer seed-parachutes aloft. (If you want the poetry of fragility, but not its helplessness, hairspray some spine into these delicate flowers!)

6-8. *A folded and rolled rose barrette, also by Suzanne Charleston.*

FOLDED LEAVES AND FLOWERS

KIMONO FOLDS AND KIMONO PLEATS

From Japan comes the concept of a particularly clever fold. We'll call it the *kimono fold*. Historically, the Japanese have an affection for cloth, treating it tenderly. Traditionally, they respect the inherent linear quality, cutting it as little as possible by sewing the kimono from rectangular panels. So revered is this national costume that ritual surrounds even the storage. A square cloth, *furoshiki*, takes on the folded kimono's form when wrapped around it, but returns to its original shape when that burden is released. I was given an antique kimono—darkest purple with fuchsia peonies—by the ladies of Takae Onoyama's Quilt School in Tokyo. They showed me how to fold the garment, bringing one wide rectangular sleeve forward, then the other. Smoothing and patting the old jacquard silk, they noted that the kimono's own weight presses out wrinkles even as the revered object rests. Finally, they placed the folded kimono on the *furoshiki*, whose opposing corners, touching like the flaps of a square envelope, were tied together.

The kimono fold illustrated in figure *6-11* holds the ribbon's point in place uniquely. After the petal/leaf point is formed by two angular folds, the ribbon tails are kimono pleated by a stylized tuck which readies a kimono waist to be wrapped by an *obi*. We'll call this clever tuck a kimono-pleat. In figure *6-12*, these folds and pleats make a shape as suitable for a petal as for a leaf. Thus romancing ribbon into a humble leaf or petal may magically spin your needleart odyssey to far-away kingdoms in the tradition-clad Orient!

DOUBLE ENDED KIMONO FOLD LEAVES WITH KNOTTED LEAF OVERLAY

These splendid leaves adorn the Gallica Rose in Project 15 and in photos 6-5 and 6-9. They combine kimono pleats with overhand knots.

1. For double-ended petal leaves, cut a 1½″ x 10″ (sz9 x 6½SQs) ribbon length, and follow steps A and B in figure *6-12*.

2. For a knotted overlay, cut a ⅝″ (15mm) x 11″ (sz3 x 17½SQs) ribbon length and follow steps C and D in figure *6-12*.

3. Center the knotted leaves over the kimono fold leaves. Use the pointillist stitch to hold them together. Figure *6-4A* from Project 15 shows these leaves framing a Gallica or Tailored Rose.

6-9. The author's Gallica or Tailored Rose is taught in Lesson Six. In this corsage, the wired ribbon rose nestles on kimono fold leaves and a cascade of overhand knots, all in Mokuba ribbon.

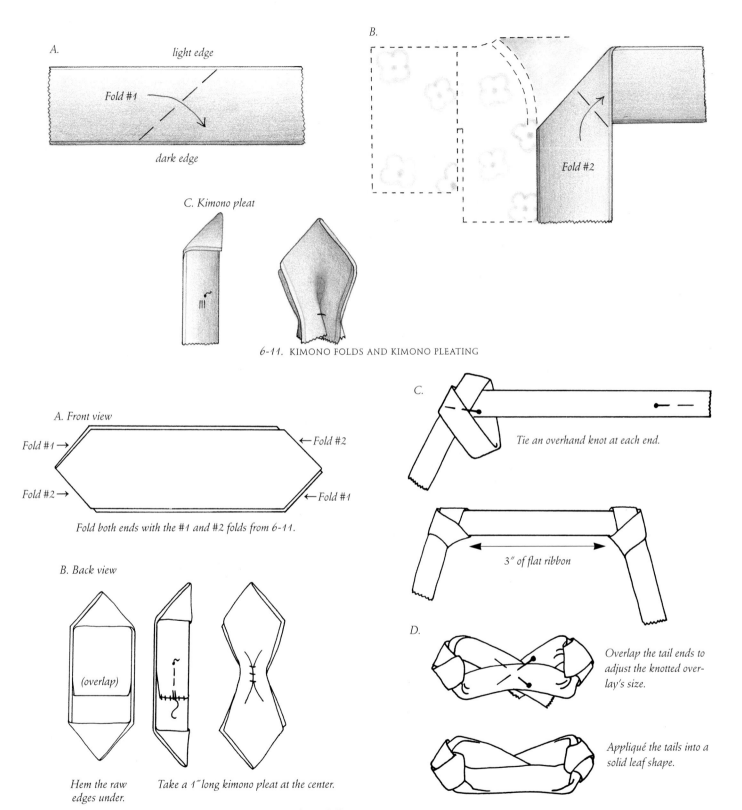

A.

light edge

Fold #1

dark edge

B.

Fold #2

C. Kimono pleat

6-11. KIMONO FOLDS AND KIMONO PLEATING

A. Front view

Fold #1 →   ← Fold #2

Fold #2 →   ← Fold #1

Fold both ends with the #1 and #2 folds from 6-11.

B. Back view

(overlap)

Hem the raw
edges under.   Take a 1″ long kimono pleat at the center.

C.

Tie an overhand knot at each end.

3″ of flat ribbon

D.

Overlap the tail ends to
adjust the knotted over-
lay's size.

Appliqué the tails into a
solid leaf shape.

6-12, A–D. DOUBLE-ENDED KIMONO FOLD LEAVES

DAHLIA

1. Cut six 1½″ x 4″ (sz9 x 2¾SQs) lengths of shaded wired ribbon for the top wreath of petals. Cut six 2″ x 4½″ (sz16 x 2¼SQs) lengths of shaded wired ribbon for the middle wreath of petals. For the bottom wreath, cut six 2″ x 5¼″ (sz16 x 2¾SQs) petal-lengths of the same ribbon.

2. To make one petal, follow steps A through C of kimono folds and kimono pleats (6-11). Make 18 petals.

3. Assemble a bottom wreath of 6 longer petals, a middle wreath of 6 mid-length petals, and a top wreath of the 6 shortest petals (6-13).

4. Make a stuffed center from Lesson Three, page 77. Appliqué it to the layered petal wreaths and bead or embroider as in 6-13.

FOLDED CHRYSANTHEMUM

1. Cut eight petals ⅝″ x 3¼″ (sz3 x 5SQs) of shaded wired ribbon. Cut ten petals ⅝″ x 4″ (sz3 x 6½SQs) of the same ribbon. Cut twelve more petals ⅝″ x 4¾″ (sz3 x 7½SQs).

2. To make one petal, fold the right and left ends forward and down at an angle as in 6-14A. Tack and secure the stitches.

3. Assemble a bottom wreath of 12 petals, a middle wreath of 10 petals, and a top wreath of 8 petals.

4. Cut a ⅝″ x 6″ (sz3 x 9½SQs) length of ribbon. Fold it in half lengthwise (from selvage to selvage). Fold the raw edges down at an angle to meet the selvages, then gather the bottom edges. Roll (from starting to finishing ends) into a roseate center.

5. Assemble the three layers topped by the roseate center. Stitch through all the layers and secure the stitches.

STAR FLOWER

1. Cut five ⅝″ x 3″ (sz3 x 5SQs) lengths of shaded wired ribbon for the wreath of bottom petals. Cut five ⅝″ x 1½″ (sz3 x 2½SQs) lengths for the top wreath of petals.

2. Fold the left and right sides of the ribbon back at an angle, away from you (6-15A).

3. Stitch across the ribbon tails (6-15C).

4. Pull to gather the stitches, then thread-wrap to tighten (6-15D). Secure the stitches. Do this for all 10 petals.

5. Assemble the petals into two same-size wreaths of five. While some stitches will be covered by the flower's center, try to hide the stitches between each

6-13. DAHLIA

6-14. FOLDED CHRYSANTHEMUM

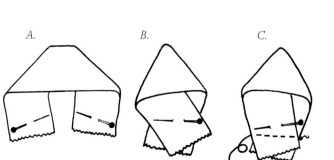

6-15, A–E. STAR FLOWER

petal.

6. Pin the smaller wreath centered on top of the larger one, with the petals alternating between the larger petals below it.

7. Top with the same roseate rolled center as taught in step 4, Folded Chrysanthemum.

THE FOLDED AND ROLLED ROSE

Modestly named, this rose has spectacular potential! Like a great actress, it can play many roles. Short lengths make delicate buds. A yard of 1½″ wide grosgrain, tightly wrapped, makes a jaunty rose sporty enough to wear on a heavy wool jacket. Softly wound around and made of shaded wired ribbon, this rose looks far more feminine (photo 6-6). A varietal, the Tailored Rose, when fashioned from Mokuba's white georgette, looks fragile, the petals translucent. This aristocratic rose consorts with opera pearls and holds in her throat the scent of wine and violets (photo 6-5).

1. To make the Folded and Rolled Rose *(6-16G)*: cut a 1½″ x 36″ (sz9 x 24SQs) length of wired or other ribbon listed at the start of this lesson.

2. Fold #1: Fold the starting end for-

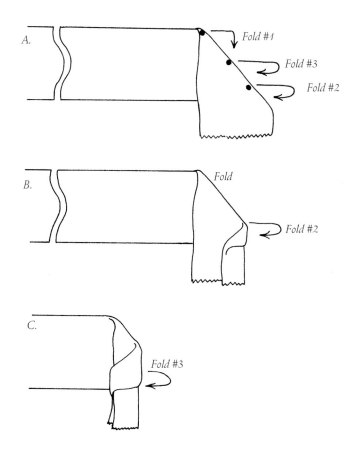

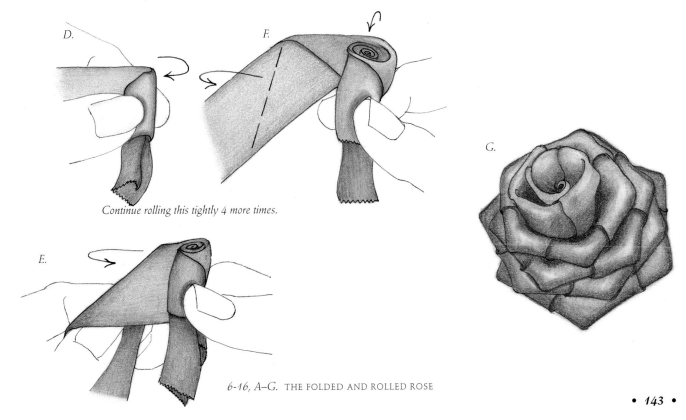

Continue rolling this tightly 4 more times.

6-16, A–G. THE FOLDED AND ROLLED ROSE

ward and down, so the raw edge extends an inch or so below the bottom edge of the remaining length of ribbon (6-16A). This forms the stem or handle.

3. Fold and roll the handle to the left, toward the length of the ribbon. Roll the handle three times (6-16B and C).

4. At the fourth fold (6-16D), stitch through all the layers at the bottom of the bud to keep it from unrolling.

5. Now begins the repetitious fold, lift, and roll rhythm by which you'll finish the rose. Fold the length of the ribbon back away from yourself and over your left thumb at a 45° angle (6-16E). Your left thumb and forefinger holds that fold lightly (6-16E), and lifts it parallel to the horizon. At the same time, your right hand rolls the bud center to the left, covering the fold's triangle. As the bud moves left, towards the length of the ribbon, it wraps the triangle's fold around itself. Your left hand guides the latest fold so it wraps around at a slightly lower level than the bud, creating a rounded rose. The motion is fluid, like waves cradled by the universe and lapping at the shore: fold, lift, roll. Just as each roll covers the folded triangle, take a securing stitch through the bottom edge of all the rounds of rolled ribbon. Then resume the fold, lift, roll rhythm.

6. When you come to the end of the ribbon, tuck the raw edge under the flower at an angle. Whip-stitch the back to secure all the whorls. Trim off any excess ribbon handle, below the stitches.

☆Art Note: An obvious bound edge on the ribbon emphasizes this rose's style more than a discreetly bound ribbon does. Similarly, a change of color like hand-dyed Hanah bias-cut silk, adds drama to this rose. Because this rose's folds catch the light voluptuously, a shiny or napped ribbon, or one with a luxurious texture, is well displayed here. Diagonal folds taken at a 45° angle, at equal intervals and in quick sequence give a tailored look. Not so with ribbon folded back at an acute angle resulting in a drawn-out fold which can be rolled quite languidly around the bud. Varying the distance between the finish of one folded triangle and the beginning of the next gives the rose a softer look and mystifies the viewer as to how it has been made. Try it! You'll find so many hybrids in this rose that only you may know how closely the cousins are related.

6-10. *Linda Gail designed this pretty and practical gift pin. Its purchased flowers are glued to a pre-cut wooden heart. Lesson Six teaches the roses' folded and rolled technique and portrays it in ribbons from inexpensive craft stores to opulent boutiques.*

THE GALLICA OR TAILORED ROSE

Gallica roses bloomed during the Roman Empire and may have been among the first civilized roses cultivated by man. A June rose so sweetly pungent that the fragrance holds long after it has dried, Gallicas have medicinal qualities both antiseptic and astringent. This same rose bears the names Apothecary Rose, *Rose du Provins*, and The Red Rose of Lancaster. So romantic, these echoes from the Gallica! Our Tailored Rose or Gallica Rose has a plumply round profile. Its easy ribbon propagation endears it to us, while its compact firmness makes it practical. Once you've nurtured this rose to bloom, the perfume will sweeten your journey. See its portrait in Project 15 *(6-4A)*, and read its history here.

1. Cut a ⁷⁄₈″ x 36″ (sz5 x 41SQs) length of shaded wired ribbon. Pin-mark the upper edge at 12″ from each end. For Project 15, cut a 1½″ x 1 yd. (sz9 x 24SQs) of Mokuba No. 4546 *Crêpe Georgette* Ribbon, color #12.

2. Follow steps 2-5 of the Folded and Rolled Rose, with one exception. For the beginning 12″, fold, lift and roll ever so tightly, wrapping the folds around the bud so the folds are level with the top of the bud, and the ribbon's lower bound edges are all in a huddle, one on top of the other. This rose's bud center will be vertical. Pin it, then stitch to hold, after the first 12″ are rolled. Make this rose's bud center hard, and at least ½″ in diameter.

3. For the ribbon's middle 12″: fold at a 45° angle, lift and roll. On these rounds, allow the rose's base to broaden so the flower's silhouette is akin to the flat, then rounded shape of a chocolate cherry cordial. Simply pin the rounds occasionally at this stage, rather than stitch them. I try to avoid any sewing until I can see this rose fully formed.

4. For the ribbon's last 12″, loosen up! Procrastinate on the folds, let them roll on seemingly forever. (Can you see that the acute angle of this longer fold also narrows these outer petal rounds, lowering the outer margins like those of an over-turned teacup?) Gentle the roll, so that the whorls have the lightness of soft meringue. The base's silhouette should be round enough to appliqué it to a marked circle.

5. Turn the rose over, tuck the end under, stitching to hold the rounds in place; then righting it, look the rose directly in the eye. Being Victorian, such an enticing rose should be less bold, more indirect. So push the flower down firmly all around, pressing her face away from you. Have her glance over her shoulder, modestly. Because the center is rolled so heavily, this can only be a subtle gesture. This same solidity also makes the rose durable. Add watercolor touches if desired. Then stiffen your rose with hair spray and wear it as a jewel.

☆ *Miniature Memo:* The Tailored Rose can be made of 7mm to 15mm silk ribbon, bound or bias-cut with a raw edge. For lush texture on a miniature scale, try these Mokuba ribbons: No. 1500 Organdy ribbon in 5, 8, or 11mm; No. 1520 Organdy ribbon in 9 or 15mm; No. 4882 rayon Gradation Ribbon in 12mm; No. 4563 Organdy ribbon in 8mm; No. 4599 Luminous ribbon in 7mm or 13mm; and No. 4597 Stripe Organdy Ribbon in 8mm. Begin with the Tailored Rose's formula of 41SQs for length and adjust to taste.

THE CENTIFOLIA ROSE, FANTIN LATOUR

A magnificent Provence rose with circular cupped blooms, which flatten on opening while retaining the cupped centre, the whole in a delicate pale pink, warmly blushed in the centre and filled with delicious fragrance.

Judyth McLeod describes this rose so exuberantly in *Our Heritage of Old Roses* that trying to reproduce it in ribbon became a delightful challenge. Fantin Latour, named for the famous flower artist, combines the Turncoat Tea Rose method with that of the Tailored Rose, producing cupped inner petals and flattened outer whorls. Its portrait appears in figure *6-17*.

1. Cut a ⁵⁄₈″ x 36″ (sz3 x 57³⁄₄SQs) length of shaded (pink to white) wired ribbon.

2. Gather the first half of the ribbon on the darker edge. Leave the second half ungathered.

3. Fold the starting end down at an angle and roll it towards the ribbon's length four or five times, keeping the bottom selvages all at the same level.

4. Make a series of petals about 1″ long. Use the Turncoat Tea Rose twist (Lesson One) to define the petals. Your thumb's first joint is a good measure for this length. Just move your thumb ahead so the last full twist is at the first joint and the next one is taken at your thumb's tip.

5. Roll the scalloped half of the ribbon up to where the non-gathered half begins. At that mid-point, pick up steps 3 through 5 of the Tailored Rose. This combination of a fluffy petaled center and a calmly rounded perimeter reflect its famous namesake, Fantin Latour of the Centifolia roses.

6-17. CENTIFOLIA ROSE

6-11.

Portrait:

Suzanne Charleston, Blooming!

Why learn to make ribbon bloom? Surely affection for nature's flowers and the artifice of ribbon offer a partial answer, but each person drawn to the craft has her own story. When a maker's romance twines with the romancing of ribbon into roses, her garden is sure to flourish! And therein lies at least part of the magic of Suzanne Charleston's art.

Photos 6-7, 6-8, and 6-11 to 6-14 dance with examples of Suzanne's work. Her colors are vivid and clear, her flowers well-defined and varied, her embellishments —from gold ribbon frayed into "straw" to baby's breath— are happily in keeping with the more prominent botanicals they ornament. Suzanne's sturdily constructed floral pieces explore all manner of ribbon flower techniques. Irrepressibly, her blossoms bud on everything from home decor items (a photo frame, a writing basket), to personal ornament—a pin, barrette, dress clip, and an evening purse. Intelligent, thorough, neat and organized, Suzanne's profession as a legal secretary is the antithesis of fanciful. One might think she chose to learn the art of ribbon flowers primarily as a relaxing, creative antidote to her responsibilities with the firm. While that does result, her compelling motive is more poetic, more adventuresome. She is honing her ribbon flower expertise to *haute couture* as she fashions her own heirloom wedding gown.

In keeping with traditions familial, Suzanne's ribbon bloom story is illustrated here, picture-album style. Suzanne's work mirrors much taught in previous lessons, and also illustrates methods taught in Lesson Six. For this reason alone, her portrait is a fitting finale to end these lessons. Reading childhood fairy tales, we smiled when the prince finally won the princess's hand. Thus Suzanne's portrait was taken by her fiancé. Flower-making doesn't get much more romantic than this.

6-12.

6-13.

6-14.

Suzanne Charleston's eye-catching original ribbonwork displays techniques recognizable throughout Romancing Ribbons.

Detail from Ribbon Appliqué

The Garden Gazebo

Needleartists

Meet the needleartists whose work is pictured in this book. Without their creativity and generosity, *Romancing Ribbons* would not have been so full of blooms. Thank you all!

Suzanne Charleston

ENCINO, CA

Suzanne's ribbonry is California bright in color, but has a style all its own. Because it showcases so many of the flowers taught in *Romancing Ribbons*, a photo album of Suzanne's work concludes Part Two, The Lessons.

Diana Dickey

SOUTH PORTLAND, ME

Diana Dickey's family business is called Artemis. Hanah, her mother, began the enterprise as a lifetime artist whose knitting, dyeing, and painting have produced an international manufacturing base and clientele. Diana's sister's "Hanah Hand-Dyed Silk" ribbon roses are pictured in Lesson One.

Susan Duffield

SIDNEY, B.C., CANADA

"I live to quilt. I'm able now to do as fine work by machine as I can by hand...I do like to push each technique to see how many impossibilities I can overcome. I've lately started working up my designs on the computer... challenging!"

Linda Gail

ROWLAND HEIGHTS, CA

"My grandmother started me 'stitchin' when I was four...I have ten grandchildren. They all like to come over and look through the trunk of ribbons and lace. I teach quiltmaking and especially love crazy quilts."

Lorraine Ryuko Fukuwa

TORRANCE, CA

Lorraine has a bold yet utterly feminine ribbonwork style which she shares in Lesson Four. By profession a technical translator (English/Japanese), interpreting instructor and writer, Ms. Fukuwa notes, "Ribbonart is a relaxing hobby, which fulfills creative urges."

Wendy Grande

APTOS, CA

Wendy is blessed with beauty, intelligence, warmth and artistry. When you couple this with the fact that she is mother to two fine young girls—and a bank vice president, you marvel at the time and creativity which have made the quilt *Ribbon Appliqué* such a masterpiece. There is also a second amazing quilt on its way, tailor-made for Wendy's second daughter.

Lisa McCulley

CHESHIRE, CN

Victoria Magazine, February 1996, features a picture of Lisa's Best of Show by Machine award-winning Baltimore Album-style quilt (1994). It is also pictured in the book, *Baltimore Album Revival!* Lisa teaches a "Baltimore by Machine" course based on a clever formula for a wall quilt. Through a layered block on point—for the center, a paper-cut block—quartered—for the corners, and a ribbon-flowered vine border, she teaches the A to Z of art needlework by machine—including R for Ribbonry!

Ruth Meyers

DHAHRAN, SAUDI ARABIA
AND EXMORE, VA

Best of Show by Hand winner at 1994's prestigious Baltimore Album contest in Lancaster, PA, Ruth's quiltmaking has gained international acclaim. She has done much commission work including this book's *Rosa Rugosa* and two classic-style Baltimores! Poetically, she captures the beauty both of old Baltimore and of Islamic tradition—always with an artist's sensitivity to their underlying passion.

Kathy Rabun

PHILADELPHIA, PA

By day, Kathy works in a large law firm, and by night, in her circa 1838 historic district townhouse, she stitches fine needlework. Her B.A. in American Studies and her artistry led to Baltimore Albums where, she writes, "Doing the appliqué makes me feel like I'm gardening, and the dimensional blooms allow me to add beads, silk leaves...etc. to truly take me beyond those beautiful classic quilts."

Katie Scott

WASHINGTON, DC

Skilled enough to be a professional *ribboneuse*, Katie is a busy high school student who puts family and study first. The time squeezed in for ribbonart seems to come when she needs a gift to say thank you, or a friend needs cheering up. Katie and her sister Christina are the admirable daughters of Denise Scott, without whose comradeship this writer's life would not be so happy!

Marge Walther

CENTREVILLE, VA

After a Baltimore Album class, Marge generously offered to make a model for the author's next book. *Maine Wreath with a Showy Bloom* is that gift. When you know that Marge works full-time outside the home and is also painstakingly making a once-in-a-lifetime Album Quilt of her own, you sense her kindness in so sharing her talents.

Pattern Transfer

BACKGROUND MARKING FOR RIBBON APPLIQUÉ

Much ribbonwork needs no pattern. Indeed for some, the pleasure is in the spontaneous creation of a piece. There is delight, though, in using a pattern to reproduce something you admire. The fabric you've chosen may determine which of the following pattern-transfer methods you can use. Beyond that, it matters most that you enjoy a given process.

TRACING A PATTERN

A photocopied or bold black ink-drawn pattern will show through from underneath on an off-white quilt block. A lightbox under the pattern is needed if the background is dark. In either case, position the pattern under the wrong side of the cloth. Prevent shifting with pins or tape. Mark the right side of the cloth with a fine lead or colored pencil, or a permanent black or brown .01 or .005 Pigma Micron pen.

DRESSMAKER'S CARBON PATTERN TRANSFER

If the background is very dark, or the fabric too thick to see through (velveteen or UltraSuede), then the pattern must be transferred from above to the cloth underneath. Sandwich dressmaker's carbon (transfer or graphite paper) transfer side down between the background cloth below and the pattern above. Use a ballpoint pen or a tracing wheel to press the pattern line into the cloth. Pre-test: if this method is messy on a napped fabric, or the lines wear off easily, use one of the following methods.

DISPOSABLE PATTERN TRANSFER

Trace the pattern onto a soft, disposable paper-like material which is then pinned or basted to the background cloth. The embroidery is stitched onto the background cloth, right through this material. The pattern is then pulled off. It should tear easily. For machine-work, Sulky's TearEasy® or Solvy® works well. For handwork, Pellon's TearAway® is more delicate and lets go more easily when pulled away from the stitching. Convenient, economical and best of all for delicate work is an old-fashioned method recalled in Yukiko Ogura's *Ribbon Embroidery* from Nihon Vogue-Sha. The pattern is traced onto white tissue paper, then crumpled mercilessly between the hands before being smoothed and pinned onto the background cloth. It is torn away when the needlework is done.

TRANSPARENCY APPLIQUÉ

Trace the pattern onto something transparent: tulle netting, a see-through interfacing, tracing paper or clear plastic. Attach the transparency across the top of the background cloth so that it can be turned back for the appliqués to be positioned and then sewn, one at a time, under it. This method works best with "freezer paper on the top" appliqué, pre-made flowers, or prepared (seams turned under) appliqué shapes. For stems and tendrils, use net or a perforated fiber equivalent. With a sharp pencil or Pigma Micron .01 pen, lightly mark brief place-ment lines right through the transparency.

IRON-ON PHOTOCOPY TRANSFER

Baltimore Beauties and Beyond, Volume II teaches how to transfer a photocopy of an engraved Album block embellishment by ironing the copy face-down to pale cloth. That method could also transfer a photocopied Album pattern for Lesson Five's Ribbon Appliqué. The process has been refined in the following ways since *Volume II* was written.

1. Stiffen the background fabric by ironing freezer paper to the wrong side.

2. Crease the block's vertical and hori-zontal centerfolds, to make registration marks. A 12½″ design image will have to be ironed on one-half at a time.

3. Work on a wooden board (a clean breadboard or press board) using a hot dry iron set at linen. The iron must be decades old or late '90's new. Because so much synthetic fiber was used, irons manufactured in the interim don't get hot enough for photocopy transfer. Caution! Rarely, freezer paper (or a photo-copy) does adhere too tightly. Never keep peeling it off into shreds! Immediately re-iron (to soften the bond)

and then grip the paper's solid edge with tweezers and pull towards the shreds. Re-warm and pull, as needed.

4. Pin the photocopied pattern to the background cloth so the print does not shift. Press hard with the iron and rotate it in a circular motion, pressing the pat-tern's carbon into the cloth. This imprint wears off with use. Don't let this knowl-edge rush your stitchery unduly. As with lead pencil, the marks grow faint over weeks, not days.

Technology has also changed since I first taught this method, and photocopies from certain new machines do not trans-fer. The question is, which machines? This 1996 e-mail letter from Beth Brandkamp of Rochester, NY provides an answer:

My husband (an engineer at Xerox®) said the Xerox laser printers use the same toner and process as the old time copiers (toner and heat fusion process). He said the way they work is to lay down a little layer of oil on the page and then fuse the toner on with heat. For that reason I would cut out only what I need from a piece of paper before ironing on. ...What he said would not work was the new ink jet printers which are the ones that are the less expensive printers with little cartridges—Canon Bubblejet®, Epson Stylus®, etc. They rely on ink, not on heat-fused toner. They are generally for home use in the $300-$500 cost range.

Thank you, Beth!

Classes

The heart of quiltmaking is community. Classes are a good place to find it! Anyone who wants to teach a class based on *Romancing Ribbons,* or to suggest that your shop or guild offer such a class may use the following course descriptions without further permission. A class participant who does not want to purchase the book can photocopy a single pattern for personal use, or trace a pattern from a borrowed book. The book's copyright prohibits patterns or any other material from the book being photocopied for class or for any other multiple-person use. Thank you for protecting my work, that of the contributing artists, and international copyright law.

One

FIVE HALF-DAY OR EVENING CLASSES: THREE HOURS PER SESSION

Learn The Pin-on Fancy Flower!
(Project 1, photo 1-1 in *Romancing Ribbons*)

Meet Elly's newest, *Romancing Ribbons,* and learn the basics of ribbon flower-making. Begin with Lesson One's straight-line gather pattern on one edge, two edges, or on the fold. Make one or more festive pin-on flowers (photo 1-2) with boat prow leaves. In class we'll take a visual "Ribbon Appliqué Inspiration Tour" of the quilts and ornament pictured in this very special book.

Skill level: All

Length: Three hours

Supplies needed: Basic sewing kit, including old scissors to cut wired ribbon, plus the supplies listed on page 24. For reference, bring a copy of *Romancing Ribbons* and any questions about other projects or classes. Make life easy! Reserve optional supply kits @ $X.00.

Master the Miniature Basket Pin!
(Project 4, photo 1-4 in *Romancing Ribbons*)

Delightfully different! Elly's 2½″ collar or lapel pin in *Romancing Ribbons* holds a basketful of learning: master split leaves, boat prow leaves, petal leaves, a posie of simple flowers with bead-stamen centers, and learn how to shape ribbon over a file card or an AidaPlus® foundation. Miniature flower ornament is fun, fast and inexpensive. The small pin style suits those who prefer a more tailored or country look. Once you make this *Romancing Ribbons*' project in class, basketsful of pansies or sunflowers are at your fingertips!

Skill level: All

Length: Three hours

Supplies needed: Basic sewing kit, including old scissors to cut wired ribbon, plus the supplies listed on page 30. For reference, bring a copy of *Romancing Ribbons* and any questions about other projects or classes. Make life easy! Reserve optional supply kits @ $X.00.

Mother/Daughter Pansy Barrette or Bar Pin Class
(Project 6, photo 2-4 in *Romancing Ribbons*)

This ribbon jewel is a delight to make! The class offers an easy but exceptionally evocative pansy technique, including leaves, embellishment, finishing the back professionally, and mounting the finished flower on a barrette or bar pin finding. This is an ideal class for a mother/daughter team or anyone wanting a product-oriented introduction to *Romancing Ribbons.*

Skill level: All

Length: Three hours

Supplies needed: Basic sewing kit, including old scissors to cut wired ribbon, plus the supplies listed on page 54. For reference, bring a copy of *Romancing Ribbons* and any questions about other projects or classes. Make life easy! Reserve optional supply kits @ $X.00.

Sunflower Necklace—A Dramatic Jewel!
(Project 12, photo 6-2 in *Romancing Ribbons*)

This jewel is a real looker! It also teaches a great deal: folded petals, boat prow leaves, beading, a padded center, a hollow armature to thread beads and professional ribbon ornament finishing. You'll complete most of the project in class, and will be ready to design heirloom jewels of your own. This is an ideal class to take with a daughter or to give as a gift to a special friend.

Skill level: All

Length: Three hours

Supplies needed: Basic sewing kit, including old scissors to cut wired ribbon, plus the supplies listed on pages 126 and 127. For reference, bring a copy of *Romancing Ribbons* and any questions about other projects or classes. Make life easy! Reserve optional supply kits @ $X.00.

A Tailored Rose and Opera Pearl Necklace
(Project 15, photo 6-5 in *Romancing Ribbons*)

Would you prefer a collar pin or corsage, rather than an opera pearl necklace rose? The tailored rose suits each of these moods to perfection! Its construction is almost fail-proof—and so easy you could make it as a gift-wrap ornament. The ribbon you choose and the foliage you stitch make all the difference. The tailored rose, kimono-pleated leaves and knotted leaves provide lots of learning on the road to this pretty adornment. Complete this project in one class! Kit available.

Skill level: All

Length: Three hours

Supplies needed: Basic sewing kit, including old scissors to cut wired ribbon, plus the supplies listed on page 133. For reference, bring a copy of *Romancing Ribbons* and any questions about other projects or classes. Make life easy! Reserve optional supply kits @ $X.00.

Two

SIX TWO-SESSION HALF-DAY OR EVENING CLASSES: THREE HOURS PER SESSION

Lisa McCulley's Blossoming Scissors-Sheath

(Project 14, photo 6-3 in *Romancing Ribbons*)

Would you like to twine Ribbon Appliqué with a touch of machine quilting—thereby mastering two hot currents in today's quilt world? You can have it all in this delightful class and come up with a finished gift in the bargain! Learn simple machine quilting and Lesson Six's folded and pleated flowers from *Romancing Ribbons*. The project's design is so quick, easy, different and useful that you'll want to make several for your friends and gift list.

Skill level: All

Length: Two three-hour sessions

Supplies needed: Basic sewing kit, including old scissors to cut wired ribbon, plus the supplies listed on page 129. For reference, bring a copy of *Romancing Ribbons* and any questions about other projects or classes. Make life easy! Reserve optional supply kits @ $X.00.

Rose Without Thorns: A Pillow or Medallion Block

(Project 10, photo 5-1 in *Romancing Ribbons*)

Something this beautiful shouldn't be so easy! We ornament a block with fused foliage, hand blanket-stitched in gold, and blooming with a ribbon rose. Bead dewdrops add a poetic touch, just as the graceful gold ribbon and carefully inked signature bespeak Victoriana. Quick and easy! The swift can get several of these made over the two-session class, or begin finishing the project into a pillow, a framed picture or even an elegant throw quilt!

Skill level: All

Length: Two three-hour sessions

Supplies needed: Basic sewing kit, including old scissors to cut wired ribbon, plus the supplies listed on pages 107 and 108. For reference, bring a copy of *Romancing Ribbons* and any questions about other projects or classes. Make life easy! Reserve optional supply kits @ $X.00.

Everlastings: A Ribbon Appliqué Motif

(Project 7, photo 3-2 in *Romancing Ribbons*)

Silk ribbon embroidery blooms even brighter with the wider ribbon flowers (Sugar Scoop Lily and Circle Posies) of Ribbon Appliqué! On a readymade base (like the apron Elly chose) or an empty quilt block (cotton, wool or velveteen),

master Elly's ribbonry techniques. A quick, delightful project, this offers heirloom adornment of wedding gift calibre for hearth and home! It's fun, easy and astonishingly fast, considering the showy results. Kit available.

Skill level: All

Length: Two three-hour sessions

Supplies needed: Basic sewing kit, including old scissors to cut wired ribbon, plus the supplies and preparation listed on pages 69 and 71. For reference, bring a copy of *Romancing Ribbons* and any questions about other projects or classes. Make life easy! Reserve one or more optional supply kits @ $X.00.

Pennsylvania Dutch Nouveau: A Ribbon Appliqué Motif

(Project 8, photo 3-3 in *Romancing Ribbons*)

Silk ribbon embroidery blooms even brighter with Ribbon Appliqué's wider ribbon flowers: delphinium, hollyhocks and daffodils! On a readymade base like the toaster cover Elly chose, or on an empty quilt block (cotton, wool, or velveteen) master Elly's Ribbon Appliqué. Delightful to stitch and astonishingly fast to complete, this project makes a thoughtful gift. Your own pleasure will grow as the one you keep becomes a treasured heirloom. Kit available.

Skill level: All

Length: Two three-hour sessions

Supplies needed: Basic sewing kit, including old scissors to cut wired ribbon, plus the supplies and preparation listed on pages 72 and 75. For reference, bring a copy of *Romancing Ribbons* and any questions about other projects or classes. Make life easy! Reserve one or more optional supply kits @ $X.00.

Create Rosa Rugosa: The Victorian Beach Rose Quilt Block

(Project 9, photo 4-2 in *Romancing Ribbons*)

The old-fashioned Rosa Rugosa grows with wild abandon along country roads. No rose is more romantic! Stitch timelessness into a quilt block, a framed hanging, or a pillow—and in no time at all! The process is pure pleasure and teaches much: fused foliage, hand blanket-stitching, silk ribbon embroidery, rake-ruched roses, and bead embroidery. This block is classic non-Baltimore 19th century Album appliqué. Simple yet stunning, it has a zesty touch of asymmetry and an open center for inked or embroidered embellishment. If enough graduates request it, we'll go on to make the wall quilt, photo 4-2, in a Master's Class of new-found friends!

Skill level: All

Length: Two three-hour sessions

Supplies needed: Basic sewing kit, including old scissors to cut wired ribbon, plus the supplies listed on pages 89 and 91. For reference, bring a copy of *Romancing Ribbons* and any questions about other projects or classes. Make life easy! Reserve one or more optional supply kits @ $X.00.

Three

FOUR HALF-DAY OR EVENING CLASSES: THREE HOURS PER SESSION

Christmas Club: Make a Ribbon Gift-a-Week!

(Begin with Project 6, photo 2-4 in *Romancing Ribbons*)

Make Lesson Two's Pansy Bar Pin (or your choice) in the first class, then make a project per week, each person choosing what she'd like to make and asking the instructor what to bring to accomplish it. The magic is in the group-learning situation, where we learn not only by what we make, but by seeing what the others create. It will be exciting, fun and garlanded by ribbons! This class is the perfect way to fill your gift drawer, prepare for Christmas in July, and review the techniques taught in Elly's newest, *Romancing Ribbons*.

Skill level: All

Length: Four three-hour sessions

Supplies needed: Basic sewing kit, including old scissors to cut wired ribbon, plus the supplies listed on page 54. For reference, bring a copy of *Romancing Ribbons* and any questions about other projects or classes. Make life easy! Reserve one or more optional supply kits @ $X.00.

Four

TEN-SESSION HALF-DAY OR EVENING CLASSES: THREE HOURS PER SESSION

Ribbon Appliqué Block-a-Month Class!

(Optional Project page 112, photo 5-2 in *Romancing Ribbons*)

Go beyond Baltimore to master classic techniques with modern freedom! Ribbon Appliqué Basket of Flowers from *Spoken Without a Word*. Then make the magical Peacock Pastorale, from *Baltimore Album Quilts*. After these patterns, chosen for specific techniques, design your own Album plan. Ribbon Appliqué® blocks fit in wonderfully with classic Album blocks. Your pace can be leisurely (one block a month) or intense. You can even continue next year in our "Album Sets, Borders, Quilting and Binding Class"! Optional supply kit available.

Skill level: All

Length: Four three-hour sessions

Supplies needed: Basic sewing kit. *Spoken Without a Word*, plus the supplies listed on pages 113–114. For fabric selection and reference, bring a copy of *Romancing Ribbons*. Kits available.

Resource Directory

Welcome to ribbonwork at the turn of the twentieth century! On an America Online Quilting Board, the author asked if readers wanted a ribbon Resource Directory included in this book. E-mail responses overwhelmingly requested a comprehensive directory for finding specialized supplies, classes and finished products.

PUBLISHERS

C&T Publishing
5021 Blum Road
Martinez, CA 94553
(800) 284-1114
Wholesale, retail, mail order. Free catalog. Publisher of nine of the author's books on applique, including Appliqué 12 Easy Ways! *and the* Baltimore Beauties *series.*

EZ International and
Quilt House Publishing
95 Mayhill St., P.O. Box 895
Saddle Brook, NJ 07663
EZ International would be pleased to send you a complete list of EZ's books, quilting tools and videos, and a complimentary Quilt House Publishing catalog, The Quilter's Essential Library.

Turtle Hill Press
5540 30th Street, NW
Washington, DC 20015
Wholesale, retail, mail order. The author's press. For Spoken Without A Word *, send check (to Elly Sienkiewicz) for $19.95 (U.S.) plus $4.50 shipping. Overseas orders should be sent to the Cotton Patch, address listed in the directory.*

CLASSES ON RIBBONRY

Elly Sienkiewicz's Appliqué Academy at the Historic Inns of Annapolis
For information write to:
Denise Scott, Director
3027 Arizona Ave. NW
Washington, DC 20016
(202) 364-2841
Workshops and lectures: Ribbon flower-making, Ribbon Appliqué, beadwork, quilting, fabric dyeing, ornament and embellishment. Three-day classes taught at the Inns by superb teachers in hand and machine appliqué.

An intimate annual (March) conference with elegant accommodations in a picturesque seaport town, 27 miles from Baltimore and Washington, DC. Sidetrips to museums to see Baltimore Album Quilts and to shop at G-Street Fabrics. A wonderful learning vacation! Send large SASE (two stamps) for a brochure.

Elly Sienkiewicz
5540 30th St., NW
Washington, DC 20015
Elly's joy is lecturing, judging and teaching, both in the U.S. and abroad. Please write for current prospectus. Advance bookings appreciated, but sometimes same-year invitations can be accomodated.

G-Street Fabrics
11854 Rockville Pike
Rockville, MD 20852
(301) 231-8998
Retail, mail order. Machine embroidery thread, oversized rick-rack, a plethora of ribbons, crepe de Chine, and a huge selection of UltraSuede. This is the author's local quilt shop where she teaches a series of one day classes once a year. Send for a course schedule.

RIBBON JEWELERS— HANDMADE RIBBON-EMBELLISHED ORNAMENT

Christa Lynn Brown
Honey Moon French Ribbon Roses
P.O. Box 5724
Eugene, OR 97405
(800) 293-5446
Retail, mail order, full-color catalog. "The rose is the heart of all our work and each one is created in a style unique to us. All of our jewelry is created in the spirit of elegance and romance." These pieces are small treasures. Beautifully packaged and reasonably priced.

Lorraine Ryuku Fukuwa
Vintage Velvet Florals
2801 West Sepulveda Blvd., Unit 3
Torrance CA 90505
(310) 782-1030
Wholesale, retail, special orders. Lorraine's work is pictured in Romancing Ribbons. If you have vintage or heirloom items you wish collaged into velvet floral jewelry, a picture frame, or Album cover, Lorraine does such commissions.

Janet Stauffacher
The Vintage Vogue Collection
712 June Dr.
Corona, CA 91719
(909) 279-9109
Wholesale, retail, mail order, and commissioned pieces. Janet's work is sophisticated, different, eye-catching, and nationally known. Her ribbonwork classes are offered at quilt symposia, national ornament conventions, and through shops and guilds.

MANUFACTURED RIBBON AND TRIM RETAILERS RECOMMENDED BY *ROMANCING RIBBONS'* NEEDLEARTISTS

Angelsea
P.O. Box 4586
Stockton, CA 95204
(209) 948-8428
Retail, mail order. A catalog so romantic it's worth ordering just to read. Victoria Magazine has featured Anglesea. (Small catalog charge. Call for current price.) Hand-dyed silk ribbon, metallic threads, vintage flowers, berries, stamens, and books. Domestic and imported ribbons.

Bell'occhio
8 Brady St.
San Francisco, CA 94103
(415) 864-4048
Retail, mail order. This is one of needleartist Wendy Grande's favorite sources. Specializing in wider ribbons, unusual woven ribbons, exceptional vintage metallic ribbons, hand-painted and hand-dyed ribbons.

Bloomers
2975 Washington St.
San Francisco, CA 94115
(415) 563-3266
Retail florist supplier famous for its fabulous ribbon selection.

The Bristly Thistle
215½ Howard St.
Petoskey, MI 49770
(616) 347-5460
Retail, will ship special orders. Silk ribbon, tubular nylon ribbon floss, threads and yarns. Also sells an inexpensive mini-drill for creating twisted cording for chatelaine or purse handles.

Britix
146 Geary St.
San Francisco, CA 94108
(415) 392-2910
Retail. A must visit for ribbon in San Francisco! Wide selection from buttons to bows.

Camela Nitschke Ribbonry
119 Louisiana Ave.
Perrysburg, OH 43551
Phone and Fax: (419) 872-0073
Wholesale, retail, mail order. Nationally known for elegant ribbons.

Dawn's Discount Lace
8655 Sepulveda Blvd.
Westchester, CA 90045
(310) 641-3466
Wholesale, retail, mail order catalog. French wired ribbon, lace, charms, flowers, stamens, velvet pods, trims, vintage 100% velvet (also pre-stripped velvet) and rayon ribbon.

Elsie's Exquisites
208 State St.
P. O. Box 260
St. Joseph, MI 49085
(800) 742-SILK
Fax: (616) 982-0963
Wholesale, retail, mail order catalog. Ribbons, trims, stamens and miniature flowers.

Hymen & Hendler
67 W. 38th St.
NYC, NY 10018
(212) 840-8393
Wholesale, retail. A treasure trove of ribbon: European and American ribbons, antique and contemporary, wire-edged, grosgrain and vintage 100% rayon velvet.

Lacis
3163 Adeline Ave.
Berkeley, CA 94705
(510) 843-5018
Wholesale, retail, shows, mail order catalog. Lace, lace supplies, ribbons and trims. Much of the metallic lace, velvet leaves and stamens in this book come from Lacis.

Quilter's Resource, Inc.
P.O. Box 148850
Chicago, IL 60614
(800) 676-6543
Fax: (312) 278-1348
Wholesale. French wired ribbon, silk ribbon, embroidery floss, trims, vintage ribbon, buttons, beads, charms and books. A wonderful supplier of ribbon exotica for shop owners.

Tail of the Yak
2632 Ashby Ave.
Berkeley, CA 94705
(510) 841-9891
Retail. An esoteric treasure of vintage jewelry, ribbon and trims.

Vaban
2070C Boston Dr.
Atlanta, GA 30337
(800) 822-2606
Wholesale. Large collection of wired and other ribbon.

HAND-DYED AND CUSTOM RIBBON SOURCES, RIBBON FOR DYEING

Artemis, "Hanah" Silk
Diana Dickey, Marketing Rep.
179 High St.
South Portland, ME 04106
(207) 741-2509
Fax: (207) 741-2497
Wholesale, retail, mail order ($10 for sample card). 100% silk and satin hand-dyed, raw-edged bias cut ribbons in an exceptional range of exquisite colors.

Jenifer Buechel
Hand-dyed Silk Ribbons
Box #118/3567
Mountain View Drive
Mifflin, PA 15122
Wholesale, retail. Unique silk ribbon beautifully packaged. Extensive colors and widths; cotton and rayon included. Jenifer also teaches Ribbon Appliquéd Baltimore Album blocks in full or miniature.

Island Fibers
Kathleen Getchius Sorensen
Rt. 1, Box 104
Washington Island, WI 54246
(414) 847-2649
Wholesale, retail, mail order. Hand painted silk ribbon, dye-painted cottons, silks and laces for silk ribbon embroidery, quilting, clothing and embellishments.

Montana Fancy
P.O. Box 9221
Helena, MT 59604
(406) 442-1864
MTFancy@aol.com
Wholesale, retail, mail order (LSASE for price list). Luscious hand-dyed and variegated 100% silk ribbons in 4mm, 7mm, and 13mm widths. Single strands, assortments, or bulk. Silk ribbon patterns for American wildflowers and other projects.

Things Japanese
Maggie Backman, Rep.
9805 NE 116th St.
Kirkland, WA 98034
(206) 821-2287
Fax: (206) 823-4907
Wholesale, retail. White silk ribbon, 2mm, 3.5mm, 7 mm, 32mm; silk dyes and dyeing instructions, and kits for dyeing. Variety packs of ribbon and ready-made roses. 100 weight silk thread in 9 colors which can also be dyed. Sells Visionart Dyes. Publisher and retail source for the book Dyeing in a Teacup.

Y.L.I. Corporation
(Yarn Loft International)
482 N. Freedom Blvd.
Provo, UT 84601
(800) 854-1932
Wholesale. Bulk silk embroidery on spools and in packets. Silk ribbon for dyeing or painting and also pre-packaged colors.

MANUFACTURED RIBBON, TRIM AND NOTIONS SUPPLIERS

Art Sale Co.
4801 W. Jefferson Dr.
Los Angeles, CA 90016
(213) 731-2531
Fax: (213) 735-3753
Trims, wholesale lace and Swiss velveteen.

Artistic Ribbon Co, Inc.
22 W. 21st St.
NYC, NY 10010
(212) 255-4224
Wholesale; catalog available.

Askren Display
2420 S. 34th Place
Tucson, AZ 85713
(602) 571-1411
Wholesale. French wired ribbons.

Bazaar Del Mundo, Fabrics & Finery
2754 Calhoun St.
San Diego, CA 92110
(619) 296-3161
Retail. Grosgrain, satin ribbons and trims; Mexican, European, and South African sources.

Beret Ltd.
328 S. Jefferson
Chicago, IL 60607
(312) 715-0404
Wholesale, mail order. Craft supplies.

Blackstone Sales Co.
5717 W. Belmont
Chicago, IL 60634
(312) 282-6668
Retail. Novelty and florist supplies.

Coco Company
300 North Elizabeth St.
Chicago, IL 60607
(312) 829-0069
Wholesale. Floral supplies and French wired ribbon.

The Elegant Needle
8747 Bronson Dr.
Roseville, CA 95746
(916) 791-5421
Fax: (916) 797-0632
Mail order catalog. Ribbons and laces, vintage and modern; specializing in miniatures for doll makers.

Europa
2330 Old Middlefield Way
Mountain View, CA 94043
(415) 969-3232
Wholesale. Trims and ribbons.

F. & S. Fabrics
10654 Pico Blvd.
Los Angeles, CA 90064
(310) 441-2477
Retail. Wide variety of ribbons and trims.

Fabric Fancies
P.O. Box 50807
Reno, NV 89513
Mail order. Bridal materials, pearl trim, ribbon and flowers.

A Fine Romance
2912 Hennepin Ave. So.
Minneapolis, MN 55047
(612) 822-4144
Retail. Vintage and contemporary ribbon and trim.

Gardner's Ribbon & Lace
2235 E. Division
Arlington, TX 76011
(817) 640-1436
Wholesale, retail. Ribbons, trims, laces, buttons, wire-edged ribbon and crushable 100% rayon velvet ribbon.

Wendy Grande, Needleartist
500 St. Andrews Dr.
Aptos, CA 95003
For information on Wendy's ribbon embellished Album block patterns, send a large SASE.

Grayblock Ribbon Co., Inc.
St. Michaels Rd., P.O. Box 967
Waston, MD 21601
(800) 847-8877
Wholesale, catalog. All sorts of ribbon: velvet, satin, grosgrain and wired.

Handcraft from Europe
1201 Bridgeway
Sausalito, CA 94965
(415) 332-1633
Retail. Specializing in needlepoint and embroidery supplies, vintage and modern ribbon, European traditional woven ribbon, wires and some silks.

Hats by Leko
14106 Ventura Blvd. #106
Sherman Oaks, CA 91423
(818) 905-8456
Wholesale catalog. Millinery trims, flowers, ribbon, stamens and accessories.

The Hobby Co.
5150 Geary Blvd.
San Francisco, CA 94121
(415) 386-2802
Retail. Reasonably priced wired ribbon.

G. Kagen & Sons, Inc.
750 Towne Ave.
Los Angeles, CA 90021
(213) 627-9655
Fax: (213) 627-1128
Wholesale. Extensive selection of trims.

Kate Webster Co.
83 Granite St.
Rockport, MA 01966
Phone and Fax: (508) 546-6462
Retail, mail order. Vintage and modern ribbon, mostly miniature.

Linen Lady
6011 Folsom Blvd.
Sacramento, CA 95819
(916) 457-6718
Retail. Ribbon and cotton lace trims.

Marin County Floral Art & Design Center
145 Tunstead Ave.
San Anselmo, CA 94960
(415) 456-6862
Retail. Imported ribbons, silk flowers and foliage.

Milliner's Supply Co.
911 Elm St.
Dallas, TX 75202
(800) 627-4337
Wholesale, retail, catalog. Extensive milliner's supplies including feathers, ribbons, flowers, standard and extra long hat pins.

Mini Magic
Patricia Road
Columbus, OH 43220
(614) 457-3687
Retail, mail order. Imported ribbons and trims.

M & J Trimming Co.
1008 6th Ave.
NYC, NY 10018
(212) 391-9072
Wholesale, retail. Decorative elastics for head and arm bands, braids, ribbons, trims, buttons, beads, beaded appliqués, tassels and passementerie.

Janice Naibert
16590 Emory Lane
Rockville, MD 20853
(301) 774-9252
Wholesale. She designs ribbons which are manufactured in France. Also imports Austrian braids and trims. Retails at shows only.

Norma Ribbon and Trimming, Inc.
48 W. 25th St.
NYC, NY 10010
(212) 206-8105
Fax: (212) 633-9189
Wholesale. Ribbons, rosettes, trims and a large miniature collection.

Offray Ribbon
C.M. Offray & Son, Inc.
Rt. 24, Box 601
Chester, NJ 07930-0601
(800) 344-5533
Fax: (908) 879-8588
Wholesale. American wire-edged ribbon manufacturer of Offray and Lion ribbon.

Paulette C. Knight, Importer
343 Vermont St.
San Francisco, CA 94103
(800) 642-8900
Fax: (415) 626-2564
Wholesale. Imported ribbons, luscious French wired ribbons, 100% acetate ribbons, metallics, all in a wide range of styles and widths.

Penn & Fletcher, Inc.
242 W. 30th St., Suite 400
NYC, NY 10001
(212) 239-6868
Wholesale. Metallic laces, embroideries, trims.

Reliant Ribbon
838 21st Ave.
Paterson, NJ 07513
(201) 881-0404
Wholesale. Wire-edged ribbon, metallics.

Renaissance Ribbons
13415 Rue Montaigne
P.O. Box 699
Oregon House, CA 95962
(916) 692-0842
Fax: (916) 692-0915
Wholesale. French ribbons and trim.

Ribbon Connections
969 Industrial Rd., Suite E
San Carlos, CA 94070
(415) 593-5221
Fax: (415) 593-6785
Wholesale. Manufacturing branch for Japanese ribbons. Large minimum quantities.

Rolf Gille Import, Ltd.
165 8th St.
San Francisco, CA 94103
(415) 552-5490
Wholesale. Ribbon, craft and floral supplies.

Sandy's Trims
7417 Knoxville Rd.
Peoria, IL 61614
(309) 689-1943
Retail, mail order catalog. Carries Janice Naibert's imported ribbons and others.

Satin Moon Fabrics
32 Clement St.
San Francisco, CA 94118
(415) 668-1623
Retail. Unusual selection of trims, tassels, buttons and ribbons.

Sherry Shallie
8732 Haskell St.
Riverside, CA 92503
(909) 688-5471
Retail, mail order catalog. Lots of ribbon geared to the doll market.

So-Good Inc.
28 W. 38th St.
NYC, NY 10018
(212) 398-0236
Retail, mail order. Lots of ribbon; satin a speciality.

Stanislaus Imports
75 Arkansas
San Francisco, CA 94107
(415) 431-7122
Wholesale. Craft and novelty supplies.

Tinsel Trading Co.
47 W. 38th St.
NYC, NY 10018
(212) 730-1030
Wholesale, retail. Specializing in vintage and contemporary metallic trims.

The Thread Gatherer
2108 Norcrest
Boise, ID 83705
(208) 387-2641
Retail. A wealth of thread, floss, yarns and more.

Lorraine Trippett
250 S. Sycamore Ave.
Los Angeles, CA 90036
(213) 939-9986
Retail. Vintage ribbons, trims and pinking tools.

Viv's Ribbons & Laces
212 Virginia Hills Dr.
Martinez, CA 94553
(510) 933-7758
Retail. Trims, ribbons, braids, laces, flower appliqués and much more!

Zucker Feather Products
P.O. Box 331
512 N. East St.
California, MO 65018
(314) 796-2183
Wholesale. Feathers, including peacock feathers.

QUILTING AND RIBBON NOTIONS AND TOOLS

Clotilde, Inc.
2 Sew Smart Way B8031
Stevens Point, WI 54481-8031
(800) 772-2891
Mail order catalog. Sewing notions galore— including Gem Tac glue, milliner's needles, Sulky invisible thread, and Clotilde's Perfect Pleater which works well on ribbon. This catalog has all the necessary findings for making ribbon accessories.

EZ International and
Quilt House Publishing
95 Mayhill St. P.O. Box 895
Saddle Brook, NJ 07663
Wholesale. A major supplier of sewing, doll-making, and quilting supplies, notions and tools.

Fiskars, Inc.
7811 West Stewart Ave
Wausau, WI 54402
(715) 842-2091
Fiskars manufactures scissors, tweezers, magnifiers and pliers for ribbon work.

VQS Supplies
7815 Antoinette Dr.
Richmond, VA 23227
(804) 266-6348
Sells Felsan Boards (felt on one side, fine sandpaper on the other side of a sturdy ¼" wooden board) in three sizes, including lap size and suitcase size. A Felsan board is a table or lap board for beadwork, ribbonwork, or freezer paper appliqué.

INTERNATIONAL RIBBON SOURCES

Midori
1432 Elliott
W. Seattle, WA 98119
(206) 282-3595
Fax: (206) 282-3431
Wholesale. Japanese ribbon, organdy, satin and taffetas.

Mokuba Co., Ltd.
Mokuba ribbons are distributed exclusively in the U.S. by
EZ International
95 Mayhill St., P.O. Box 895
Saddle Brook, NJ 07663
(201) 712-1234
Fax (201) 712-1199
Mokuba ribbons are available wherever fine ribbons are sold.

Mokuba Co., Ltd.
18 Rue Montmartre
Paris, France 75001
45.08.80.02. Fax: 45.008.16
As complete a retail stock of Mokuba as you'll find anywhere— Trés romantique!

PRINTED FABRICS, HAND-DYED YARDAGE

The Cotton Patch
1025 Brown Ave.
Lafayette, CA 94549
(800) 835-4418
Retail. Excellent international mail order service on all quilt-making supplies, including freezer paper, notions, quilt books, (including all of the author's books), the Elly Sienkiewicz Baltimore Beauties for P&B Textiles designer collection, and an enviable selection of silk ribbons and wider ribbons.

Daffodil Dye Works
10111 Davis Ave.
Woodstock, MD 21163
Retail, mail order, special orders and a vendor at quilt shows. Artfully dyed 100% cottons which work wonderfully as backgrounds for ribbon pieces.

P&B Textiles
1580 Gilbreth Rd.
Burlingame, CA 94010
(800) TLC-Bear
Manufacturer. Wholesale. Call for the shop nearest you carrying "Baltimore Beauties by Elly Sienkiewicz" designer fabrics. The line includes a rich selection of ombres and excellent prints for use as backgrounds for Ribbon Appliqué. This is the source for Elly's Baltimore Beauties "Calligraphy Cloth". A word from this cloth is reverse appliquéd into Lesson Four's "Maine Wreath with a Showy Bloom." The other fabrics in that block are also from the Baltimore Beauties collection.

DYE AND FABRIC FOR DYEING

Cerulean Blue
P.O. Box 21168
Seattle, WA 98111
Retail, mail order. Dye, fabric paints, and dye tool supplies. Color charts available.

Dharma Trading Co.
P.O. Box 150916
San Rafael, CA 94915
Carries everything for the dyer, including color charts for these dyes: Setacolor, JonesTones, Dr. Ph. Martin's, Spectralite, DeKa Permanent Fabric Paint, DeKa Print, DeKa Series L Dyes, Tinfix on Silk, Peintex on Silk.

Rupert, Gibbon & Spider
P.O. Box 425
Healdsburg, CA 95448
(800) 442-0455
Fax: (707) 443-4906
Retail, mail order. Natural fabrics ready to dye. Dyes, paints, pigments, color remover and dyeing tools. Silk, cotton, rayon and silk jacquard.

Salis International, Inc.
40393 North 28th Way
Hollywood, FL 33020
(800) 843-8293
Fax: (305) 921-6976
Wholesale, retail. Specializing in liquid color for almost any fabric dye, or any fabric painting use, including air-brushing and watercolor. Nine different lines of color.

BEAD SUPPLIERS

General Bead
317 National City Blvd.
National City, CA 91950
(619) 336-0100
Fax: (800) 572-1302
Wholesale, retail, mail order. A king's ransom in beads and the best buy nationwide on cylindrical Japanese Delica beads.

Shepherdess
2802 Juan St., #14
San Diego, CA 92110
(619) 297-4110
Fax: (619) 297-9897
Retail, mail order. A bead store filled with unusual components and ethnic treasures. Classes, seminars.

TWE Beads
P.O. Box 1128
Denville, NJ 07834
(201) 586-3844
Retail, mail order, vendor at quilt shows. Speciality beads, bead books, and Czech glass seed beads.

PLEATING AND QUILTING SERVICES

A-1 Pleating
8426½ W. 3rd St.
Los Angeles, CA 90048
(213) 653-5557
Custom pleating, belts, buttons. Send for price list with descriptions.

ACME Button and Pleating
404 S. Wells
Chicago, IL 60607
(312) 922-0096
Custom buttons, button covering, and pleating service.

Advance Pleating and Button Co.
750 Florida St.
San Francisco, CA 94110
(415) 648-3111
A wealth of services from pleating, smocking, ruffling, trimming, rhinestoning, computerized embroidery, and attaching snaps and rivets.

Mona Cumberledge and Joyce Hill, hand quilters
HCR 74, Box 106
Alma, WV 26320
(304) 758-2530
Individual, professional hand quilting service. They have done exceptional hand quilting for the author for years. Write, describing your quilt, then call to discuss.

Ruffles and Flourishes
242 Greenview Dr.
Richland, WA 99352
(509) 627-5906
Victorian pleating of up to 4" wide ribbon. Also sells pre-pleated ribbon.

San Francisco Pleating
425 2nd St.
San Francisco, CA 94107
(415) 982-3003
Send for brochure giving types, sizes and prices: crystal, accordion, mushroom, box, knife and circular pleating.

An original Album block design by Wendy Grande from her quilt, Ribbon Appliqué.

About the Author

All her life, Elly has been "making things." The imagination which characterizes her work has been evident throughout her versatile quilting career. The popularity of her exceptional needlework designs and her lavishly illustrated books attest to Elly's originality, curiosity, humor and fascination with the human story.

From 1978 to 1992, she was a Teaching Fellow at Glen Echo National Park, where her solo exhibition, *Eleanor Sienkiewicz: Textile Art—A Retrospective,* was presented. In 1979, three of her works were exhibited in the group show, Wellesley's Artists, at the Textile Museum, Washington, D.C. A recognized quilt artist by 1978, Elly continues to exhibit widely, as well as teach and lecture throughout the United States and around the world.

In 1983, she published her first book, *Spoken Without a Word,* which is still in print today. That she has ten additional titles to her credit reflects her versatility and energy as a writer, teacher and designer. Elly confirms she is happiest in the classroom, where her charm and willingness to share contribute to a teaching style greatly admired by her students.

With a Bachelor of Arts in History from Wellesley College, and a Master of Science in Education from the University of Pennsylvania, Elly's academic background lends historical enrichment to her teaching and writing.

At home in Washington, D.C. with her husband and their three children, Elly continues to enjoy "making things." Many recent creations enhance the pages of this book.

Books by Elly Sienkiewicz:

Romancing Ribbons into Flowers

Papercuts and Plenty, Volume III of Baltimore Beauties and Beyond, Studies in Classic Album Quilt Appliqué

Baltimore Revival! Historic Quilts in the Making

Appliqué 12 Borders and Medallions! A Pattern Companion to Volume III of Baltimore Beauties and Beyond, Studies in Classic Album Quilt Appliqué

Dimensional Appliqué—A Pattern Companion to Volume II of Baltimore Beauties and Beyond

Design a Baltimore Album Quilt, A Design Companion to Volume II of Baltimore Beauties and Beyond, Studies in Classic Album Quilt Appliqué

Appliqué 12 Easy Ways! Charming Quilts, Giftable Projects and Timeless Techniques

Baltimore Beauties and Beyond, Studies in Classic Album Quilt Appliqué, Volume II

Baltimore Album Quilts, Historic Notes and Antique Patterns, A Pattern Companion to Baltimore Beauties and Beyond, Volume I

Baltimore Beauties and Beyond, Volume I

Spoken Without A Word—A Lexicon of Selected Symbols, with 24 Patterns from Classic Baltimore Album Quilts